Buddy Boys

Buddy Boys

When Good Cops Turn Bad

MIKE McALARY

G. P. PUTNAM'S SONS / NEW YORK

G. P. Putnam's Sons
Publishers Since 1838
200 Madison Avenue
New York, NY 10016

Library of Congress Cataloging-in-Publication Data

McAlary, Mike.
Buddy boys.

1. Police corruption—New York (N.Y.).   2. Corruption
investigation—New York (N.Y.).   3. Brooklyn (New York,
N.Y.)   I. Title.
HV8148.N5M24   1987   364.1′323′097471   87–19040
ISBN 0-399-13295-3

Printed in the United States of America
1   2   3   4   5   6   7   8   9   10

Acknowledgments

Unfortunately, this is a true story.

An investigation in the dealings of corrupt police officers in Brooklyn's 77th Precinct first appeared in the pages of *New York Newsday*. My colleagues in the newsroom—City Editor James Hairston, reporters Marianne Arnenberg, Bob Drury, Richard Esposito and Sandra Widener—combined sweat, legwork and a selfless determination to breathe life into a simple list of thirteen names, the roster of the suspended police officers. They combined day after day to tell the story of the 77th Precinct in compelling detail, with accuracy and fairness, under intense deadline conditions. I am forever in their debt.

My agent, Flip Brophy of the Sterling Lord Agency, deserves equal credit for the completion of this book. She believed in the story from the start and kept a late-night ear available for a first-time author's frenzied telephone calls.

Finally, I would like to thank my editor at Putnam, Chris Schillig, for the use of her critical eye and practiced hand. At the point of Schillig's No. 2 pencil, *Buddy Boys* made the startling transformation from unruly manuscript to polished book.

For my wife Alice, New York's finest

Contents

Buddy Boys

Prologue

Henry Winter lay in bed, dreaming. He was sleeping late, again.

In spite of all the recent developments in the New York City police officer's life—a period of betrayal, deception and fear—Henry Winter had amazed even his own wife with his ability to fall asleep during this time of unrest. He didn't tell his wife that the only time he felt unburdened now was when he slept. He didn't have to record his dreams. Henry found sanctuary in slumber.

Crooked Brooklyn street cops were free from harm in Henry Winter's dreams. They could speak freely without fear of punishment. No one played Henry's dreams back on a little tape recorder, listening to them on a headset.

No one plugged them into a videotape recorder either, watching them on a television. No one dissected the ghetto cop's dreams, pulling out names and addresses, marking down dates and times of crimes committed by other members of the New York City Police Department.

Much later, Henry Winter's dreams would turn to nightmares. Sometimes he would awaken in a cold sweat, his bedclothes sodden, his body twitching uncontrollably. Betsy Winter would be holding her husband, trying to shake him free of some unseen torment.

"It's happening again," she would say. "Isn't it?"

Henry Winter would grab a cigarette from the pack of Newports on his nightstand and strike a match to it. Mentholated smoke would fill the couple's tiny Valley Stream, Long Island bedroom. Then Henry would run his fingers through his blonde hair.

Yes, it was happening again, Henry would realize. And then the conversations—the headings on the tapes he was recording on a small machine he carried hidden in a pocket of his bulletproof vest—would come back to him. The conversations always began with the same introduction.

On some darkened and desolate Brooklyn street, Henry Winter and a faceless investigator from the Police Department's Internal Affairs Division would meet in an unmarked car, huddled over a tiny metal machine.

And it would begin again.

"At this time I am testing an Olympus microrecorder, model number L200, serial number 211417. This recorder is to be used to record conversations by Police Officer Henry Winter during a tour of duty on this date in the Seventy-seventh Precinct. Officer, do you realize that once this recorder is activated it will record any conversations by you or directed towards you?"

"Yes," Henry would reply in a dead, colorless voice.

"Officer, are you willing to record all conversations of your own free will?"

"Yes."

"Have you been instructed on the proper use of this recorder?"

"Yes I have."

"This is the primary recorder to be used during your tour of duty. I ask that you have nothing in your pockets that would interfere with that recording. Is that understood?"

"Yes."

"End of this portion of the tape."

On the morning of June 22, 1986, Henry woke to the sound of a telephone ringing at his bedside. The phone sounded like an alarm. At first Henry was confused; a shaft of midmorning summer light shone in his eyes. He grappled with the phone, lifting the receiver with one hand and pressing a small button on a recording machine with the other. It was a practiced maneuver.

Brian O'Regan, forty-one, another police officer from Henry's Bedford-Stuyvesant command—the 77th Precinct—was calling. O'Regan wanted to talk about the job. He had just finished working a midnight tour, and he was excited.

Brian O'Regan was about to engage in the single most important conversation of his life. It would be replayed before a special grand jury hearing evidence in the most widespread case of police corruption in New York City since the days of the Knapp Commission. One morning phone call to Henry Winter's bedroom would ultimately lead a corrupt cop to the most desperate of acts.

"We had a very good night last night," Brian said.

"Ver-ry goo-ood," Henry replied. Now he needed to get

more information. His role as an undercover cop demanded specific dates and times.

"What happened, Brian?"

"Oh, we got a job, Twelve-sixty Pacific Street, man with a gun, we had a complainant and all."

"Twelve-sixty?"

"Yeah. Above the Chinese restaurant, Pacific and No-strand. Last night we had a gun run there. And we met a complainant who's the superintendent of the building. You would have loved this one—a Rastafarian man with all the dreadlocks, but he don't want anybody in the building with no guns. And he says, real quiet like to me, 'They're dealing cannabis in the second floor right apartment.' So Junior bangs on the door and they let him and the other guys into the apartment. Billy Gallagher's there. Sammy Bell. Billy Rivera. They're looking all over the place. Looking and looking. Don't find anything.

"I'm outside, just standing there in front of the building, finger up my ass as usual, thinking, 'What the hell's the story? What are they doing in there?' I look up at the fire escape. And ho-ly shit, there's a fucking wad of money sitting on the fire escape."

"On the fire escape?"

"I hauled ass upstairs. 'Junior! Junior!' I grabbed him. 'Go to the front. The fire escape near the left window. All the way in the corner. Look, and get out there as fast as you can, some of the money is blowing away.'

"He goes out there. He calls me out in the hallway. He says, 'Come here.' He says, 'What the fuck are we going to do with all of this?' There's a big wad of ones, tens, twenties. I says, 'Oh, shit. We're gonna have to voucher some of this.' They had one hundred and seven nickel bags of marijuana. So I bring the money inside another room. I tell Junior,

'Gimme the shit.' And then I started shoving some money in my pocket, shoving it in my socks and everywhere else."

"Beautiful," Henry said.

"I grabbed Sammy and said, 'Look, I found it.' He says, 'Oh man, there's a lot there.' So I vouchered one hundred and eighty dollars. One-eight-oh."

"One eighty?"

"One-eight-oh," Brian said. "We did nine-six-oh. Apiece."

Henry was stunned. The cops had hit a jackpot.

"Nine . . . You did nine hundred and sixty dollars apiece?"

"Yep."

"Nine-sixty for you, nine-sixty for Junior?"

"Yep."

Henry needed to know about the other cops now. Had they been given a share of the stolen money?

"And did you throw Sammy or Billy anything?" he asked.

"We couldn't."

"Oh yeah, because you don't know how good they are." Henry sounded disappointed.

"That's it. I mean, hey, naturally we would, but I'm afraid, you know. I don't know anything about these guys. What am I gonna do, Henry? If you don't know who you're with, you can't just go, 'Here's yours.' "

"No, Brian, you can't."

After a pause, Brian began again.

"Yeah. Then we did Classon Avenue."

"Classon and where?" Henry wanted to know.

"Between Dean and Bergen."

"Yeah, how did you do there?"

"Very bad. Seventy dollars and some of that funny stuff."

Henry would have to be careful here. He would have to know how much drugs had been stolen and what kind. He would offer to fence the stolen drugs for O'Regan. Then he could turn them over to a prosecutor.

"What's funny stuff?" Henry asked, already realizing that Brian had stolen crack, a mutant form of cocaine that is smoked in a pipe.

"The funny stuff in the capsules."

"Oh, the crack."

"Yeah."

"And I got fifty-eight for you, Henry."

"Fifty-eight what?"

"Funny things in capsules," Brian said. "You want them?"

"Yeah, Brian. You want me to get rid of them for you? I can ask my guy and see if he wants them."

Brian sounded nervous. "Is he safe?"

"He's good. Don't worry about him, Brian. He's excellent. Figure on getting about four hundred dollars."

"Are you kidding me?"

"No. He generally takes a third, so I give you two-thirds. I'll give him a call tonight."

"All right. Anything on stereos, televisions, VCRs?"

The prosecutors were up to their ears in electronic equipment. They wanted stolen drugs and guns. There are more headlines in New York City cops stealing drugs and guns, Henry had heard them say.

"No, that's dead," he said.

"So we shouldn't even worry about taking that stuff no more?"

Henry hesitated. He didn't want to be in the position of asking cops not to steal.

"Let me try and call this guy Tuesday and see what's happening," he said.

"Okay. So we only came out of Dean and Classon with seventy dollars. Plus we got eight no-responses."

In other words, the dispatcher had tried to reach O'Regan

18

and his partner on eight separate occasions at twenty-minute intervals. O'Regan and Gallagher had spent close to a third of their tour robbing people, Henry calculated.

"That sucks," Henry commiserated.

"Yeah. But I told them we were on a job at Bergen and Nostrand. We covered there. That was no problem."

"Hey, tell them to scratch," Henry said.

"That was that. But while we were at Classon I was talking to a guy upstairs. And I told him we're coming down on this crack. And he told me, 'Why don't you go down to Pacific and Classon. The all-night candy store. They're dealing heavy there."

"Oh, very good."

"It might be a place you guys could do. He says he thinks it's crack and reefer."

"Pacific and Classon. Oh yeah, I think I know the place. It's got the game machines in front?"

"You got it, Henry."

"Oh good. Then we'll take a look at him. That's all. Take a look and see what the hell goes on."

"It was a good week for us."

"Okay Brian, I got to go. I got to jump in the shower."

"Okay. See you in the morning."

"Right-o, Buddy Boy."

Henry Winter hung up the phone and switched off the recording machine. Then he looked up to find his wife standing in the bedroom doorway, staring down at him. Henry rewound the tape and played it for her. The conversation was a good one, an incriminating one. The special state prosecutor would be very pleased with Henry Winter's work.

If Brian O'Regan had actually done everything he had just told Henry Winter about, O'Regan had talked his way into an indictment.

1

"We have a deal."

Henry Winter was in the mood to catch some blues.

Out in Jamaica Bay and Long Island Sound, schools of bluefish were already starting their summer spawning run. By early summer, the waters would be bubbling with frenzied schools of bluefish traveling in hunting parties half a mile wide and an eighth of a mile long.

They are a strong, pugnacious breed—a fish that can weigh as much as thirty pounds and fight twice its weight. Built like missiles, bluefish have long, sharp, and irregular teeth, delicate blue scales, and a thin backbone. Fishermen regard them as demented fish—hunters that lose all self-control in the presence of too much of a good thing.

When the blues are running, a school will slam into a

fisherman's boat, flopping against the sides and devouring anything he throws into the bait slick—chopped-up mackerel, butterfish, cigarette butts, paper, even beer bottle caps. Excited bluefish will eat, vomit, and eat again. They think nothing of taking single bites out of passing fish from their own school. And if a fisherman keeps a small bluefish on the line too long, a larger one will come along and gobble it up. Once you get a school of bluefish in an eating frenzy, it is impossible not to catch them.

The blues were Henry Winter's favorite fish. He liked the fight in them, and the fact that although they traveled in great blue waves, they were really only interested in preserving their own individual lives. Bluefish even reminded Henry of the cops he worked with in Bedford-Stuyvesant's 77th Precinct. Once the blue-jacketed cops had worked themselves into a stealing frenzy, their adrenaline pumping, there was no stopping them. They stole whatever was put in front of them on the streets—money, drugs, cars, electronics equipment, garbage cans, cigarettes, batteries, beer, and newspapers. It would be impossible not to catch them.

Henry woke shortly before 7 A.M. on May 23, 1986. It was Friday, the first day of a three-day weekend for him. The morning dawned clear, crisp, and bright, a fisherman's day, a day to bag your limit.

He dressed quickly and quietly, careful not to wake his wife and their two daughters. He slipped into a pair of shorts and pulled white jogging pants over them. The elastic band was just slightly uncomfortable. At thirty-four, the six-foot cop was developing a new plumpness.

Looking like a sailor in white pants, a white T-shirt and white sneakers, Henry emerged from his house. He headed for the garage and packed up his fishing gear, loading it into the back of a blue 1982 Ford pickup truck, then returned to the house and the refrigerator, filling a small plastic cooler with ice and seven-ounce bottles of Budweiser. He placed the cooler in the back of his boat, an eighteen-foot Cobia christened *Bolt Action,* and secured his outboard motor, a water-cooled, seventy-horsepower Mercury. Then he hooked up the boat trailer to his truck and headed out.

Henry never even noticed the maroon Buick following him—a car filled with the kind of cops who bait city streets for a living, waiting for crooked cops to bite. His movements on that day are well documented. He drove west along the Belt Parkway, breaking off the highway at the exit for Cross Bay Boulevard in Howard Beach, Queens, continuing south across a toll bridge that led to the narrow strip of Queens called the Rockaways.

Stopping briefly at a delicatessen, Henry ordered a bagel with cream cheese and peppers to go, with a chocolate Yoo-Hoo soda. Then he stopped at a bait shop to get something for the blues—a two-and-a-half gallon container of chum, a box of butterfish, and fourteen sickly looking mackerel.

On Beach Channel Drive in Rockaway Henry put his boat in the water at a public launch, leaving his truck and trailer parked in a lot across the street from a McDonald's restaurant. Within an hour after leaving his home, Henry was on the water, motoring through an inlet and out into the Atlantic Ocean until he reached the Ambrose light tower six miles out.

There were already several boats in the area by the time he arrived. Some of them were drifting, a sure sign that they were fishing for fluke, a flat fish that looks sort of like a flounder with the measles.

Henry spent the rest of the morning chumming for bluefish, and caught three ranging from six to ten pounds. Before noon he headed back toward the inlet, drifting for fluke but continuing to bounce a butterfish along the ocean floor in hope of catching one more blue. He landed a dozen flukes but none of them were fourteen inches long—big enough to keep.

The watcher studying Henry Winter through binoculars was surprised at the patrolman's display of lawfulness. It was odd that the same Henry Winter who took bribes from ghetto drug dealers would not steal from the sea. The watcher wondered what set of rules guided this cop's life.

By two o'clock Henry had packed up his gear and headed back in. Judging by the size of his catch, some might have said that he had had a bad day fishing. But he was happy. He regarded any day on the water as a good one. He hardly even noticed his sunburn—or the group of men in sports coats scrambling for their cars as he pulled up to the landing.

After loading *Bolt Action* onto the trailer, Henry secured his gear and engine and headed back home. He stopped briefly as he entered Howard Beach to inquire how some men fishing off a bridge with drop lines had fared with the fluke, then he continued onto South Conduit Avenue. He had traveled about three-quarters of a mile when he heard a car horn behind him.

Checking his rear view mirror, Henry saw two white men in a maroon Buick waving at him frantically, a red, flashing dome light on the dashboard between them. He didn't hear a siren, but then he knew what the cops wanted. Police Officer Henry Winter was driving an unregistered boat trailer. He would have to talk the traffic cops out of writing him a forty dollar ticket.

The Buick pulled up along the left side of Henry's truck. The man in the passenger seat waved a gold shield out of the car's window.

"Pull over," the cop yelled.

"Ah, shit," Henry thought. "Haven't these traffic humps got anything better to do?"

He parked his truck on the shoulder and got out. As he walked to the back of the pickup, two more unmarked cars pulled up in front of the truck. Now Henry was surrounded by three sets of badges. Two cops wore bulletproof vests over their sports coats.

"What's the problem, guys?"

"I'm Lieutenant Andrew Panico from Internal Affairs Division," a man said. "I'm placing you in custody."

"What for?"

"Official misconduct and three counts of bribery receiving," Panico answered.

"That's bullshit."

"Turn around and put your hands behind your back."

Henry put his arms back. A cop stepped forward and snapped handcuffs around his wrists.

"Where's your gun?" Panico demanded.

"Under the front seat of the truck."

Winter was dazed. For the first time in his life, someone had put handcuffs on him. He had done the same thing to other people a thousand times. Now he felt disoriented, violated, humiliated. A cop led him by the arm to the Buick.

"What about my truck?"

"We'll park it for you, officer."

"The fucking car is my car," Henry exploded. "It's a clutch. You're talking about moving a truck. I got a boat on the back of it. I've got an expensive fishing rod. The gear alone in that truck is worth more than your fucking car. Let me park my truck."

"No, we'll move your truck."

The officers put their prisoner in the back of the Buick. Henry knew the routine. Any minute now one of the cops would start reading him the *Miranda* warning from a small card. "You have the right to remain silent . . ."

But there was no warning, no words.

"What's going on?" Henry finally asked as the car shot along the Belt Parkway on Brooklyn's underbelly.

"Don't say anything," Panico said. "We're not talking to you. You're not talking to us."

Henry shifted back in his seat. He tried to fill the car with an air of coolness. "They're just cops," he thought. "Cops can't frighten me." But then, as happens with all cops who suddenly find themselves wearing handcuffs, he thought of the worst possible scenario. This was going to make the six o'clock news, he realized. Betsy Winter was going to see her husband walk across a television screen in handcuffs.

"I've got to call my wife," he said. "I want to make my phone call."

"No phone calls," Panico said.

No phone calls? Now Henry's head was reeling. And his confusion only deepened as the Buick headed into Manhattan, passing through the Brooklyn-Battery Tunnel. Once free of the tunnel, the driver made a sharp right turn, parking on a deserted side street near Battery Park.

"Look, we're taking the handcuffs off you," Panico said. "Don't be foolish. Just do what we tell you to do."

"No problem. Look, I'm not a bad guy. I'm not here to hurt you or myself. Let's just do what we have to do."

Henry believed he was being taken to One Police Plaza and Central Booking. He expected to be suspended from the force, arrested, his fingerprints taken, and jailed until his arraignment. Instead, the cops led him down a street in the opposite direction from police headquarters. They escorted him into a towering stone office building at Two Rector Street—only a short distance from Wall Street.

Surrounded by four cops, Winter walked into the unmarked building and took the elevator to the twenty-third floor, where he spotted a sign—Office of the New York State Special Prosecutor for Corruption.

"Oh shit," Henry thought to himself. "These guys are serious."

The cops escorted Henry down a narrow corridor and left him alone in a small room for what seemed an eternity— approximately ten minutes. Two officers spied on him through an open doorway from across the hall. They did not want their prisoner jumping out of a window. Henry Winter was too valuable to lose now.

Men in suits, smelling of fine cologne, made short visits to the room. They spoke in soft, agreeable tones. Henry made them for lawyers.

"Can I get you any coffee, Henry?" one asked. "Coffee, cigarettes, or anything?"

"No."

Henry had played the role of good cop to his partner Tony Magno's bad cop routine long enough to know what was happening now. The investigators were loosening him up, looking for a soft spot. It was like a game after a while. He would ask to make a phone call. The lawyers would deny him access to a phone. Men paraded into the room one by one, saying essentially the same thing.

"You have to think of your family now, Henry."

"Henry. Now's the time to think of your wife and kids."

The strategy was working too, because by the time State Special Prosecutor Charles J. Hynes entered the room an hour later, all Henry could think about was his family.

"Come here," Hynes said gruffly, never even bothering to identify himself. "I want to show you something."

Hynes led Winter into a large adjoining room where a group of twelve men sat around a rectangular table. Each man had a small pile of papers stacked neatly in front of him. Henry was told to sit facing a television, a videotape recorder, and a tape recorder.

"I don't want you to say anything," Hynes said. "I just want you to listen and read." One investigator handed Henry a set of headphones. Another produced a typed transcript for him to read.

He recognized the first voice on the tape instantly. It belonged to Benny Burwell, a forty-eight-year-old cocaine and marijuana dealer from Bedford-Stuyvesant. Benny had a drug operation set up in the 77th Precinct near an area patrolled by Police Officers Henry Winter and Tony Magno—Sector Ida-John. Benny had been paying Henry and Tony to protect his drug operation for months. The cops had never actually done anything to protect Benny, but they had taken regular payments from him. Lots of cash. Lots of times.

Then in early 1986 Benny was arrested by another cop in the 77th Precinct who wasn't renting out his shield, and who caught Benny with close to a pound of cocaine. Major weight. Felony weight. Benny knew he was going to jail. So he told his probation officer to get in touch with the Brooklyn district attorney. Then Benny sat down with the prosecutor and said the magic words.

"I can give you cops. I've been paying off cops in the Seventy-seventh Precinct for years."

When pressed, Benny mentioned the right names—Henry Winter and Tony Magno, two cops already suspected of taking bribes. Elizabeth Holtzman, the Brooklyn district attorney, turned the case over to Hynes, a special prosecutor with close ties to Governor Mario Cuomo. Working in conjunction with the Police Department's Internal Affairs Division, Hynes outfitted Benny Burwell with a tape recorder and supplied him with payoff money. The dealer had been out on the streets trying to bribe cops since February.

Henry wasn't really shocked. Not at first, anyway. "All right," he thought. "They wired Benny. They turned a mutt drug dealer to get us. They got me and Benny talking and they got Benny giving me money. Okay, that's good. But how are they going to prove it?"

A former city fire commissioner who had made his name as an investigator during a statewide nursing home scandal, Hynes had carefully orchestrated this entire production. He seemed to be reading Henry Winter's mind.

"Now look up," Hynes said in his most dispassionate voice. "On the television screen."

An investigator reached past Henry to push a VHS tape into the recorder. Henry's image, wearing his blue uniform, appeared on the screen alongside Benny, who was holding up a brown paper bag full of money. Benny handed the bag to Henry.

"Thanks," Henry heard himself say.

The investigators produced two other tapes of Henry and Benny. Each contained the same critical scene, the one where the cop accepts the payoff from a man he knows to be a drug dealer. Henry watched, but he did not see. He knew they had him. But every once in a while someone would ask him, "Had enough, Henry? See enough yet?"

Finally Henry took off his headphones.

"I saw enough."

"Don't say anything," an investigator said. "We don't want to know anything. Just think of your family."

He was led to a room and left alone again. He asked to make a phone call.

"I got to call my wife. She's going to be looking for me."

"No phone calls," he was told again. "You can't call any-one."

By now it was close to five o'clock. Henry's wife was getting ready to contact the Coast Guard. His brother-in-law was already out looking for him. The people Henry loved were concerned about him. But he was beginning to worry about someone else.

"Where's my partner?" he thought. "How could they grab me and not Tony?"

While he waited, a lieutenant from the Internal Affairs Division suddenly entered the room.

"We have a problem," the cop began. "We've been sitting outside your partner's house since seven o'clock this morn-ing."

"So?"

"Well, we got to get him out of the house. He's been in there all day and only came out once to walk the dog. It's up to you to get him out."

"Up to me?"

"Yeah."

He was told that he had to come up with a plan to get Tony out of his house. "We don't want anybody to know we're grabbing him, we don't even want his wife and kids to know we're taking him."

"Let me go get him. You drive me out there, park, let me out at the corner, I'll call and tell him my truck broke down. He'll come out. But promise me first that you'll give me a second to talk to him before you grab him."

The investigators, lawyers, and prosecutors all agreed to go along with Winter's plan for taking his partner into cus-tody. They piled into four cars and headed back through the Battery Tunnel into Brooklyn. The Borough of Churches. And confessions.

* * *

29

Tony Magno was cursing, again. Standing on the toilet bowl, he was trying to hang silver and white foil wallpaper on his bathroom wall. The paper slipped and crinkled under his hands.

"Goddamn it," Tony yelled. "Hanging this shit is like trying to nail fucking Jell-O to a wall."

A seventeen-year veteran of the force who had spent his entire career in the 77th Precinct, Magno rarely left the sanctuary of his home on his days off. During the work week it was different. Tony drank beer with his buddies in the backs of grocery stores—called bodegas in the ghetto whether they were owned by Hispanics or not—and held court in the precinct locker room. He was liked by younger cops and veterans and was considered to be a leader who knew the ins and outs of the job.

Some cops even idolized Tony Magno. He knew when to slap on the handcuffs and when to let someone go. He could handle a domestic dispute one minute, calming down an irate husband who started a fight with his wife after finding hot dogs on the dinner table instead of meat loaf, and the next minute grab a loaded gun out of a robber's hand. He was considered to be a cop's cop—had assisted on thousands of arrests, grabbed bad guys, and delivered babies. Just a cop. Just another Constable on Patrol in the city of New York.

But Magno also had a bad temper. And his tendency toward violence had led other cops to nickname him Tony the Jack years earlier. He always liked to say that when he swung his nightstick it was a pure act, a movement untainted by either prejudice or favoritism. Other cops took this statement to mean that Tony the Jack would strike any prisoner anywhere, anytime the spirit moved him.

A stately six-foot-two, 190-pound Italian, Tony had dark

brown hair that he combed straight back. He was the picture of good grooming, given to wearing starched shirts and creased slacks. A neat black mustache accentuated an even neater set of teeth. And whenever Tony Magno smiled, the whole 77th Precinct seemed to light up.

But he wasn't smiling now, and he wasn't dressed very well. He had gobs of plaster in his hair and wet streaks of wallpaper paste on his old black chinos and white T-shirt. He had spent his entire day in the bathroom, a cold can of Budweiser at the ready, wondering why he had ever agreed to spend the first day of his three-day swing hanging foil wallpaper.

Keeping a careful distance from her frustrated husband, Marianne Magno had just put dinner on the stove when the telephone rang shortly after 5 P.M. Henry Winter was calling. And Henry Winter rarely called Tony Magno at home.

Marianne was no fan of her husband's partner. She had heard a lot of rumors about him. Frankly, she didn't trust him, and she didn't trust her husband when he was with Henry. So now, Marianne rolled her eyes and handed her husband the telephone.

"It's him," she said. "Your partner."

"Tony, I got to talk to you," Henry began.

The cop's voice was low and filled with concern.

"Are we in trouble?" Tony asked immediately.

"Yeah, in a way. I got to meet you."

"Jesus, I'm in the middle of hanging wallpaper in the bathroom."

"I got to meet you."

"Is it that important, Henry?"

"Yeah."

"Okay, when do you want to meet?"

"Right now," Henry said.

"Well, where are you?"

"Right here. Right in the pizzeria on your corner."

"Ooooh shit," Tony said.

"Yeah, it's important. I got to talk to you."

"Okay, I'll be right down."

Tony hung up the phone and turned to face his wife.

"What's the matter?" Marianne asked, her voice already boiling with suspicion.

"I have to meet Henry. He's right on the corner. I'll only be a few minutes. He's just got to tell me something. I'll be right back for dinner."

"All right," she said. "But don't forget I'm cooking."

Magno walked out his front door wearing dirty chinos, a blue rag hanging out of his back pocket. He hadn't bothered to take his wallet or a pack of Pall Mall cigarettes off his bedroom bureau.

Tony walked a block over to the corner of McDonald and Avenue N where he spotted Henry sitting inside Vinnie's Pizzeria, gobbling down a slice of cheese pizza and finishing off a Coke.

"What is it, Henry?"

"They got us."

"What do you mean they got us?" Tony asked, gesturing wildly with his hands.

"Internal Affairs got me. I'm under arrest, Tony."

"Ho-ly shit."

Tony paused for a second, afraid even to mouth the words of his next question.

"What about me?"

"I guess you too."

"Oh, God."

Tony's hands shook. He scanned the room, wide-eyed,

searching the booths and counter seats for undercover cops.

"Tony. Now don't do nothing. Don't say nothing. Don't try to run. Don't do anything. But they're all around us."

"Where?"

"Right outside, Tony. Calm down."

"Okay Henry. All right. All right."

As the partners walked out of the store, a half-dozen police officers in plain clothes descended upon them, leading them off to separate unmarked cars.

"Have you got your gun, Tony?" Lieutenant Panico asked.

"I got nothing. I don't even have a penny in my pocket."

Tony was placed in a car along with two lieutenants and a police officer from Internal Affairs.

"We want you to come with us," Panico said. "We want you to see something. The special prosecutor wants to talk to you."

"Just let me call my wife and I'll go anywhere you guys want me to go."

"No. No phone calls."

Magno pleaded with the investigators to let him call his wife. He asked to go home and change his clothes, to be able to tell his wife where he was going.

"Am I under arrest?"

"Technically," Panico said.

"You can't do this. This is illegal."

"Believe me," Lieutenant Panico replied evenly. "We can do it. The guy sitting next to you, Lieutenant Frohme, is a lawyer. You can't ask for a lawyer. You can't ask for union representation. Think of your wife and kids on this."

Tony was frightened and confused. In all of his days of arresting people he had never heard of anyone being "technically" under arrest. Either you were under arrest, or you weren't. Finally, as they sat in the parked car debating the law, Tony spotted his thirteen-year-old son, Anthony, Jr., rounding the corner. The boy was searching the neighborhood for his dad, who was already twenty minutes late for supper. Tony watched his son shrug his shoulders after checking the avenue stores and then head back home. He wanted desperately to be out there with his son again. His eyes filled with tears.

"That's my son. He's looking for me. Please, let me go home."

"You can't," Panico said. "You got to trust me. You gotta do it this way. They just want to talk to you. See what they have to say."

"Okay, let's go," Tony decided, finally.

During the ride to the special prosecutor's office in Manhattan, Tony began to relax. The cops explained that he was not being arrested just yet and that he might even be able to call his wife soon. One of them mentioned that they had been sitting on Magno's house all day, waiting for him to come out.

"The least you guys could have done was come up and help me finish hanging the wallpaper," Tony Magno replied.

He was led into the building and then up to the twenty-third floor, past a smaller room where Henry Winter sat. Tony walked into the big conference room where the men in ties sat around the large table and television. The headphones and transcripts came out again.

"All we want you to do is listen and read," an investigator said. "Listen, read, and watch."

Tony also recognized Benny's voice right away. Henry had told him they were in trouble, and Benny's voice confirmed it. He heard himself accept a payoff from Benny. On the screen, he saw his lips moving.

"Gee, Benny. We missed you for Easter."

On another tape, Magno watched Henry take a bag of money from Benny.

"Yeah, if anybody gives you any trouble, just let us know," Henry said. "We'll take care of it."

A third tape focused on an incriminating conversation between Tony and Benny at the door of the squad car.

"Any of the guys giving you a hard time, Benny?" Tony heard himself say.

He only noticed two things about the incriminating evidence: The television picture was clear and the voice on the tapes was unmistakably his own.

"Oh yeah," Tony thought to himself. "I remember these scenes like yesterday."

As the last tape concluded, Hynes suddenly stood up, introducing himself as a special prosecutor for the state of New York and a deputy attorney general. Still playing the bad cop role to his assistant's good cop act, Hynes stated, "You saw yourself. That's you on that tape there. We know what's going on in the Seventy-seventh Precinct. We've been after that precinct for a long time. And now we have you. We want your cooperation. If you have anything for us that we could use in this investigation, it could benefit you."

Hynes paused a moment, like an auctioneer preparing to drop the hammer.

"If you don't cooperate with us, I will personally prosecute you to the full letter of the law. I'll make the terms run consecutively. You'll be doing nine years."

Tony's hands and knees shook. An investigator handed him a filtered cigarette. Tony snapped off the filter and lit the remainder of the sawed-off cigarette, puffing madly as he smoked.

"Can I talk to my partner?"

"Yeah, you can talk to your partner," a lawyer said. "We want you both to make the same decision. And whichever way you go, that's the way things will go."

The investigators led Tony to an adjoining room where he was joined by his partner. Hynes had already told Henry that he might not have to go to jail if he agreed to cooperate.

"We're going to leave you two alone to talk things over," an investigator said.

The two men sat across a table from each other, smoking cigarettes, trying to make a decision that would determine their own fate and ultimately the fates of nearly twenty-five other New York City cops.

"Henry, what are we going to do?"

"I don't know. It's up to you. You're senior man."

"Look Henry, I don't want to go to jail."

"Well I don't want to go to jail either."

"Do we cooperate with them, Henry?"

"I don't know. Do we?"

And that's the way it went—Tony asking questions and Henry repeating them.

"I want to go home tonight, Henry. Do you want to go home tonight?"

"Yeah, I want to go home too."

"Then I guess we have no choice, Henry. I guess we'll cooperate."

"Whatever you want to do. You want to cooperate, Tony, we'll cooperate."

"We got to do this together all the way, Henry. Not that bullshit where they stick you in one room and me in another room and pretty soon we're going at each other."

"No," Henry agreed. "We got to stay together through the whole thing."

"Okay. Then we'll do it that way. As long as we're together, then I don't give a fuck."

Henry and Tony returned to the conference room and sat down at the table. There wasn't an available seat in the room. Hynes sat on the opposite side of the table, his shirt open and his tie askew. Henry remembered that the prosecutor's hands were folded. Tony would recall that Hynes looked priestly.

"We agree to cooperate with you," Henry said.

"We'll do whatever you want," Tony added.

Hynes stood up.

"Okay," he said firmly. "Now I want names."

Henry and Tony were startled. They were being asked to give up other cops, to identify other cops as criminals, right now. Tonight.

At that point, Tony spotted two piles of photographs stacked on the table across from him. An investigator started thumbing through a smaller pile of pictures.

"William Gallagher." He held up the cop's picture for everyone to see. "What does he do?"

"He would take things," Tony began.

"Brian O'Regan. What would he do?"

"He will steal things," Henry volunteered.

"Robert Rathbun. What would he do?"

"He'll steal drugs." Henry and Tony both agreed.

"Crystal Spivey. What does she do?"

"I think she does drugs," Henry said.

And so it went, with the prosecutors producing photographs and asking questions and the frightened cops giving up information. They worked through the smaller pile and then into the bigger pile. Winter and Magno identified approximately twenty-five of their fellow officers as men and women who would rob drug dealers, break into apartments, take money from dead bodies and use drugs. They spent the better part of an hour identifying their fellow police officers as robbers, drug users and car thieves.

At one point a lawyer left the room to get an even larger stack of photographs. One by one, the police officers offered information—either good or bad—on every cop in their precinct, roughly two hundred people.

After Henry and Tony had finished identifying the suspected criminals in the 77th Precinct, the investigators filed out of the room taking their photographs with them. Oddly, neither man felt shamed by what he had just done. The words had come from their lips freely.

"Do you realize what we just did?" Tony asked.

"What else could we do?" Henry said. "I ain't going to jail."

"Me neither. Let's just tell them what they want and get the hell out of here."

A moment later Hynes reentered the room with his aides. He offered his hand to Henry and Tony. The three men shook hands.

"We have a deal," Hynes said, smiling.

Henry and Tony remained expressionless. They were going home. Later Hynes explained that the men had been "unarrested." He told them they would have to wear recording devices during the investigation and meet secretly with Internal Affairs operatives in the middle of the night. They were given a special telephone number to call day or night, something called a "hello number." An investigator manned the phone twenty-four hours a day during the investigation, answering incoming calls with a simple, "Hello." If discovered, the telephone number could not be traced.

"You can't tell anybody about this investigation," an aide said. "That means friends, family, and other cops. You can't even tell your wife about this unless you can trust her. If word gets out, all bets are off. You go to jail."

Henry and Tony were advised that they would have to testify in court against the cops they caught stealing, probably some of their friends. Later, they would be asked to catalogue every crime they had ever committed. They would be given full immunity for all past crimes but murder.

In exchange for their cooperation, Henry Winter and Tony Magno were given a simple deal.

"No jail," Hynes promised. "No jail time whatsoever."

An investigator slid Henry's gun and shield to him across the table. The officers were still on the job. They were told to report to work in the 77th Precinct on Monday morning.

They left the building shortly after 11 P.M. Henry was driven back to his truck, which was parked at a motel near John F. Kennedy Airport. All of his fishing gear had been taken off the boat and packed into the truck. The only things missing were the three bluefish. Someone had stolen the day's catch.

Still shaking, his body drained of emotion, Henry started to drive home. He pulled off to the side of the Belt Parkway and cried. Then he took out his gun. He stared into the barrel for a moment, pondering what he had just done and what he would have to do in order to stay out of jail.

But Henry Winter could not shoot himself. He wasn't strong—or weak—enough for that. He was just dazed, an unfeeling hollow man. He would never again be the same cop who had left his house nearly sixteen hours earlier in hopes of catching some fish and sun.

The fisherman went home and made up a story. He didn't

want his wife to know her husband was a rat, at least not yet. So he fabricated a tale about a broken propeller and being marooned at sea for eight hours. Betsy believed him.

Henry Winter was already starting to live a lie.

A police officer assigned to the Internal Affairs Division, Al Pignataro, drove Tony Magno back to Midwood.

"There are guys that have been in worse positions than you," Pignataro said. "You'll be okay."

But Tony wasn't even thinking about what he had just done. He was thinking about what he was going to tell his wife.

He knew he was in trouble the minute he walked in the door. Marianne was standing by the kitchen with a drink in her hand. And Marianne is not a drinker.

"You no good son-of-a-bitch," she said, figuring that her husband had been out partying somewhere with his partner for the last six hours.

"Please," Tony whispered. "Wait until the kids go to bed."

"If you want to be with Henry Winter so much, why don't you just leave us and move in with him?" Marianne yelled.

"Look, I'm in trouble."

Marianne hesitated, pausing in midcurse.

"Marianne, I'm in a lot of trouble. Wait until the kids go to sleep."

He walked to the refrigerator and grabbed a beer.

"Come on, honey," Tony said. "Help me hang another piece of wallpaper."

Later that night the couple sat on their bed. Suddenly it seemed huge. Marianne sat on one corner waiting to listen, and Tony sat on the other corner waiting to talk. He didn't know how to explain without making himself sound like a crook. He did not want to lose his wife now.

"Look," he began. "I don't know how to tell you this, but I was arrested."

"What?"

"Technically I was arrested. But not really arrested."

In time, Tony revealed everything, explaining how he had accepted bribes, broken into apartments, and robbed drug dealers. He just sat on the corner of his bed, telling his wife that the cop she had married was really a thief. Marianne sat smoking a cigarette, pretending that her heart wasn't really broken. But the tears gave her away.

"Didn't you think of me and the kids?"

"It may sound crazy, but I was thinking of you and the kids."

Marianne looked at her husband like he was crazy.

"How can you say that?" she said, her voice cracking. "You were thinking of me and the kids when you were taking money from a drug dealer?"

"Yeah. Remember the money squabbles we used to have all the time? You were always running short of cash? You were reaching into the house money?"

"So what? Did I ask you for extra money? Did I need extra money? I didn't care about money. We were happier when we had nothing. I should have realized that something was going on in the last couple of years. You changed. There was something different about you. I don't know what it was. But I knew it had something to do with him."

"I'm not gonna blame Henry. It's not his fault. He didn't put a gun to my head. But now there are a couple of things I can do. I can go to jail or I can cooperate. If I cooperate some guys could go to jail. Guys you know. What do you want me to do?"

Marianne looked at her husband like he had six heads—all of them empty.

"What do you mean, what do I want you to do? I'm not going to tell you to go against your friends. But I don't want you to go to jail. I don't want you to do anything. This is something you got to live with. These are your friends. You've got to live with this the rest of your life."

"I'm not making any decision until you tell me what you want me to do."

Marianne finished the discussion at 4 A.M. "All I'm telling you is that I don't want you to go to jail."

Tony Magno knew exactly what he would have to do. The most trusted and popular cop in the 77th Precinct would have to help send his friends to jail. He would remain Henry Winter's partner. And they would become the first partners in the history of the New York City Police Department to turn against an entire precinct.

2

"Some of you will be arrested."

When Henry F. Winter was born on July 29, 1952, a group of nurses in a Queens hospital gathered near the infant's bassinet. With his turquoise-colored eyes and curly wisp of amber hair, little Henry was the talk of the maternity ward.

"Get a load of Blondie," one nurse was heard to say. "He's the most perfect baby in here."

The child's father, Henry H. Winter, felt his chest inflate when he heard these words. Earlier that year, Winter, a floor supervisor with a Schlitz beer distributorship in Brooklyn, had moved his wife and two children out of a tiny New York City apartment and into a suburban world of polished cars, manicured lawns, and commuter trains. For $8,500 he bought a two-story, wooden frame home with a finished basement and one-car garage in the Long Island village of Valley Stream, turning his back on the big city and its problems.

There was a comfortable world awaiting little Henry Winter. And at that moment, no one could have imagined what the name Henry Winter or the nickname Blondie would mean to drug dealers and crooked police officers in Bedford-Stuyvesant, Brooklyn's black ghetto.

Mildred Winter doesn't remember the first time her son Henry uttered the word "cop." But she can recall his fascination with guns and badges, and the many times he imagined himself a miniature Eliot Ness or a pint-sized Joe Friday. There was even a day when ten-year old Henry sat his mother down at the kitchen table and interrogated her with a plastic gun.

"Just the facts, mom," he insisted.

As a kid Henry liked three things—cops, guns, and hunting. He grew up catching things, using a pole to pull carp out of a pond behind Central High School and tracking down rabbits with a bow and arrow in a field near his house. Henry liked to imagine the scurrying animals as fleeing felons. There was no place to hide from a fledgling twelve-year old New York City police officer named Henry Winter.

In the mid-1960s when other kids gathered to play catch on neighborhood baseball diamonds and talk about their idols Mickey Mantle and Whitey Ford, Henry retired to his father's basement den. He would stand before a mirror and push live .38-caliber shells into his father's handgun.

"Freeze!" he'd yell, assuming the classic combat position and pointing the gun at his own image. "Police officer!"

Certainly Henry knew right from wrong at an early age, having attended a Catholic grammar school, Blessed Sacrament, from first through sixth grades. He also learned about trust in school. His best friend was Jimmy Hoffman, a neighbor and classmate. Regarded as the class hellions by the nuns, Hoffman and Winter spent a good portion of each school day sitting outside the principal's office, begging forgiveness.

One day the nuns caught Jimmy Hoffman painting a mustache on a hallway statue of the Virgin Mary. Statues of Jesus and Saint Joseph had been similarly defaced. Hoffman had signed the art work with the letters "J" and "H." Suspecting that Hoffman had an accomplice, the nuns called in Henry Winter for questioning. Henry feigned innocence, insisting that the letters "J" and "H" stood for Jimmy Hoffman. In another room, the nuns were threatening Jimmy with a priest. The word "Hell" was mentioned several times during the interrogation. Fearing eternal damnation, Jimmy Hoffman finally told all—confessing that the letters "J" and "H" really stood for Jimmy and Henry.

"The nuns never even offered Jimmy a deal," Henry remembered years later.

When they were thirteen, Jimmy and Henry were picked up by a team of Nassau County detectives as they walked along a pipeline in a wooded section of Valley Stream, taking potshots at squirrels with a BB gun. The cops, responding to a "man with a gun" call on the radio, surrounded the youths as they emerged from the woods at dusk, pulling their own weapons and yelling, "Freeze!"

Hoffman and Winter literally wet their pants. The equally shaken cops drove the kids home, warning them to be more careful.

At fourteen, Henry was in trouble again. He was driving to school one morning when he turned the corner and struck a fifteen-year-old boy riding a bicycle. The boy flew over Henry's car, breaking his leg. Cops led Henry away.

Although the charges against Henry were later dropped because of his age, Millie Winter's insurance company had to pay a sizable claim. Henry neglected to tell the cops investigating the accident that the car was actually his, or that his mother had registered and insured it for him.

The first time Henry Winter got near a cash register, when he was fifteen, he shortchanged it. Working in the sporting goods section of a Times Square department store near his home, he started running his own sales. Winter's buddies got an automatic 50 percent cash discount on everything from baseball gloves to fishing poles. Usually, anybody shopping in Henry's department got a bargain.

He watched intently one day as a black child tugged on his mother's arm, begging her to buy him a Giants helmet and shoulder pad set carrying a twenty-five dollar price tag.

"How much do you have," he finally asked the woman.

"Ten dollars."

"Sold. Bring it over here."

A store detective spying on the transaction later led Henry into a back room, where it was determined that he was both underage and working under an assumed name—Bruce Winter.

"I'm really only fifteen," Henry said confidently. "That makes me a youthful offender." The manager threw up his hands and fired the underage thief.

Henry graduated from Valley Stream Central High School in 1969. A card-carrying member of the National Rifle Association, he boycotted his graduation ceremony rather than join in a student demonstration.

"Everyone was supposed to refuse to stand during the national anthem. It was being done in high schools all across the country. But I argued about it because I thought we should stand. It's our country." Henry went fishing on graduation day.

As the first kid in his class with a car, Henry was very popular. He drove a 1956 Chevy Bel Air that his older sister Millie had painted over with large red roses and white daisies. A huge smiling face with two eyes stared out from the front grill. With his shoulder-length blonde hair and an interest in marijuana cigarettes, Henry was known on the streets of Valley Stream as Flower Power Hank.

In high school he had the rare ability to get along with both jocks and hippies. There was an incongruity in his life-style. Henry seemed as comfortable smoking a line drive single to center on the baseball diamond as he did partying after the games. Henry batted cleanup on the baseball team and played shortstop. He hit close to .600 in his junior year and spent a lot of time listening to Crosby, Stills, Nash and Young records as a senior. He especially liked a protest song entitled "Chicago"—a song that commemorated the 1968 riots involving young people and Chicago police in a park outside the Democratic National Convention.

"We can chaaange the world," Henry would sing, an eight-track tape blasting in his car. "Chi—ca—go. If you bee—lieeve in justice. Chi—ca—go. If you bee—lieeve in free—dom. Chi—ca—go. It's start—ing . . ."

But the thing that Henry Winter loved most about high school was love itself. As a fourteen-year-old sophomore, he met a seventeen-year-old senior named Betsy Bassett at a New Year's Eve party in his parent's basement. Henry's older brother, Bruce, on leave from the Air Force, had invited Betsy and one of her girlfriends to the party. Henry and Betsy milled around a polished pine bar in the basement, chatting quietly over beers while Bruce got drunk with Betsy's girlfriend upstairs.

When the party ended, Henry offered to walk Betsy home. But he ran out of sidewalk—she only lived three blocks away—and conversation.

"I was interested," Henry recalled. "But she was three years older. She seemed bored by the whole idea of me."

Three weeks later Betsy invited Henry to a high school sorority dance. Sometime during the night, she suggested that Henry join a fraternity. At first he balked at the idea— he didn't see much sense in hanging out with other guys when he could be dating girls—but he later joined a frat in order to pacify his new girlfriend.

Winter, who even years later rarely hung out with other cops while off-duty, came to be regarded by the brothers of Alpha Omega Theta as one of their sorriest pledges. He refused to be hit with a paddle, never shined anyone's shoes, and rarely brought seniors their coffee and bagels in the morning. One time the brothers succeeded in holding Winter down and paddling him for refusing to get a haircut. A week later, when the brothers threatened to paddle their long-haired pledge again, Winter quit the fraternity.

"It was either my ass or my hair," he recalled. "I decided to keep both."

In the process, Henry lost Betsy Bassett. She graduated that summer, leaving Flower Power Hank to patrol the high school parking lot by himself.

With Vietnam pounding in the distance, seventeen-year-old Henry Winter decided in 1968 that he would join the Army along with several high school buddies who had been drafted. The family threw a going-away party for him, bestowing on him a knapsack-load of address books, razors, and shaving cream. At 7 A.M. the next morning, Henry's mother dropped him off at the Army recruiting station in Fort Hamilton, Brooklyn. Henry was met by fourteen other scared-looking inductees and a muscle-bound sergeant with a square jaw.

"We are your mothers now, and anyone who doesn't want

to stay here can leave," the sergeant roared, pointing towards the door.

Henry turned and made eye contact with a black recruit standing next to him.

"I don't want to be here," the black teenager said.

"I've got to stay," Henry whispered. "They had a party for me and everything."

The two teenagers smiled, then walked out the front door, taking their address books, razors, and shaving cream home, missing the Vietnam War. Henry hitchhiked back to Valley Stream and threw himself a welcome-home party.

An Army recruiter continued to call his home for the next few days, but neither Henry nor his parents, who needed to sign a permission slip, would budge. Most of his buddies went off to war. Some of them even made it back home.

Henry spent most of his summers upstate and became an avid hunter. He especially liked deer hunting. And like the character played by Robert De Niro in the film *The Deer Hunter*, Henry abided by a single commandment in the woods. One deer. One shot.

He hunted with a single-shot 7 × 57 Ruger rifle. If he missed hitting the deer with his first shot, the animal was free to escape. He never reloaded. Amateurs reloaded. Henry also had another odd habit. Sometimes he would just chase a doe through the woods, screaming crazily, until he lost sight of the animal.

The hunting ritual caused a rift between the Winter brothers and their father. Henry's father would have liked to take both of them hunting, but Bruce preferred the ski lounges and the fireplaces.

The Winters soon noticed that their sons didn't seem to like each other much. Although they shared the same friends, the boys rarely shared each other's company. They did occasionally meet by accident on the streets, where their disputes quickly became neighborhood legend.

Living in a house with a one-car garage and three cars, the Winter brothers often raced each other home in order to get the only parking spot off the street. One day Henry, driving an Opel, arrived at one end of Washington Avenue just as Bruce, driving a Capri, rounded the corner at the opposite end of the block. The brothers zoomed down the block, each determined to reach the parking spot first. As neighbors watched, the cars smashed into each other head on, metal and glass flying. Henry and Bruce jumped from their steaming wrecks and proceeded to pummel each other in full view of their horrified parents.

"My father stuck up for the hunter," Henry remembered. "My mother stuck up for the designer clothes."

Eventually the brothers decided that neither the house nor garage was big enough for both of them. After graduation, Henry began to spend more and more time in a small upstate New York town called Cochecton Center, staring across a table at a girl named Kathy Costello. A part-time waitress and maid in a boarding house where Henry worked chopping wood and clearing brush, Kathy served him heaping piles of pancakes in the morning and hearty stew at night. She changed his sheets and vacuumed his room. The couple took moonlight walks on country roads and attended her senior prom.

Kathy was everything Henry ever wanted in a girl. Her family owned half a mountain. He began to dream about living in a world where a man could roll out of bed in the morning and hunt from dawn to dusk without ever stepping off his own property. The couple became engaged.

"My father was in favor of marriage," Henry said. "He couldn't imagine a more qualified bride. He sat there and said, 'Tell me about the land again.'"

Late in December 1969, Henry invited Kathy and her mother down to Valley Stream to do some weekend Christmas shopping in Manhattan. On the night they arrived, Henry was lounging in the remodeled basement watching television when the telephone suddenly rang.

"Hello, Henry Winter?" said a woman with a vaguely familiar voice. "This is the Dime Savings Bank in Valley Stream. We just wanted to notify you that your checking account is overdrawn."

"Good try," Henry said, recognizing the caller as Betsy Bassett. "But I don't even have a checking account at the Dime Savings Bank."

They spent the next half hour reminiscing. Betsy had left the sorority and taken a job as a bank teller. Henry was working on the back of a village garbage truck and thinking about taking the entrance examination for the New York City Police Department.

"I hear something about you getting married," Betsy said.

"You hear wrong."

The couple made a date to meet later that night on a deserted neighborhood corner.

"I'll wear a pink coat," Betsy said. "You wear a white carnation, so I'll be able to recognize you."

Henry hung up the phone and went upstairs to find Kathy Costello sitting on the couch. Mildred Winter and Kathy's mother were sipping tea in the kitchen.

"Let me see that ring I gave you," Henry said nonchalantly.

Kathy pulled the ring from her finger and handed it to him. He closed one hand on the ring, grabbed his coat with the other, and headed for the front door.

"I don't want to get married," Henry was heard to say.

Henry returned home two days later. Kathy Costello and her mother were long gone, having returned to their side of the mountain.

Henry and Betsy spent their evening in her Corvair station wagon parked on a road alongside the village garbage dump. After three years, there was a lot to talk about. They laughed long into the evening, agreeing that Betsy had phoned Henry at precisely the right moment in his life.

The couple talked about buying land together and one day possibly even opening a joint checking account at the Dime Savings Bank. Finally, Henry held up the ring and said, "I got this."

Earlier in the year Henry had taken the first job of his adult life, joining the Valley Stream Sanitation Department as the tail man on a garbage truck. He got the job through a hunting buddy named Jimmy Leavy who wound up working on the same truck. By coincidence, they had been assigned a route that included both their homes. Henry was thoroughly unprepared for the physical strain of lifting twenty-five hundred garbage cans into the back of a truck. An hour into the job it seemed to him that a lot of people were throwing away cement with their trash. And at 10 A.M. when the truck stopped in front of his home, he tore off his uniform and ran into the house.

"I quit!" he yelled.

Winter refused to come out of the house until Jimmy promised to let him ride in the truck while he finished off the rest of the route. It took a week before Henry was able to work an entire shift without threatening to quit. By that time he and Jimmy were moonlighting as junk dealers. Sifting through their neighbors' garbage for something they called "mongo," the garbage collectors came up with copper, other metals, and wood, which they later sold. Eventually, they graduated to a route in an even nicer neighborhood, finding toasters, stereos, and an occasional working television set in the morning trash.

Although they had their problems, Henry and Betsy continued to date over the next four years. Henry worked on the garbage truck but he really wanted to be a New York City cop. And on an August night in 1973, his brother-in-law, Dennis Caufield, a city cop working with an undercover anticrime detail in Brooklyn's 75th Precinct, invited Henry to join him on a midnight tour.

Henry drove into the city and met Caufield on a corner, sitting in a yellow cab with his partner.

"What's this?" Henry asked.

"Our cover," Caufield explained.

As he accompanied the cops on their tour of a bleak neighborhood named East New York, he gazed at rows of gutted tenements and tilting brick buildings. He saw wooden planks nailed over windows and sheets of steel bolted over apartment house entrances. Henry watched intently when a group of blacks scattered from a Pennsylvania Avenue storefront as the Checker cab—with three white men inside—drove past.

"They seem to recognize you guys," Henry noted.

"Cockroaches," Caufield replied.

"Skells," the partner added, using the catchall nickname used by cops when referring to ghetto pimps, prostitutes, drug dealers, robbers, muggers, junkies, and other lowlifes. Henry remembered thinking, "Why would anyone from the suburbs want to come and work in a ghetto?"

By the middle of the midnight tour, as the undercover cops raced from robbery to burglary, answering radio calls of "shots fired," and "ten-thirteen—officer needs assistance," Henry had changed his mind. He wanted to work here. He watched in amazement as Caufield and his partner rushed into a building after hearing gunshots, kicked down a door, and finally emerged from an apartment with a black man in handcuffs.

"Is it always like this?" Henry asked, staring at a loaded .357 magnum the officers had taken off the gunman.

"No," Caufield said. "Most of the time it's busy."

Henry settled back into the deep Checker cab seat and smiled.

"Fuck the garbage truck," he thought.

Having passed an entrance examination for the department in 1970, Henry Winter was finally told to report to the New York City Police Academy for a physical in June 1974.

Along with half a million other suburban commuters, he rode the Long Island Railroad to work, pushing and shoving his way onto the train each morning for the ride into Penn Station, then boarding a bus for the ride to the Police Academy, nestled between Second and Third Avenues on East 20th Street. He was happy and nervous. Soon the same Henry Winter who had pretended to be Joe Friday as a kid would be pulling his very own .38 and telling real bad guys to freeze. He would be a New York City cop—a member of a department known throughout the world as the Finest. He could hardly contain his excitement. His father, the same Henry H. Winter who left the city for the suburbs twenty-two years earlier, was already telling the fathers of Nassau County cops he drank with in a local bar, "Your sons aren't real cops. Not like my son Henry, anyway. He's a city cop."

In July, Henry invited Betsy out for dinner at the Lincoln Inn in Rockville Centre, Long Island. It was the first restaurant he had ever been to where someone parked your car. Betsy was similarly impressed. She ordered chicken cordon bleu. Henry got the veal. Over appetizers, he popped the question: Would she be interested in becoming a cop's wife? By the time a waiter rolled the dessert cart over to the table, the couple had agreed on a May 1975 wedding.

From the start, Henry liked the military atmosphere and the feeling of confederacy at the academy. But it wasn't too long before he spotted a way to circumvent certain rules and regulations. All recruits, he noted, were given three yellow "gig cards." They were to be carried at all times in a uniform shirt pocket. If a recruit with dull shoes or a stained uniform was spotted by a supervisor, he had to surrender a gig card. If he lost all three cards, he got a reprimand from the captain. Repeat offenders faced expulsion.

Although Henry Winter lost twelve gig cards during his four-month stay in the academy, he was never disciplined. He and the other recruits always seemed to have enough gig cards, even though they often weren't in the right names.

In October, Henry graduated from the Police Academy. There was no official ceremony, just a party at an East Side Italian restaurant. He was assigned to the 25th Precinct, a Spanish Harlem command housed on East 119th Street. The day before leaving, the class watched a training film that included a message from a member of the department's Internal Affairs Division, the unit which polices the police.

"Don't ever forget that we're out there watching," said an IAD investigator.

As the film ended and the lights came on in the auditorium, a sergeant stood at the podium, scanning the faces of recruits.

"There are a few of you out there who won't make it as cops," he said, holding up a pair of handcuffs. "Some of you will wind up being arrested."

The words meant nothing to Henry. He had the gun and he had the silver badge. He was the good guy and had a blue uniform to prove it. That night, he went home and had one of the most powerful dreams of his life. Henry dreamed he was standing before hundreds of bad guys with his gun drawn and his badge sparkling.

"You're all under arrest," the patrolman said in his dream. Before awakening, Henry Winter dreamed he had every bad guy in the city wearing handcuffs.

The voice of Henry Winter:

"My first day on the job and I'm standing on the corner of Lexington Avenue and East One Hundred and Twenty-fifth Street with my thumb up my ass on a foot post when I suddenly get a call on the radio. It's a ten-two. I didn't even know the police radio codes yet, so I just ignored the call. A few minutes later a sergeant pulled up to my foot post in a car. He said, 'Hey, Winter. Didn't you just get a ten-two?' I said, 'Yeah sarge. Should I call the station house or something?' The sergeant looked at me for a second and then said, 'You dumb rookie hump. You don't call the station house on a ten-two. When you get a ten-two, you return to the station house, pronto.'

"So I ran back to the station house and reported to the front desk. The sergeant there is smiling and holding up my license plate. I said, 'Oh, did it fall off the car or something?' The sergeant said, 'No. And don't get excited now, Winter, but, ah . . . this is all that's left of your car.' I was stunned. The sergeant had to put a hand over his mouth to keep from laughing.

"It turned out a drunk cab driver had smashed into my car on One Hundred and Nineteenth and Park, pushing it up against a pole. The car looked like an accordion when I got there. It was a beautiful car too—a 1972 Grand Torino with white leather interior and a midnight blue paint job. The car had a 351 Cleveland, a four-barrel engine. I couldn't believe it. My first day on the job and some drunk turned my car into an accordion. I cried.

"I made my first collar in October on a burglary. It was a radio run—we responded to a call over the radio. We came up the street with our lights off and arrived at a warehouse on the corner of East One Hundred and Eleventh Street and Second Avenue. When we got there a sixteen-year-old kid was swinging down off the roof on a rope with a knapsack full of radios. He looked like Batman. He hit the ground and we arrested him. He was real surprised to see us.

"Later I took him to the old Central Booking at One Hundred Centre Street. In those days you stayed with the suspect right up until his arraignment. The whole process could take thirty hours. Anyway, in the hallways, there were all these empty lounge chairs. Some had little pieces of cardboard tacked to them with names on them. I thought they were police department property, so I fell asleep in one. Finally I wake up and there is this oldtimer kicking at my feet, yelling, 'Get the fuck out of my chair.' By the next week I had my own lounge chair. I used to keep it in my car and then grab it out of the trunk whenever I made a collar. I did a lot of sleeping on the job back then.

"I didn't see much corruption in the beginning. The biggest thing was that we'd go into a store and get a free sandwich. I didn't think that was wrong. Probably the worst thing I saw was two days before Thanksgiving in 1974—my second month on the job. The city pulled a tractorload of turkeys into the precinct one night and parked it on the corner of Park Avenue and One Hundred and Twenty-fifth Street. They were going to give the turkeys away to the poor in the morning. I got the foot post guarding the turkeys, to make sure nobody broke in and stole them. But throughout the night I got sergeants, lieutenants, captains, and borough commanders driving up to the truck and demanding free turkeys. I'm just out of the academy. The supervisors are yelling, 'Hey kid, let me have a turkey.' What am I supposed to do? Say, 'Excuse me, Captain, but you can't have a turkey?' No, I give him the turkey. If I don't give him a turkey, my ass is grass.

"But that was a good job too, because the next day when we started giving out the turkeys, a line formed. It was good. Blacks, Hispanics, whites, all the poor people from the neighborhood were coming out to get a free turkey. One of us was supposed to hand a person a bag of potatoes while the other guy handed him a turkey. But it got crazy. People started grabbing us and pulling us off the truck, just to get another turkey. And then they'd sell them. On the next corner there were guys selling frozen turkeys for five dollars apiece. So we threw them out at the people, yelling 'Here's a turkey for a turkey, here's a turkey for another turkey.'

"The same thing happens today with the cheese the government gives out. In a ghetto area like the Seventy-seventh Precinct, you can go into any bodega and you'll see packages of cheese, honey, and butter stamped 'U.S. Government, not to be sold.' But in every bodega they've got them for sale. I guess once you slice cheese and put it on a piece of bread, it doesn't say 'Not for sale' anymore.

"The cops were just as bad as the skells, though. A sergeant in the Seven-Seven and two other guys went down to a Catholic Charities cheese giveaway. They pulled up and said, all somberlike, 'There are some disabled people on the far side of the precinct who can't get over here to get the free cheese. If you can give us some, we'll gladly distribute it amongst the poor and handicapped.' A priest gave the cops the cheese, said 'God bless you, officers,' and sent them off with a trunkload of free cheese. The cops drove right back to the precinct and split up the cheese among themselves."

On March 10, 1975, as rumors persisted that there would soon be massive police layoffs because the city was facing a fiscal crisis, perhaps even bankruptcy, Henry arrived for work in the 25th Precinct only to learn that he had been transferred from Spanish Harlem to the 100th Precinct in Rockaway, Queens. He was surprised by the move—he had only spent five months in his first command—but he was happy because his commute to work would be cut from an hour to just under fifteen minutes. But soon Henry learned that there was no rush to get to work anyway—there was no work to be done. Throughout the city, young police officers facing July 1975 layoffs had simply stopped arresting people.

"They told us not to make arrests, because we'd have to go to court and if I'm laid off why should I go to court? The word was: Don't give out summonses, don't make arrests, don't do anything. Just be in Limbo. I went about three months without making an arrest. Nobody was.

"It got so that we'd just go out, drive around, and if we saw somebody committing a crime, we'd just pick up the radio and say, 'Anybody catching collars tonight?' If nobody answered, we let it go. Just drove away.

"I remember one time I was up on One Hundred and Sixteenth Street in the One Hundredth Precinct and I see two mutts pull up in a green Comet. I said to myself, 'They don't belong in that car.' So I put the plate number over the radio to see if it had been reported stolen. My partner was an oldtimer. He was in the bank, cashing his check when I spotted the car. He came out and got in the car just as the central dispatcher came over the air and said, 'One hundred [sector] David, that's a ten-sixteen [stolen car], wanted by Yonkers.' My partner just looked at me. So I said, 'Hey, we got a stolen car here with two guys in it.' He just looked at me and said, 'Kid, you think that I'm going to make the arrest?' And I said, 'Well, I ain't making the arrest either. I'm getting laid off.' He said, 'And I'm too old to make arrests.' I picked up the radio and said, 'Wrong plate, Central.' We let them go. We just let them drive away, go to the beach and do whatever they wanted to do. I didn't give a shit."

Betsy and Henry were married on May 30, 1975 in Valley Stream's Blessed Sacrament Church. But even as the couple sat on the dais, toasting the future, Henry was worried about losing his job. Mayor Abe Beame was already preparing police union officials for the biggest layoff in the history of the New York City Police Department. The wedding guests, some of them cops, pushed envelopes containing checks and money into Henry's hands.

"Sorry about the job, kid," people said, offering condolences on what should have been the happiest day of his life.

Three weeks later, Henry came home from his honeymoon to the bad news that he didn't have a job. He walked into the precinct house in late June only to be handed a teletyped message by a desk sergeant. The message listed all those police officers in the department being laid off on July 1, 1975. Henry found his name, tax registry number, shield number, and command listed with the W's near the bottom of the sheet. It was official. Henry Winter had become an ex-cop three-quarters of the way through his rookie year on the job.

"That was it. The words were there. We weren't supposed to work, we didn't work. Actually, they wanted our guns as of July third, but everybody had it up to here. We said, 'Fuck you, take my guns, take my shield, take my patrol guide, take everything now,' and that's what we did. We went to the desk and turned everything in. Why should I work? I was getting laid off in three days. I wasn't going to go out and get shot up on the day before I got laid off."

"Being laid off was like a kick in the pants, because I made good collars. I didn't cause anybody headaches. If they told me to do something, I did it. I was the type of cop who, if I thought you were dirty and you were in my sector, I would fuck around with you or get you to come after me until I could get you. There were times when, if I saw a stolen car parked on my foot post, I wouldn't budge. I'd hide, wait for somebody to get in the car, and then pounce just to make a collar. But now, why should I do stuff like that? I'm getting laid off. My benefits were going. When I was in the Two-Five, there was a cop who just got out of the academy, but he was getting laid off. He went to answer a call on One Hundred and Tenth Street with a day or two to go on the job, and a bomb went off. He lost an eye and his job. The department didn't do anything for him until the story hit the newspapers.

"Anyway, we all went up to Dingy Dan's on One Hundred and Eighth Street and Beach Channel Drive and had a party and a half. It was a good place, a cop's place, and he put out a spread with pitchers of beer. It was all for free. Officially, we still had three days left as cops. We weren't civilians yet. Dingy Dan knew that. He didn't make us pay for anything."

Disappointed, Henry headed back permanently to his apartment in Valley Stream. Soon he was collecting unemployment and working part-time making deliveries for Gus's Pizza Shop on West Merrick Road. He continued to look for police-type work, applying for jobs with a variety of security firms that guarded warehouses at night and accompanied armored car deliveries of cash. Ordinarily, an ex-cop like Winter—one with no criminal record and two commendations—would have been snapped up by a security firm. But the timing was all wrong. There were literally hundreds of laid-off New York City police officers vying for security jobs. Henry's application got lost in a flooded job market.

Within a year of his firing, however, Henry was already

developing a reputation in the New York City and Long Island newspapers as something of a heroic figure. He was delivering a pizza for Gus shortly after 10 P.M. on March 7, 1976 when he noticed a car with six black men in it parked in front of a Merrick Avenue bar, the Club 600. The car was running, but the lights were off.

Henry parked his delivery van about sixty feet behind the suspicious car, a beat-up Chevy Impala. He watched one man get out and enter the bar, spotting a gun butt sticking out of the man's waistband.

His cop instincts working, Henry jotted down the car's license number and headed off to a nearby corner where he knew he would find a Nassau County Police call box. Instead, he met a uniformed Nassau County patrolman and neighborhood acquaintance, Vincent Joaquin, sitting in his patrol car.

"Follow me," Henry said. "There's six black guys holding up the Six Hundred bar."

Joaquin, recognizing Henry as the ex-cop turned pizza delivery man, asked, "OK, but have you got your gun?"

"Nah. I left it home."

The men reached the scene just in time to see the suspect jump into the car and speed off, heading west into the city.

"I just got a call on the radio," Joaquin screamed to Henry. "They robbed the bar."

Winter jumped into the delivery van and Joaquin sped off in the patrol car, chasing the robbers across the city line into Queens. Henry raced into oncoming traffic, cut off the Impala and jumped from the van. He ran to the passenger's side of the Impala, pretending to reach behind his back for a gun.

"Freeze, motherfuckers!" he yelled.

No one dared move.

"Now shut the car off and put your hands on the dashboard."

One pair of hands, the one closest to Henry, placed a gun on the dashboard. He reached into the car, grabbed it and held it on the suspects until Joaquin arrived with his backups. "Is that your gun?" asked one of the arriving officers, Larry Robinson, another Nassau County cop, who recognized Henry as the ex-cop from the pizza parlor.

"No, this is their gun. My gun is at home."

"You mean you took these guys without a gun?"

Henry laughed. One of the suspects began to curse.

"I told you we should have wasted the dude. He's a pizza man. We got nabbed by a pizza man."

The Long Island cops scratched their heads.

"All yours, officers," Henry said. "I got a pizza to deliver."

Two days later, the New York *Daily News* carried an account of the arrest on page seven. The article, headlined, "With a Hunch and a Bluff, Laid-off Cop Corrals Six," ran at the top of the page and explained Winter's exploits in detail. The lead to the story included a curious error, however.

"A young ex-cop, a casualty of New York City's fiscal woes, ventured from his Valley Stream home in quest of a pizza pie to share with his wife and wound up helping to bag a carload of robbery suspects by bluffing that he had a gun, Nassau County police said yesterday.

"Police said Henry Winter, 23, laid off from the city Police Department last July, spotted five men and a juvenile in a car near the Club 600 bar at 600 Merrick Road, Valley Stream at about 10 P.M. Sunday while he was driving to a pizza parlor."

Years later, Henry recalled: "All I knew was that these guys robbed a bar and they had to be caught. That's all I cared about. But when the *Daily News* reporter called me, I realized that I had to tell him I was driving to the pizza parlor rather than delivering pizzas. I couldn't have it printed that I was working for a pizza parlor, because at that time, hell, I was still collecting unemployment checks from the city."

In April, Henry made the city newspapers again.

This episode began shortly before 1 A.M. as Gus Sakellarios, Henry and a teenaged waitress named Jan Tragner prepared to close up Gus's Pizza Shop. Henry was at the front counter, counting his tips, when a black man entered the store. The man walked to the back of the shop and then returned to the front counter.

"Where's the bathroom, man?" he asked.

"Out of order," Gus replied.

The man then left, but Henry, wearing a small revolver in an ankle holster, felt the hair on his arms stand up.

"Gus, we're going to be robbed."

"Henry, won't you ever stop being a cop?"

"I'm telling you, Gus, it's going down."

Two minutes later, the man returned to the parlor with a friend.

"Two slices," he said.

As Gus put the slices on the counter, the man pulled a nine-millimeter automatic from his waistband and pointed it at the owner's head. The other man grabbed Jan, holding her in a choke hold.

"Open the register," they shouted at Henry. "Move!"

Henry hit the 'No sale' button and the register drawer popped open. One of the men dug his hand in, stuffing dollar bills into his pocket.

The gunmen then pushed all three workers into a back room and closed the door. For a split second, Henry thought about pulling his gun. Then he thought again. Jan was still in his line of fire. He heard the men run back to the front of the parlor, a bell jingling as they opened the door to the street.

"Don't follow or else."

As the door closed, Henry ran out of the shop and into the street. He caught a glimpse of the license plate on the red Oldsmobile getaway car as it pulled away from the curb. He raced fifty feet to the corner, where his brother-in-law, Douglas Caufield, a Hempstead cop, was waiting in his car to drive Henry home from work.

Douglas and Henry took off after the robbers, chasing them at high speed across the city line. They lost track of the car in Queens, but stopped to give a description of its occupants and the license plate number to a patrolling team of city cops. They put out a radio call, alerting Nassau County officers, who later caught up with the fleeing robbers near the Nassau Expressway in North Lawrence. The cops recovered an automatic and fifty dollars, arresting two robbers and a driver.

Two days later, *Newsday* and the New York *Daily News* carried reports on Henry Winter, the cop without a police department. The *News* was really impressed this time, headlining the article, "Laid-off City Cop Helps Nab 3 in Store Robbery."

The lead to the story read: "Stickup men who ply their trade in Valley Stream are on notice to watch out for Henry Winter. The 23-year-old laid-off New York City cop played a hero's role for the second time yesterday in the arrest of three Far Rockaway, Queens men who allegedly held up a store where Winter has a part-time job."

Henry recalled, "I was gonna drop the guy with the gun. I wanted to shoot him dead. But I couldn't take a chance. The other guy was holding Jan. He could have been armed. Gus was still very happy, though. I was the best delivery boy he ever had. After that, I could eat anything I wanted in the store. Veal cutlets. Meatballs. Shrimp. Finally, I even said to Gus, 'Hey, did you ever think of putting lobster on the menu? I really like lobster.' Gus just shook his head. He figured if I didn't get a job with a police department soon, I was going to eat him out of business."

Henry Winter's big decision:

"I sent résumés out to various police departments in different parts of the country. The union told us that other police departments were looking to hire laid-off New York City cops. So I sent a résumé out to Arapahoe County, Colorado, about twelve miles east of Denver. They called and asked me to come out and take a lie detector test. I flew out at the end of June in 1976, just about a year after I got laid off. I met this sergeant in personnel, Reynolds. He gave me the lie detector test.

"It consisted of three questions: Did I ever steal anything? Did I ever cover up a felony? Did I ever have sex while I was on the payroll as a New York City police officer? Did I ever steal anything? Yeah, everybody steals. You take a little money out of your mother's pocketbook when you're a kid and you steal money from other kids when you're in school. Did I ever cover up a felony? The answer to that was no. I had never covered up a felony. Did I ever have sex as a member of the New York City Police Department? I answered yes to that one too. They didn't specify on duty or off duty. The sergeant says, 'All right. We'll be in touch.' I figured, that's it—I flunked the damn thing.

"The following Wednesday I get a phone call. This guy said, 'Henry Winter? This is Sergeant Reynolds, from the Arapahoe County Police Department in Colorado. We went over your application and we'd like you to work for us.' So I said, 'Oh, fine. I'm interested. But it will take me about a month or so to get squared away here. I have a wife and child. When do you want me to start?' He said, 'Monday.'

I said, 'I have no place to live. I can't just drop everything.'
He said, 'They're going to waive everything, all the learning
and the academy.' They were going to set me up in the
police barracks until I could find a place. I'd have to learn
the new gun laws and things like that. He said I could look
for my own place and eventually move out of the barracks.
I talked it over with Betsy and she said, 'Yeah, go out and
try it.'

"So I loaded up our 1971 Volkswagen bug, and took
off. I drove all the way out to Arapahoe County in three
days. I went in, met the guys, everything was fine. They
said, 'Here's your hat, here's your shirt, here's your pants,
here's your boots, here's your gloves, here's your jacket,
here's your leather goods, here's the keys to your car.' The
keys to my car? Turns out the car was mine twenty-four
hours a day. We got to take the car home at night. That
was nice. I didn't even need my Volkswagen out there.

"So there I was. Deputy Sheriff. Deputy Dawg. They called
us 'Pepsi cans'. Our cars were red, white and blue with red,
white and blue lights on the top. You had a bluish pair of
pants, highlighted with a red stripe down the sides and a
white shirt. We even had Smokey the Bear hats. The town
was beautiful. It was the great outdoors. Every other store
was a sporting goods store. Everybody carried guns. They
were legal as long as you didn't conceal them. I called up
Betsy that night and told her it was really nice, clean.

"Eventually they found me an apartment in the nice section
of town. It was four and one-half rooms, fully furnished,
for one hundred forty-five dollars a month and five dollars
more a month in the summer for air conditioning. An indoor/
outdoor swimming pool. Tennis. I mean, really nice. It was
excellent. I would ride up to Jefferson County, stand by
the side of the road and see a deer crossing the field.

"After two months, I called Betsy up and told her, 'I like it here. It's really nice country. Come on out and tell me what you think of it.' She said, 'No, Henry.' I said, 'What do you mean, No?' 'I thought about it and I don't want to leave Valley Stream. I don't want to leave my family.' I told her, 'Betsy, I'm your family. We're married now. Come on. I think this is going to be good out here.' But Betsy wouldn't budge. She told me, 'No, it's too big a move. Come home.' So she put it, not in these exact words, but something like, 'Make up your mind. Do you want to stay in Colorado or do you want me?' I said, 'Okay, I'll be home.'

"I didn't even think about the decision. I just loaded up their cruiser, went into work, and handed everything back in. I even apologized to Sergeant Reynolds. I told him that I liked it there but I couldn't stay. He said that he understood. I wasn't the first New York City cop to do this to them. I got into the Volkswagen and drove nonstop back home. From Arapahoe County to Valley Stream in thirty-seven hours.

"Now I don't even think about what it would have been like if Betsy had come out to Colorado. I don't bring it up too often. I don't bring it up too often because that was me then, Colorado was Henry Winter. It was a hunting town where I could work as a cop. Arapahoe County was me and I left it.

Henry returned home in late August 1976, taking a job at a 7-Up plant in Mineola, Long Island. He drove a truck dispensing cases of soda pop on a route that included Queens, Brooklyn, and eastern Long Island, including some of the same streets his father had driven twenty-five years earlier while distributing beer. Henry's boss turned out to be a gun freak who liked cops. He wanted to hear all of Henry's stories, and Henry was only too happy to embellish. He and his boss started taking off from work early to drive to the Nassau County Police range, where they fired guns and listened to more cop stories. When the company started to lay off workers in the winter of 1977, the boss made Henry management, giving them even more time to fire guns and tell cop stories.

Henry didn't allow himself to think about Arapahoe County much. Mostly he just worked and waited. The city had started hiring back some of the laid-off cops. And then finally, in November 1978, Henry got a letter from the New York City Police Department asking him to report to the Police Academy for a two-week retraining session.

Blondie was getting his service revolver and silver shield back.

3

"I'm from Bed-Stuy. Do or die."

"First I went to the academy for two weeks. Then they put me in something called the Neighborhood Stabilization Unit. We were housed in the Six-Nine Precinct on Foster Avenue in Canarsie, Brooklyn. The NSU was a new thing for rookies that was formed while we were laid off. Now they made rookie cops spend six months in NSU before assigning them to a precinct. None of the guys coming back from the layoff wanted to be in NSU. We were already cops. We knew what the game was. NSU was an insult. We all felt the same way. We came out of the academy with a class of rookies, but we weren't rookies. There were guys in my unit with three and four years on the job. So I couldn't take the Six-Nine. I was there for about a month, walking a beat on Avenue

L, and I just couldn't deal with this precinct. It was a white precinct and I couldn't deal with white people. I had worked in Harlem and East Rockaway. If you arrested somebody in Harlem, they stayed arrested. If you took somebody off the street in the Six-Nine, the bad guy's lawyer would beat you back to the station house. Then the phone calls would start. Some political guy would call your captain or a lieutenant from another precinct would get you on the phone and say, 'That's my cousin Sal you got there. What can you do for him?' I used to wonder what the hell was going on. I wanted out.

"I had a dynamite boss there named Frank Bunting. He came from the Seven-Five out in East New York—my brother-in-law Dennis Caufield's precinct. One day Bunting told us, 'Look, we got a foot post open in the Seven-Five on Pitkin Avenue. It's a badass place. Does anybody want it steady?' I jumped for it. I took care of Pitkin Avenue from Crescent and Pine to Euclid, that whole section of East New York. And I loved it there, because now I was back with the skells, the guys who, when you collared them, they stayed collared."

For most of the next year and a half, Henry Winter walked a beat on Pitkin Avenue, swinging his nightstick, grabbing crooks and developing a reputation as an active cop. He made good collars, harassed drug dealers, and just generally broke the bad guys' chops. When other cops hesitated to chase an armed robber into an abandoned building, Henry charged past them. It never dawned on him to be actually afraid of something in the street. After all, he had a gun and a badge.

Steadily, Henry became more streetwise. Unlike other white cops in the precinct, he actually seemed to like the people on his beat. Hispanic kids on the block taught him Spanish words and the black kids gave him lessons in cool. It was not uncommon, supervisors noted, to find Police Officer Henry Winter dancing in the streets with kids. He was given an excellent rating in their reports.

Back in the precinct house, where Henry's brother-in-law was still working a plainclothes assignment with an anticrime detail, cops were beginning to take notice of his arrests.

"That kid brother-in-law of yours is pretty active out there," cops told Caufield. "What's he trying to do, arrest the whole city?"

If nothing else, Henry had an active imagination when it came to making arrests. One day he noticed several men lining up outside a building on the corner of Pitkin Avenue and Pine Street. Sitting on a step across the street, Henry watched the men ring an apartment doorbell and then slip dollar bills into a mail slot. A second or two later, the slot reopened and a hand passed out a small white envelope. Henry ambled across the street, rang the doorbell himself and pressed his face close to the peephole, so the people inside couldn't see his uniform. When the mail slot opened, Henry took five dollars from his wallet and pushed it into the opening. A hand passed back a nickel bag of marijuana.

"Bingo," Henry thought.

He waited a half hour until a backup unit arrived before kicking down the front door of the apartment. Rushing in with his gun drawn, he arrested two men and found a large supply of cash and fifty nickel bags of marijuana.

Henry then returned to the precinct with his two suspects and the confiscated cash and drugs. He told his sergeant how he had just made an undercover drug buy while in uniform and the sergeant, who years later would wind up working with him in the Internal Affairs office, shook his head. "Winter, you're going to become a legend in your own time if you keep this up."

Henry vouchered all the confiscated drugs and money with the exception of his own five dollars, which he casually reclaimed once the sergeant left the room.

Soon he was doing his own stakeouts. Finding it virtually impossible to make any more undercover drug buys in uniform, Henry started bringing binoculars to work. He hid in abandoned homes across from buildings he suspected of being drug spots and waited for something to happen. When he spotted a drug deal, he'd rush to the street and make an arrest. Neighborhood dealers soon referred to the new blonde cop on the beat as 'the Invisible Man.' "

Not everyone appreciated Henry's tactics however. One night as Henry walked his beat on a midnight shift, a green car suddenly leaped the curb and tried to run him down. Henry jumped out of the way at the last moment, escaping injury. As the car passed, he swung his nightstick, shattering the rear window. Henry reported the license number and threat on his life to his superiors.

Three months later, an alert team of patrolling cops spotted the car and gave chase, running it off the road. The suspect, having tried to murder a cop with a car, took one look at the officers surrounding him and realized his own life was probably in danger. By the time Henry arrived on the scene to identify his attacker, the suspect had defecated in his pants.

"You want to lock him up or take care of him yourself?" a supervisor asked Henry.

"Ah, just lock him up. I don't want a piece of him. He's in enough trouble."

Six months later, the man who tried to kill Henry Winter with a car agreed to a plea-bargain arrangement with the

Brooklyn district attorney's office. The arrangement called for the man to pay a fifty dollar fine.

The foot patrolman tells his secrets:

"I must have made eight or nine good robbery and drug collars in the Seven-Five using the binocular trick. If you sit in a room and stake something out, it's easy to see what's going on. Nobody sees you.

"There was this one family named Garcia up on Pitkin Avenue. They were heavily into drugs, especially the woman, who had blonde hair. And I loved breaking their chops. I just missed getting her good one day too. I had just come on duty when one of the kids ran up to me and yelled, 'Henry. Henry. Henry.' I liked it better when they called me 'Henry.' It was a little easier to deal with people when they said my name rather than 'officer'. So the kids yelled 'Henry, Henry, Henry. You just missed something. The blonde lady just came out and got in a fight with one of the girls. Then she pulled out a little .25 automatic.' So I stayed there and watched because I wanted her so bad. But she was good. I couldn't get her. I got her husband, but I never got her.

"One day she even invited me and my partner, Al Haymen, up for coffee. She knew I was giving her business a beating. So she says, 'Well, we'd like to buy you a new hat.' I'm thinking, I got a hat, what does she want to buy me a new hat for? Then the light went off. Bribe. So I went back and told Frank Bunting about it. He told Internal Affairs. That night the IAD guys came down and wired me up, put a tape recorder on me. Then I went out and tried to make contact with her, but she was too slick. She must have gotten word back, somehow. She wouldn't even stand on the same side of the street with me.

"That was the first time I wore the wire. I wore it just that one night on her. And it was the only time I ever wore a wire where I didn't get some type of conversation."

Traditionally, city cops pay little heed to rumors about pending investigations, particularly investigations of cops by other cops in high crime areas. Like bad guys without badges, crooked cops tend to see themselves as somehow beyond the reach of the law. It's always the other guy that gets caught.

In the 75th Precinct, a group of four crooked cops in an elite detail called the Anticrime Unit were positive that they could continue to burglarize apartments, rob drug dealers, and steal money off dead bodies whenever they wanted to. They would assure each other: If we can't catch the robbery and burglary suspects out here in this jungle, how are other cops—spit and polish Manhattan cops, who don't know the area—ever going to catch us dirty. You'd have to be one of us to catch us.

These officers who had been at the top of the precinct's overtime list, suddenly quit working extra tours and making arrests. One began wearing a lot of gold jewelry. Another drove a brand new Cadillac to work. Two others bought expensive new homes. Lumped together, these signs had the effect of raising a giant red flag over the 75th Precinct.

In 1979 rumors flew through the locker room of the station house on Sutter Avenue. Cops began whispering to each other that there was a big investigation of guys in Anticrime going on. It was even said that cops were going to jail.

Police Officer Henry Winter heard the rumors too. But he couldn't have imagined how the truth would effect his own career. All he knew was that he wasn't dirty. Sure, he bent the rules a little to make a good collar here and there, but he never stole anything. He wasn't what Internal Affairs would call "a player."

Then on a humid night in August something happened that threw a fright into Henry Winter. A team of four cops assigned to the Anticrime detail were driving an unmarked car through the precinct when they noticed another car following them. Curious, the driver of the Anticrime car suddenly threw his car into reverse, getting behind the suspects. This maneuver, called double tracking, enabled the Anticrime cops to get the drop on the people tailing them, and they surrounded the chase car with guns drawn.

"Get out of the car," the cops yelled.

"We're on the job," the men answered.

"What job?"

"None of your fucking business what job."

The cops escorted their suspects back to the precinct house and searched their car.

"Hey look at this." One of the cops held up a stack of photographs he had recovered from the front seat. "These guys have got a picture of every guy from Anticrime here."

During questioning it became apparent that the men trailing the Anticrime officers were investigators assigned to the office of the special state prosecutor for the New York City criminal justice system. Their investigation had been blown. It was like a twenty-megaton bomb had gone off in the 75th Precinct.

Henry Winter was in shock too. But he was also in for an even bigger surprise. Not only was there a state investigation into corruption in the 75th Precinct, but his own brother-in-law, Dennis Caufield, an eleven-year veteran of the force, had been wearing a wire for the last eighteen months, secretly recording conversations with the corrupt cops he worked alongside.

Henry Winter's own brother-in-law was a bona fide rat.

* * *

"I would call Dennis's house and my sister would say, 'Oh, hold on.' or 'I'll call you right back.' I didn't know it then, but their phone calls were recorded. So she would shut the recorder off and then call back. I found out that Dennis was wired when I went over there one day and there was a police department radio and recorder right on top of the television in the living room. I knew then that Dennis had to be working undercover. And that was it. I never brought it up with him until after the arrests came down in the precinct.

"The day after they grabbed the guys from Anticrime I went into the Seven-Five and a couple of guys came up to me. They asked, 'What's the story with your brother-in-law? What's the matter with him? How come they picked up Dennis and his partner last night and only Dennis's partner is locked up.' I said, 'I don't know anything.' I couldn't say anything because I knew they'd kill Dennis. So I just kept my mouth shut. But later I called Dennis and asked him what the story was. He told me he was working undercover for Internal Affairs and the special prosecutor's office. He and his partners were hitting drug locations, robbing the dealers and then splitting up the money and the drugs. Dennis was turning the drugs back in. That was his job. He was undercover. I said, 'Okay.' and hung up the phone. But things weren't okay. I felt about him the same way people feel about me. Cops don't turn in other cops. Rats turn in cops.

"The cops in the Seven-Five were thieves. They were doing the same thing that was going on in the Seven-Seven. Hit the place, take the money, take the drugs, sell the drugs, sell the guns. Same exact thing. I should have known, really, what was going on. They would go in and hit a place and all the bad guys would run out the back door. I always thought it was kind of stupid that with four guys in an

Anticrime car they never sent two of them to cover the back. All four went in the front door, and I'd be standing there watching these dealers flying out the back and escaping over a back fence or something. Sometimes I'd even chase them and come back and say, 'I tried to catch that guy.' And the cops were probably saying, 'Whew, glad he didn't catch him.' Guys would just look at me. 'Okay, all right. Nice job, Henry.' In the meantime, Dennis was standing there wired, rolling tape on me. I didn't know.

"I still called Dennis but I wasn't as friendly as before. If he had just told me from the beginning, I would have felt a lot better. But he didn't and I talked to him at times when he was wired. That made me think. What would have happened if I had done something wrong? I would have been screwed too.

"I know this only too well, now. If you do something and it makes the tape, you're fucked. The guys listening to the tapes don't care about family or friends. They care about indictments. They think, 'He's a cop. He said and did something illegal. Take him. He's gone.'

"If I had come up dirty on those tapes, Dennis would have had to help send me to jail. It doesn't matter who you are. If the tape gets you, you go. And if you don't believe me, ask Richard Nixon about that."

Dennis Caufield was made a hero. The Police Department called two press conferences on November 30, 1979, the day after a special state prosecutor for corruption, Roderick Lankler, announced the indictment of four cops from the 75th Precinct's Anticrime detail. The first press gathering focused on the undercover investigation. Police Commissioner Robert J. McGuire pointed out that cops who stole were being caught, that safeguards implemented by his department in the wake of the Knapp Commission investigation into police corruption were working. The so-called Blue Wall of Silence was cracked, he insisted. Cops were turning in other cops. Cops were getting other cops arrested.

"The system is working," the Police Commissioner said as the television cameras focused on a set of indictments in his hands.

Charged in nine overlapping indictments involving thirty-seven counts of bribe taking, attempted extortion, and burglary were officers Frank L. Beltrani, 32, Daniel Buckley, 31, Joseph Fina, 30 and William Roberts, 30. The indicted cop's supervisor, Sgt. Anthony Canilleri, was suspended. The four men, all of whom had between nine and eleven years on the job, lived in suburban Long Island towns. They had come to the city to rob people in the ghetto.

All four either pleaded guilty or were found guilty at a jury trial. They had accepted bribes, resold stolen guns and burglarized apartments. On one occasion an officer had even called 911, the police emergency number, disguising his voice. He reported that there was a man with a gun inside a Brooklyn building. This practice—called "dropping your own dime"— enabled the Anticrime officers to report on a bogus gun run when they really entered the apartment to search it for narcotics and money.

Later in the day, the police brass gathered to pay homage to Dennis Caufield during a promotion ceremony. The Commissioner handed Caufield a gold shield and announced that the department's newest detective was being transferred out of East New York and reassigned to a Manhattan command on the swank East Side. McGuire didn't say that this was being done to protect Caufield from angry cops in the 75th Precinct.

John Guido, chief of the department's Inspectional Services, stood at the podium and said, "Detective Caufield represents the new breed of New York City police officer," and cited the detective for his extraordinary courage. Newspapermen rushed to their computer terminals, proclaiming Caufield the second coming of Frank Serpico.

"There were times when I thought my cover had been blown," Caufield told the reporters. "But as to the danger— I didn't want to think about it."

Like Serpico—the legendary cop who reported criminal activities of fellow cops in the Knapp Commission investigations—Caufield had broken the Blue Wall of Silence.

"I think anytime a police officer sees a crime or crimes like those that occurred in the Seventy-fifth, he should come forward. I feel sorry for the position these guys put themselves in, but they think they are smarter than the police department."

And for a while, Dennis Caufield even felt like a hero. Some detectives actually talked to him. But then, a year or so later, rumors about Caufield began to circulate in the 17th Precinct where he now worked.

"Caufield saved his own ass," the cops and detectives whispered. "He was just as dirty as the rest of them out in the Seven-Five. Only they caught him first and he agreed to turn."

Dennis Caufield became a pariah. He spent more time in the Valley Stream volunteer fire house, where he had recently been named chief, and less time in the police station. He couldn't fight rumors—even false ones. He got tired of telling people that he had only turned on the other cops because he had seen wrong and wanted to right it. Considered to be a man of conscience, Caufield's conscience began to bother him. Although he never left Valley Stream, Dennis changed his residence several times.

He didn't seem comfortable anywhere, anymore. It seemed that everyone was watching him. In the sanctuary of his home, Dennis screamed and punched walls. Sometimes Henry's sister Millie came home and found her husband sitting in a darkened room, sobbing. Dennis began to have loud arguments with his wife and kids.

Finally, in 1984 he turned in his gold shield and gun. Dennis Caufield, hero cop, couldn't stand the agony of being a policeman anymore. Right or wrong, other cops believed that he had done a terrible thing. He had turned in other cops and they had gone to jail. One day those cops would all be out of jail, but Dennis wasn't sure if he'd ever be free again. He took a better-paying job with the village of Valley Stream.

Still on loan from the 69th Precinct, Henry Winter was finished as a cop in the 75th. All of his fellow officers in East New York were in total agreement: If Henry's brother-in-law is a rat, then Henry must be a rat too.

Within days of Caufield's press conference, Henry was threatened by other cops. They put cheese in his locker and made rodentlike sounds whenever Henry walked into a room. Supervisors were getting scared. The roll-call sergeant told the desk lieutenant that something bad could happen to Henry Winter if he was allowed to remain on a foot post in the 75th. At One Police Plaza, the decision was made to take him out of the precinct.

Henry got new orders. He was put on a foot post at the Canarsie Pier, back in the 69th. Henry hated his new beat. He couldn't hide in buildings on a pier. He couldn't use binoculars to spy on drug deals, kick down doors, or make undercover arrests in uniform anymore. He was with white people again. He was dealing with lawyers again. And he was bored.

But then on April 5, 1980, after a four-month stint on the isolated Canarsie Pier watching waves lap at his feet and young lovers smooch in parked cars, Henry got new orders again. He was going back to a crime front, back to a neighborhood where lawyers rarely ventured and where, if you arrested people, they stayed arrested. Henry was going to the Police Department's dumping ground. He was going to Bedford-Stuyvesant, a neighborhood where young thugs like to brag upon being arrested, "I'm from Bed-Stuy. Do or Die."

Henry had been transferred to the 77th Precinct.

"The funny thing about it was that my nickname was Seven-Seven. I always drank Seagram's Seven Crown and Seven-Up back then. In the Six-Nine we used to go over to the VFW Post on Conklin Avenue after work and I would drink Seven and Seven. When the orders came down, I was out on my post. So this cop I used to drink with who knows my nickname gets a copy of the orders and calls me on the radio.

" 'Seven-Seven. Know where you're being transferred to?'

" 'No.'

" 'Seven-Seven.'

"I waited a moment and then asked him again. 'Where am I going?' He gets back on the radio and says, 'Seven-Seven, I just told you. Seven-Seven.' I came back to him again. 'Okay, quit fucking around. Where am I going?' He comes back, 'Seven-Seven, Seven-Seven.' It went on like that for about ten minutes before I realized that I was going to the Seventy-seventh Precinct. It was like that old Abbott and Costello routine, 'Who's on first?' "

The morning of Monday, April 8th, 1980 was gray and rainy. Henry left Valley Stream with his gear packed in a blue duffel bag lying on the car seat beside him. He had his uniform draped over a hanger in the back. Henry was headed for his first day of work in the 77th Precinct. The big news blasting from the radio that morning focused on a week-old strike of 33,000 New York City bus and subway workers. The traffic on the Belt Parkway was bumper-to-bumper. Thousands of people were walking to work in Manhattan from Brooklyn, strolling across the Brooklyn, Manhattan, and Williamsburg bridges. Mayor Koch was out there somewhere, asking the stragglers, "How am I doing?" A few commuters even told the mayor how he was doing. The embarrassed mayor trudged back to City Hall surrounded by bodyguards on at least one occasion.

Elsewhere in the city, drivers were picking up hitchhikers in three-piece suits throughout Queens and the Bronx to join them on the slow commute into midtown Manhattan. Some of the strangers would develop life-long friendships. Other people made their way to work on roller skates, bicycles, and fishing boats. In a time of crisis, the city of New York seemed to be getting along for once.

Driving the back streets through Queens and Brooklyn to avoid traffic, Henry reached the southwest perimeter of the 77th Precinct an hour after leaving his home. He drove west on Eastern Parkway, a six-lane street with a tree-lined mall separating the traffic, heading towards the 77th Precinct station house.

Once Eastern Parkway had been one of the great Brooklyn addresses—a polite Jewish neighborhood of nineteenth-century brownstones and elegant limestone townhouses. Doormen in white gloves and maroon caps stood sentry at expensive apartment houses. Howard Cosell and thousands of other little kids had grown up here. They attended local synagogues, studied in the Brooklyn Public Library, stood in awe of the Egyptian exhibits in the Brooklyn Museum, took romantic walks through the Brooklyn Botanical Gardens and watched parades under the dramatic arch in Grand Army Plaza near Prospect Park.

But in the late '50s and early '60s something that urban sociologists labelled "white flight" hit Eastern Parkway and the surrounding neighborhoods of Crown Heights and East Flatbush. Poor blacks from Brownsville, East New York, and Bedford-Stuyvesant, seeking to escape the ghettos, moved into these neighborhoods. Rents and real estate prices plummeted as blockbusters went to work integrating them. Jewish merchants began to close their shops on Nostrand Avenue and flee to suburban Queens and Long Island, abandoning their Eastern Parkway temples and yeshivas.

Soon the brownstones stood scarred, abandoned, and gutted, sheets of steel bolted to windows and doorways. Black Baptist ministers transformed the temples into churches, hanging wooden crosses outside stained glass windows shaped like the Star of David. Other ministers opened storefront churches in old dress shops on Nostrand Avenue. Liquor stores replaced Jewish delicatessens on Utica Avenue. Dry cleaners closed up, making way for little Spanish grocery stores called bodegas on St. Johns Place and Troy Avenue.

Bedford-Stuyvesant, like Eastern Parkway, had once been a predominantly white area filled with doctors, lawyers, and merchants. As one of the first neighborhoods to gain subway service to Manhattan in the late nineteenth century, the enclaves of Bedford and Stuyvesant had become prototypes for the modern suburb. Rich people who wanted to get away from the rat race lived there, and commuted to work in the city.

The neighborhood underwent a dramatic change during World War II when the Brooklyn Navy Yard hired black workers from the South who had never been welcomed in a white area before. They soon integrated the neighborhoods of Bedford and Stuyvesant, shortened to Bedford-Stuyvesant in 1944. The war ended and many of the blacks stayed, unable to get jobs, and eventually joined the city's burgeoning welfare rolls. By 1960, 51 percent of the residents living in Bed-Stuy were black. And as city services declined and new low-income housing developments went up, the crime rate soared. Another mass exodus of whites occurred after a series of race riots in the late '60s. By 1970, 84 percent of Bedford-Stuyvesant's residents were black. It had become to Brooklyn what Harlem was to Manhattan—a raging ghetto.

The neighborhood's remaining whites left following the blackout on a sweltering July night in 1977, when the streets teemed with rioters and looters. By then the area was known as Black Brooklyn. The only white people who walked the Eastern Parkway mall were cops from the 77th Precinct, and a good portion of them drove in to work from their Long Island homes. The neighborhood served by the police officers of the 77th Precinct was now the home of pimps, muggers, robbers, rapists, and drug dealers.

The station house itself, located at 127 Utica Avenue was a two-story, red brick structure surrounded by an eight-foot brick wall. The complex included the station house, a parking area, and a private filling station, and was a block wide and half a block deep. An American flag waved high above the building on a flagpole dwarfed by a sixty-foot radio-communications antenna. As he drove up the block that first day, Henry Winter decided that his new command station looked like a fort.

And, in truth, there was a war being fought in the streets surrounding the 77th Precinct. Henry was now stationed at a sort of domestic Vietnam where each year some 230 cops logged as many as 80 murders, 100 rapes, 400 shootings and more than 2000 robberies. For their part, the 77th Precinct cops kept the Civilian Complaint Review Board bogged down with almost 100 reported cases of police brutality, abuse, discourtesy, and ethnic slurs each year.

The 77th Precinct's detective squad came to be known as some of the sharpest homicide minds in the city. They caught and cleared more murders in one year than some other squads dealt with in a decade. In 1979, the year before Henry arrived, eighty-two people were murdered in the 77th—more murders than in the entire city of Boston for the same period, or in all of England. And all this carnage took place in an area about half the size of Henry Winter's hometown of Valley Stream.

To make a bad situation worse, the Police Department had a secret policy of fighting Black Brooklyn's crime war with what amounted to a "black sheep squadron." Although there were certainly good, decent, law-abiding cops in the 77th, the house had been dubbed a police dumping ground years ago. Henry's new command included a locker room full of drunks, duty shirkers, wife beaters, drug addicts, rule benders, and discipline problems who were not quite bad enough to fire. An officer would screw up somehow in a cushy command, only to find himself dressing at the 77th on the following day.

"What are you in for, kid," the veterans would ask new arrivals. "Murder, rape, or robbery?"

On the day he arrived Henry had only one mark against him, but it was the mark of Cain. His brother-in-law was a rat who had helped send other cops to jail. Henry Winter had to be a rat too. And so from the day he stepped through the precinct's metal doors and walked up a flight of steps to introduce himself to the duty captain, Henry was someone whom other cops ignored, distrusted, and avoided.

* * *

"My name got there before I did. The word had come down that I was Dennis's brother-in-law and that I was a rat. Nobody would talk to me. There was one guy, a cop named Larry Bolliack. Larry was a little wacky. He wore an earring with a little number 77 on it. I guess he really liked the precinct. He said his girlfriend had given him the earring. I had been working with Larry for a little while and he came up to me one day and said, 'Look, I just got to find out what the hell is going on here with you. I hear you're a rat. I know your brother-in-law is a rat. He worked for IAD. I want to know if you're working for IAD. That's why the guys aren't talking to you here.' I said, 'Look, Larry I'm not working for IAD. What my brother-in-law did was what he did. We're two different people.' Larry told me, 'Well Henry, that's why guys aren't talking to you.'

"All the guys on the midnight tour shied away from me. Some of them were into serious shit before I ever got to the precinct. The first time I got involved with it was with the sergeant, Gallagher, and Gallagher's partner. There happened to be money missing on a job they went on, and the guy who lost the money came into the precinct bitching. It was a set-up job. It wasn't a real radio run. They had dropped a dime on the guy. They had called 911 themselves and then responded to the bogus call to get inside the building. The owners were selling drugs out of an apartment in the front and running a dice game in the back. So the cops went in to hit the place, I happened to swing by. It was on Schenectady Avenue.

"Later the guy who got ripped off came into the station house bitching that money was missing. The sergeant met the guy outside. In the meantime, I had to go out on a car accident with a DOA. When I got back, Gallagher came up to me and said, 'There's a guy in the precinct bitching about money being taken.' I said, 'What do I give a fuck? I didn't take any money from him. Let the guy bitch all he wants.' At that time, it was 1981, I was a year in the precinct. I didn't take money then. I didn't know these guys on the late tour were grabbing money left and right. Anyway, apparently they gave the guy some money back. But later the guy came around and started bitching again about money being taken. I don't know if they gave him money the second time or just took him for a ride. He was gonzo alonzo [gone] after that.

"That night the late-tour guys said they wanted to talk to me. They caught me in the garage. Gallagher and his partner were there, talking about the situation. Finally, they said, 'Look, not that we don't trust you, but your brother-in-law was a rat.' And then they tossed me—checked me for a wire. Jesus, I was pissed. We almost got into a fight. I said, 'You don't have to fucking toss me. If I tell you I'm not wired, I'm not wired. What the fuck is going on here?' Gallagher's partner said, 'Nothing against you, but I don't talk to anybody unless I toss them first.' I said, 'Yeah. Okay. No problem.' And from that day on, because they knew I knew something had happened and I didn't open my mouth, I was accepted. I wasn't accepted to the point where they took me in with them—but at least they talked to me. The rest came later."

4

The Alamo

At the New York City Police Department's headquarters at One Police Plaza in Manhattan—a fourteen-story building dubbed "the Purple Palace" by the city's rank and file cops— the 77th Precinct had acquired a reputation as an "unmanageable" precinct with an acute integrity problem.

Just as a riotous command in the South Bronx had been named Fort Apache, Brooklyn cops referred to the 77th Precinct as the Alamo. A detective's wife who knew a little about silk screens even designed a blue and white T-shirt, with a drawing of the real Alamo and the words "77th Precinct. The Alamo. Under Siege." The shirts—approximately 150 of them—were snapped up at $7.50 a clip within a week after they went on sale. Most of the cops liked the new nickname. It was much better than that of an adjoining Brooklyn precinct that had been overtaken and trashed by a group of angry Hasidic Jews after a mugging—Fort Surrender.

"We were just thinking of a fort. There were four of us. Me, my partner Al, Larry Bolliack and another cop named Frankie. We were parked side by side in a playground just off Atlantic Avenue. One guy says, 'We got to name this place and its got to be a fort like Fort Apache.' We were talking about Indians, war and being surrounded. Bolliack wanted to call it Alienated City. Then somebody said it. The Alamo. And the next thing you know it was painted on the wall outside the precinct in orange Day-Glo paint. Alamo. That was the only place it was painted and I did it myself. I pulled up in my car on a midnight tour, and I just went out and wrote in big letters with a spray can: A. L. A. M. O. Alamo. My partner Al kept going, 'Did you spell it right?' He was nervous about that. He didn't want to be party to a misspelling.

"The next week, something happened at the precinct and the name hit the newspapers. The story said, 'The Seven-Seven Precinct, sometimes referred to as the Alamo . . .' But some precinct in the Bronx sent us a teletype message, saying, 'Hey, we're the Alamo. We're the original Alamo.' One of the guys sent them a message back too—Fuck you.

"About the same time a Communist Party group came in to the precinct, trying to rile the blacks up. They came around and started breaking the windows in the station house. They had us surrounded. And that's when our captain said on the news, 'We were like a fort under siege.' That did it. They came out with the T-shirts right after that. 'The Alamo. Under Siege.' Everybody bought the shirts. Didn't Brian have his on when he did what he did in the motel?"

No one liked wearing the new T-shirts better than some of the cops working the precinct's midnight shift. Some of the officers would put the shirts on under their uniforms and then set out to wreak havoc in the precinct—drinking beer, robbing the dead, stealing from the scenes of past burglaries and holding up drug dealers. It seemed to the officers on the midnight tours that almost everyone knew about these extracurricular activities except the people in charge of stopping corruption—an apparatus that included the precinct's Integrity Officer, the Internal Affairs Division, the Field Internal Affairs Unit, the Brooklyn district attorney and the state special prosecutor.

Sergeant William Stinson, who supervised the midnight tour, always asked precinct detectives, "So, what do you hear?" When detective Frank Duffey told him, "I hear you guys on the midnight tour are out there robbing everybody blind," Stinson replied, "I think I'll retire." But when he put in his retirement papers, and realized that the department was actually going to let him go, he rethought his position. Stinson went back to work, telling friends, "If they're going to let me retire, that means they don't have nothing on me."

Peter Heron, another new cop in the 77th Precinct who got transferred there after pulling his gun on the day he graduated from the police academy and shooting a neighbor in the head during a hallway scuffle, was fired from the department after he started snorting heroin on the job. Heron, an active cop if there ever was one, got into no less than four shootouts with drug dealers and robbery suspects during his first six months in the precinct—a remarkable achievement when you consider that most city cops retire without ever having fired their guns in the heat of battle.

In an interview with a newspaper reporter years later,

Heron even admitted shooting an unarmed man in a Manhattan park during an argument over heroin. He dropped a knife at the fallen man's side before police arrived. The arriving cops then charged the victim with attempted murder. Eventually Heron—nicknamed Peter Heroin by the cops in the 77th Precinct—was arrested for attempted murder. He defended himself saying the stress he experienced in the precinct had led him to use drugs and had ruined his life. In earlier years, Heron had taken Brian O'Regan and Henry Winter aside and warned them that a routine of mayhem and misery could change one's perspective on life.

"Get out of this precinct while you still can," he advised them.

"Pete Heroin and I worked together for awhile when I first got there. One night we were over by the Albany projects and a robbery went down. A guy with a gun had just ripped a lady off. The guy took off into a building and Pete and I ran after him. He ran to the roof and we could hear him, he was always like one landing ahead of us. When we got there we couldn't find him. We're the only people on the roof. I go to check the other entrance and it's locked. Where the hell could this guy go? We searched the top of the air shafts. We checked the elevator shaft. Nothing. Finally Pete spotted the guy's fingers. He was hanging over the side of the building waiting for us to leave, but before we could get there he lost his grip. He had been hanging there for at least five minutes. It's a standard ghetto trick, but he fell.

"We both thought the same thing. Fort Apache. The Bronx. We could see the headline: 'Cops hurl suspect to death from rooftop.' There's no witnesses. We're both going to jail. We ran downstairs and found the guy moaning in the courtyard. He hit a tree on the way down, breaking his fall. A crowd gathered and somebody was already yelling, 'You cops threw

him off the roof. We saw you do it.' We rushed the guy off
to Kings County Hospital. He came to in the emergency
room. We didn't know if he was going to make it. A doctor
asked him, 'What happened up there?' And the guy said, 'I
lost my grip. I fell.' Then he blacked out. But we were all
right—he had told the truth. Everybody heard him. But imagine if he comes to and makes a dying declaration, something
like, 'The cops pushed me off the roof.' The funny thing
was that we never found the mutt's gun. I think somebody
stole it off him when he hit the ground.

"Pete and I were on another robbery in the Albany projects.
I arrived on the scene as the backup. I saw a guy come
running around the corner with Pete chasing him in a patrol
car, driving his car like a cowboy with his gun out the window.
Pow. Pow. He's shooting away. Pete dropped the guy with
a shot in the ass.

"I did a lot of strange things in my time. But Pete, he
was the weirdest of the weird. Like I wasn't afraid of anybody.
If I had a job to do, I'd do the job. If a guy was six-foot-
six and weighed 260 pounds, I would take the diplomatic
approach. I knew I couldn't take him out right away, so
I'd bullshit with him a little, bullshit with him a little more,
try to get behind him, and then cold-cock the son of a bitch
with my jack or nightstick. Pete would go right up to them.
He was an ex-Marine. Every situation was Tripoli to him.
He would go face-to-face with them. And lose. Get his ass
kicked. He's the type of guy who would say, 'Give me a
ten—eighty-five [backup] with two units and call an ambulance.' And then he'd walk in on the guy and fight him.
Instead of doing it the sneaky way, trying to get behind
him, and hit him with the stick or something, Pete would
just call in the troops, call in the medics, drop the radio,
and go to war."

* * *

Even a casual visitor to the 77th Precinct could see there was something inherently wrong at the station house. In a neighborhood where cops were literally stepping over dead bodies and running into robbers on the streets, the most that anybody in a position of authority wanted to know was why the number of traffic summonses was down and the precinct's overtime up. The bigger questions went unresolved.

"I believe crimes are being committed by Members of the Service in uniform," wrote Captain Donald T. Bishop, the precinct commander, to his zone commander shortly after taking over the 77th Precinct in February 1982. "There's a good possibility that late tour personnel are committing larcenies at the scenes of past burglaries."

Bishop's warning, like those of a previous zone commander, went unheeded. Police officers assigned to the precinct sensed that most of their supervisors simply wanted to get their time in and move on before a major scandal broke. The department seemed to care little about the 77th and even less about what cops did in the neighborhood. Henry Winter was about to discover that a cop in the 77th Precinct could pretty much do whatever the hell he or she wanted.

Henry Winter got in trouble with his superiors shortly after he arrived. Oddly enough, he got "jammed up"—a cop phrase meaning in trouble—after he caught a bad guy who was supposed to be a good guy, driving a stolen car through his sector.

One night in 1981, Henry was teamed up in a squad car with a rookie, patrolling a section near Eastern Parkway, when he looked over to his right and saw a black man with wild-looking hair and a ragged shirt driving a beat-up Ford. Henry studied the man's car for a moment and then spotted a portable radio on the dashboard.

"Hey," Henry said to his partner, "that looks like a police department radio."

Edging up, Henry finally got close enough to read the insignia on the side of the radio—NYPD. Henry was excited. This guy couldn't be a cop.

"Look, I bet we got a member of the Black Liberation Army here with a stolen radio," Henry said. This imaginary scenario wasn't so wild. Recently, two members of the black supremacist gang had jumped from a van on a quiet Queens street and fired more than twenty shots at two police officers trapped in their radio car. Neither cop had time to get his gun out of his holster—one was killed, the other critically wounded. The surviving cop's father had a heart attack in the hospital and later died. The shooters, although later captured and convicted of murder, were still at large.

The light turned green and the driver took off. Henry followed, running the man's plate over his own portable radio. Within seconds the plate came back as a ten-sixteen (stolen). Henry reported his location over the air, hit the siren, and started to give chase. He felt good, too, figuring he was chasing a fugitive with a stolen police radio in a stolen car. He was going to be praised as one alert cop when this was all over.

Henry continued chasing the car and finally pulled it over at an intersection. He and the driver got out of their cars at the same time. Henry looked at him and felt sick. They were both wearing standard issue police trousers, shoes, and gun belts. Henry had caught a cop.

"What are you doing?" the driver yelled. "I'm a cop."

"What do you mean you're a cop?" Henry yelled back. "Show me something."

Henry was mortified. Any second now there would be a half-dozen other police cars converging on the scene.

"What are you doing in a stolen car?"

"Ah, the car's not stolen, man."

"Don't bullshit me. I just ran the fucking plate. You're in a stolen car."

Henry looked to his left and saw the radio cars closing in, their lights flashing. He had to make a quick decision, a fateful decision. Should he or shouldn't he rat on a fellow cop?

"All right. Get the fuck out of here now."

The cop sped off just as the first radio car arrived, carrying a sergeant, no less.

"What happened?" the sergeant asked. "I thought you had a stolen car."

Henry tried a smile. "No. I must have put over the wrong plate because he's got papers for that car and everything. I just let him go."

"All right," the sergeant said.

But things were not all right. The sergeant had caught a glimpse of the fleeing car and had written down a plate number just as he arrived. He called the dispatcher to ask what plate number Henry Winter had given over the air. The two numbers matched. Henry was in a lot of trouble.

They took his gun and shield away pending an in-house investigation. But later that night, following a meeting in the precinct captain's office between two borough commanders and members of the Field Internal Affairs Unit, they were given back. Henry insisted he had made a mistake, that he had put over one number and seen another on the car and registration. Essentially the department decided to look the other way. Henry was given an official reprimand; a yellow sheet was placed in his file.

The cop whom Henry let get away was assigned to watch prisoners at Kings County Hospital. He had taken an impounded car from the parking lot of his precinct during his break and was on his way to see his girlfriend when Henry pulled him over. As punishment for unauthorized use of the car, the cop was transferred to another precinct and given a foot post.

There was no reason to transfer Henry Winter anywhere else. He was already assigned to a dumping ground. Only now Henry wasn't going to get out of the 77th Precinct. Ever.

Originally, Henry had been dumped in the 77th because the department didn't know what to do with a cop everybody thought was a rat. Now he was anchored to the Alamo, a yellow flag sitting in his personnel folder, all because he had refused to turn in another cop. Life was strange, Henry Winter concluded.

"I never really did much in the beginning. Maybe little things. You know, if you go into a burglarized apartment and there's money left, you put it in your pocket. But then I worked with Gallagher—we called him Junior—one night in 1983 and I got started.

"At that time, Gallagher was looking for a partner. His partner Artie had left the precinct to join the highway patrol, and Junior was auditioning for his replacement. He was the precinct union rep. He had his ear to the ground. Gallagher always knew what was going on. He asked me to be his partner but I just didn't want to work steady midnights—I couldn't take working from midnight to eight in the morning. But Junior told me, 'Midnights are good. Get any days off you want. Nobody is out here watching you.'

"We had stopped outside a place on Rogers Avenue— there was a social club upstairs. Junior said he had to go and see this guy Robbie for a minute. I said, 'All right. I'll stay down here with the car.' Junior insisted, 'Come up.' So I went up to the club with him.

"It was a Jamaican club. Junior was talking to a guy off on the side and having a beer. So I ordered a beer just to be sociable. Then after a few minutes, we went back to the car. Gallagher handed me a ten dollar bill as we pulled away. I said, 'What's this for, Junior?' He replied, 'This is from my friend. Every once in a while he gives me a couple of dollars just to stop up and say hello. I give half to the guy I'm with.' I said, 'Oh, all right, thank you.' I didn't even think about it. It was like found money. You really weren't stealing money from anybody. I'm used to working on the back of a garbage truck. Everybody pays a garbage man.

"Later on that night, we were on patrol up on Fulton Street. We spotted a guy with a paper bag, standing in a vestibule. The guy saw us, did a double take, and dropped the bag. Boom. We got out and grabbed the guy and put him in the car. There was a pound of smoke, marijuana, in the bag. Junior asked the guy for identification, and he handed over his wallet, with a couple of hundred bucks in it. We never even looked at the guy's identification. He could have been Son of Sam for all we knew. Junior kept looking in the wallet and then back at the guy. Then Junior told him, 'You know, there's a lot of smoke here in this bag, pal. You could go to jail.' Back and forth. I looked at Gallagher and said, 'Ah, come on, we'll take him in.' Gallagher said, 'Wait a minute. Wait a minute.' So at the end of the story, what happens is that Gallagher takes money out of the guy's wallet and then hands it back to him. Then he says, 'This one is on us.'

The guy was overappreciative. Super-appreciative, in fact. We even drove him home. We drove him home, let him out of the car, and that was it. I think we split fifty dollars apiece. We left the guy some money. Junior took the smoke. He said, 'I'll take care of this.' I wasn't hip to what was going on back then with the drugs. Today I know what he did, though. He resold the drugs to a drug dealer in the neighborhood. But back then, Gallagher just held up the bag and said, 'I'll get rid of this. Don't you worry about this, buddy boy.'"

It can be argued that never in the history of the New York City Police Department has there been a precinct quite like the 77th. Certainly there has never been a more raucous locker room than the one in the bowels of the Utica Avenue building—a large but comfortable room roamed by misfits and supervised by uninterested sergeants.

The locker room and an adjoining lounge were alternately used by some of the two hundred-odd cops in the precinct as a gambling den, target range, bar, and flop house. It has also been said that on any given day there were more cash transactions made in the 77th Precinct locker room than in any Bedford-Stuyvesant bank.

The most legendary figure ever to work the room was an aging veteran named Johnny Massar, a man everybody loved and respected as a father figure. A thirty-five-year veteran of the force, Massar was one of a dying breed, a dinosaur who had worked the streets for twenty-five years and now rarely left the precinct grounds. A beer drinker without peer, Massar served as the precinct's gas attendant, cell attendant, and assistant station house officer until finally leaving the department in 1985 on a medical disability. His principle responsibility was to keep a ready supply of cold beer on hand.

Throughout the years Massar distinguished himself in a series of astonishing incidents. One day he was given the assignment to fill in for a sergeant's regular driver. Massar proceeded out to the garage and began warming up the sergeant's car. Somehow he put the car in reverse and then stepped on the gas pedal instead of the brake. The car hit a metal pole and flew through a set of steel doors, stopping in the precinct's vestibule. Massar is said to have shut off the engine, left the car, and walked calmly into the captain's office. Then he saluted and said, "I just got into a car accident, sir, and I want you to know I wasn't even drinking."

Young cops were particularly fond of blackening out the white numbers on Massar's combination lock with a marking pen. As he squinted at his lock, the young cops would yell, "Why don't you go home and get some new glasses, you old fart?"

On one occasion he finally decided to end his frustration. He pulled his service revolver and shot the lock off his locker, and then shot the locks off several others as well.

On another night, Massar took exception to the volume level of a radio in the lounge. He asked the young cops to turn the music down, insulting their taste in rock and roll. A young cop responded by cranking the volume even higher.

"I'll show you," Massar suddenly yelled, pulling his gun. "Take that!"

He fired a single shot into the heart of the radio, knocking it from a shelf to the floor. To his amazement, the radio continued to play.

"You can't kill rock and roll," the young cops shrieked. "Rock and roll lives!"

On the nights when he wasn't conducting gun battles in the lounge, the immensely popular Massar spent most of his tour drinking and cooping—sleeping on duty. When he worked as a cell attendant, he did more drinking than guarding.

One night, after Massar pounded down several cans of beer, police officers found him asleep in the lounge on a bench borrowed from Prospect Park. Ordinarily, the cops might have seen fit simply to wrap him up from head to foot in toilet paper, as was their custom. But on this particular night, the cops harassed him to the point where he felt compelled to check on his prisoners.

Massar entered the cell area and walked to the end of the row by himself. Then he walked back out of the room— his face the color of chalk.

"What's wrong, Johnny?"

Massar could not bring himself to speak. "Ahh," he said, pointing to the cell.

Henry Winter and two other cops rushed past Massar into the cells, discovering a young Hispanic man hanging from the door by his shirt. The man's lips were blue and his face contorted. As Massar looked on in silent shock, Henry grabbed hold of the man's waist and lifted him up while another cop cut the prisoner down.

Feeling a slight pulse in the man's wrist, Winter and the other cops worked frantically to revive him. They poured ammonia on his clothes and slapped his face. Finally, after a minute or two, he stirred.

"Are you okay?"

"Yeah, yeah, I'm okay."

Henry and the other cops sat back, breathing a sigh of relief.

"He's gonna make it, Johnny. Relax."

At this point Massar emerged from his nearly catatonic state and rushed towards the prisoner. "I'll teach you to try and kill yourself on my watch!" he screamed while beating the man. "I'll kill you. Nobody dies on my watch."

"Going to one of our outings was like taking your life into your own hands. I went to two functions in the Seven-

Seven and both of them blew up. The first one was the precinct picnic in 1983 at Eisenhower Park. They told us don't ever come back. We even had to pay damages. The problem was the tug-of-war. One of the guys tied his end of the rope to a water fountain. All of a sudden the water fountain is down, we've broken the pipe, and there's water all over the place. We're laughing like hell, rolling over. We're all stewed. Even the wives are looped. Then as we're leaving, I see one cop coming along with a Harley Davidson and another cop coming right at him with a brand new Mustang. They're both drunk. Boom. The guy hits the Mustang broadside, the other guy's gun comes out. One cop is threatening to blow the other cop away. Shots fired in the air. I said, 'Goodbye.'

"The other outing was a fishing trip. I'm in my boat, and a cop named Billy is in his boat with another guy named Jimmy. We were fishing for fluke off Riis Park. We were drifting, three boats together. These guys over here are drinking, these guys over there are drinking, I'm not drinking because when I fish, I don't usually drink. All of a sudden, I pulled a nice fluke up out of the water. Boom. Boom. Boom. They're shooting. I'm here with my boat, I got a fluke out of the water and there's this cop trying to shoot the fish off my line. I look at him, 'What are you, fucking crazy?' Boom. Boom. Boom. I dropped my rod. Both guys go after my pole. One guy gets his outriggers tangled up with my line, loses his outriggers, his engine floods. It's pure insanity. I said, 'So long.'

"But, then again, sometimes I liked the madness. I remember one time I had a black powder gun in the locker room. A rifle—a .45-caliber monster. A guy wants to see how it's shot. Okay. So I go to the locker room and load the sucker up. I didn't put the ball in, I just loaded up a charge. Then I go back to the lounge and yell, 'Ah, you motherfucker." Boom. The whole lounge. Ka-boom. Then I went into the bathroom after a few guys went into the stalls, cocked the hammer back and let it go again. Ka-boom. It was like an ash can went off. The room filled with smoke. The guys are screaming. It was beautiful. Then I went upstairs and the lieutenant says, 'Heard a little tremor downstairs men. What was it?' We said, 'Nothing, Nothing, don't worry about it.'

"That was good but not as good as when Gallagher got the whole roll call to wet their pants. We made believe we were having an argument. Gallagher took his real gun out of the holster and replaced it with a starter's pistol—you know, blanks. So the sergeant is in the middle of the roll call and Junior suddenly stands up. 'I've had it with your fucking shit, Henry.' And I'm in the back. 'Fuck you, Junior. Your wife says this—' He screams, 'Oh yeah, your wife and your brother-in-law—' 'Yeah, well, you son of a bitch.' He pulled the gun from the holster and then: Boom. Boom. Everybody in roll call hit the ground. And after he shot, I went, 'Aaaaggghh,' and bent over, like I've been hit. One sergeant, a young one, he turned white. Sergeant Jervas was there too. His nickname was Nervous Jervas. He was beyond white. He was absolutely bloodless.

"It really didn't go over too well, though. It was funny later when everybody sat down and laughed. But Jervas, he was pissed. He said, 'You could have been blown away. These guys, they don't know you. They could have shot you.' He got over it though. Eventually, no matter what you did in the Seven-Seven, the supervisors got over it."

* * *

During the summer of 1982, a sergeant named Jerome Schnupp was transferred into the 77th and made it known that he had every intention of straightening out the misguided troops. Schnupp worked around the clock getting to know all of the precinct's cops by face and putting a hit list together. Within weeks of his arrival, the cops had a nickname for their new supervisor that epitomized their feelings for the do-good leader. They called him Sergeant Schmuck.

In January 1983 Schnupp went to the precinct captain, Donald Bishop, and reported what everyone else had known for months. A lot of cops were robbing bad guys instead of arresting them. Schnupp filled out a report that was later delivered to Internal Affairs in which he named cops on the late tours whom he suspected of committing larcenies, cooping, and visiting girlfriends while on duty. A police officer with friends in Internal Affairs got hold of a copy of the report and circulated it in the precinct locker room. A few days later, Schnupp walked into the muster room to oversee roll call only to discover a dead rat pinned to the blackboard. The rat wore a name tag too—Sgt. Schmuck.

Schnupp left the room and ran to see the captain, complaining that the men were, well, using rodents to challenge his authority. By the time Schnupp returned with the captain, the rat had disappeared.

"What's the problem here, men?" the captain wanted to know.

"No problem, sir."

"Was there just a rat in here?"

"A rat in here? There aren't any rats in the Seven-Seven, Captain. Everybody knows that, sir."

Within two years, the misfits drove Sergeant Schnupp out of the precinct, if not his mind. He spent a lot of his time out in the parking lot after work, changing flat tires on his car.

"I must have went over that pothole too hard," he once told Henry.

"Yeah," Winter replied, pointing to three fresh puncture wounds in the tire. "And there must have been a pitchfork in the pothole."

5

"You killed that guy for ten dollars?"

New York City Police Department regulations specify that any officer suspected of taking drugs must submit to a test called a Dole Urinalysis within twenty-four hours of being so ordered. If an officer tests positive for drugs, he's immediately suspended and ordered to face a departmental trial where he's usually fired. If a policeman is suspected of taking drugs and refuses to submit to a test, he's also usually fired.

Certainly the 77th Precinct had a drug problem. Some officers smoked marijuana in their patrol cars on the late tour and snorted cocaine in the locker room lounge. Many more used drugs off duty, snorting cocaine with girlfriends they had met in the precinct while working. It was not at all unusual for a cop in the 77th Precinct to leave his wife and kids in the suburbs for a prostitute in the slum.

One June day in 1983, a black woman and her husband walked into the precinct and demanded to see a lieutenant. The husband had apparently come home unexpectedly the night before and discovered his wife smoking marijuana with Thomas Texiera, a veteran cop from the 77th with a reputation for a quick trigger finger and an insatiable appetite for women. The husband insisted that Texiera be tested for drugs. Immediately.

A black cop who was preparing to retire soon, Texiera was given to combing his hair straight back and wearing a lot of gold jewelry. "Tex" was widely feared on the street and was said to have dropped four armed suspects during shootouts. Shortly before his current problem, Texiera was sitting in a friend's apartment when he heard a noise on the fire escape. A burglar broke through the apartment window; Tex shot him dead. The incident went into the books, as the cops like to say, as a good shooting.

After hearing the husband's complaint, which was corroborated by his wife, the officer's girlfriend, the desk lieutenant notified Internal Affairs. A cop who overheard the conversation rushed to warn Texiera, who was watching a chess tournament in the lounge.

"Who wants to go across the street for me?" Texiera suddenly asked.

"What do you need?" asked Henry.

"Do me a favor. Here's two dollars. Get me a bottle of vinegar from the store across the street."

Henry returned with a bottle of cooking vinegar minutes later. Believing falsely that the acidic vinegar would somehow help him pass the drug test, Texiera guzzled down the bottle in front of his friends. He then walked out of the lounge to be met by investigators and members of the Health Services Department, who administered the drug test. Tex tested positively and was dismissed from the force, never to set foot in the 77th Precinct, or the woman's apartment, again.

"I used to smoke some marijuana. Not every day, religiously, but if I went to a party, and all of my friends were there smoking reefer, I'd join them. They'd say, 'Aw, you're a cop? What are you going to do—lock up your best friends?' We grew up with drugs. 1969. Woodstock. Everybody does it. So I do a joint over here with close friends, that's it. I never touched coke until I got to the precinct. And I just wanted to see what the hell it was. I wasn't an addict or anything. It's like—say you're doing an eight-to-four tour, you wind up going through the four-to-twelve to the midnight-to-eight, then you come back, you work and do another eight-to-four. You're tired. You do some coke. It was a nice feeling. Kept you up, kept you aware, kept you awake.

"Much later, if we hit a place and got drugs, I might have dipped into the package. I can look back and say I was stupid because you don't know what the hell you're getting from these people. But if we got a lot of coke, I'd open up one package in the car, taste it, snort maybe a little bit, and say, 'Yeah, this is good stuff, we'll get good money for this.' Then I'd be ripped the whole rest of the night. I'd say, 'Yeah, let's go do this job. Let's go do that job.'

Elsewhere in the precinct, cops were getting suspended or demoted by department brass after committing perjury on the stand or overextending their police powers in the streets. Some were so busy ripping off drug dealers and breaking into apartments that they were no longer interested in making arrests or working overtime. Essentially they were moonlighting as thieves while working in uniform.

Steadily, a small circle of 77th Precinct cops began giving more and more of their arrests away to other cops. Odd radio chatter filled the 77th Precinct airwaves.

"Who's catching tonight?"

"I am."

"Who's looking tonight?"

"I am."

"All right, Nostrand and Park."

One set of cops in a patrol car would then rush to the corner of Nostrand Avenue and Park Place where they would discover another set of cops standing next to a burglary or robbery suspect in handcuffs. The cops would then hand over the suspect and the case to the arriving officers, who returned to the precinct and fabricated arrest reports. If the case ever went to trial, the cops took the stand and perjured themselves, entertaining the judge and jury with a false story of how the arrest was made.

In September 1984, Stephen Christiano, a police officer who worked the late tour, was fidgeting in the witness box in a Brooklyn court, under heavy cross examination from a defense counsel. A burglary suspect insisted that when he was arrested months earlier, Christiano had not been at the crime scene.

"Where was the defendant standing, Officer Christiano, when you entered the apartment."

"How the hell would I know?" Christiano screamed. "I wasn't even there."

The case was thrown out of court and Christiano was suspended for seventy-five days for supplying false information on an arrest report.

By now, some of the supervisors in the 77th were having trouble staying clear of the mayhem. Morton Lavan, a probationary sergeant, drove past a corner one summer day and spotted a group of dice players arguing over a pile of money.

As Lavan approached, the men stepped back, leaving money piled up on the sidewalk. Lavan bent down and picked it up.

"Whose money is this?" he asked.

The dice players, reluctant to admit ownership of the cash and risk imprisonment, said nothing. Lavan shrugged. He looked across the street and spotted four or five kids on a corner. He called them over and handed them the money. The neighborhood kids were ecstatic. The police department regarded the act as a robbery. Sergeant Lavan, suddenly regarded on the streets as a Robin Hood, was demoted to the rank of police officer.

Internal Affairs investigators watching the 77th Precinct were intent on catching members of the late tours who were breaking the law. In July 1983, a team assigned to the Field Internal Affairs Unit set up an "integrity test". The investigators drove two nondescript vans into the precinct one night, parking one across from a firehouse and the other a half block away. The first van, which was left unlocked, with the side door open, contained several cases of Newport cigarettes. The second van contained two police officers, armed with enough movie equipment to start a small film company.

While the surveillance team trained their cameras on the bait van, another investigator took control of the radio and ordered two police cars into the neighborhood. According to police records, the operation had been designed to test the integrity of Sergeant Stinson and police officers William Gallagher, David Williams, and Joseph (Zeke) Zayas. The officers—particularly Zayas, who smoked Newport cigarettes—might have gone for the bait but they were forewarned of the test by a friend in Internal Affairs earlier that night.

Gallagher later told friends that he was the first to notice something fishy.

"Why do they keep sending us down this street?" he asked, after passing the open van and its poisoned cargo for the third time. "They must think we're stupid."

Eventually Sergeant Stinson noticed the surveillance and parked down the street from it. He motioned to a friend on the street.

"How long has that van been parked over there?" he asked.

"About a half hour."

"Did you see anything?"

"Yeah. The van pulled up. Two guys jumped out and got into the back. A third guy from the van got into another car and pulled away."

Insulted, the four officers then approached the surveillance van. They began rocking it back and forth, banging on the doors and prying at the windows.

"Come on out, you scumbags."

"We know you're in there."

The integrity test ended with the officers taking the bait van back to the precinct, where they vouchered it according to the book. One of the officers even added an extra pack of cigarettes to the confiscated cargo to further confuse the frustrated investigators, who arrived at the precinct hours later to reclaim their bait.

News of the bungled test swept through the precinct. The cops made the investigators look like idiots, everyone agreed. Amid much laughter, it was decided that the 77th Precinct cops were untouchable. They were just too street-smart. Their moles in the Internal Affairs Division and police union kept them well insulated. "Hell, guys," they told each other, "We're practically bullet proof."

* * *

Henry Winter was feeling equally immortal. He had just survived his first two shootouts, dodging bullets aimed for his head as he patrolled the Bedford-Stuyvesant streets.

"I was coming back from court in downtown Brooklyn one day. I had gotten off the subway and was walking up Utica Avenue to the station house when I spotted this badass kid named Melvin Blunt standing across the street. I know this kid is trouble because he's got numerous arrests in the city for robberies. He always carries a gun. I had just reached the intersection of Sterling and Utica when I looked across the street and spotted Melvin talking to a group of kids. So I keep my eye on him. I got up a little closer and spotted a kid showing Melvin a silver gun. I thought, 'I'm going to sneak around and just grab the fucker.' But the kids saw me and took off.

"I chased them to Sterling Place and onto the roof of a building. Suddenly this other kid, Richard, turned around and took a shot at me. It surprised the hell out of me. The shot missed me by a foot or two. The kid had turned and fired from about twenty feet in front of me. I peeled off the chase and called for a backup. I wasn't afraid, just pissed. The cavalry came out after that. The guys found Melvin Blunt about three buildings down. The shooter got away.

"Not too long after that I had the second incident with a guy named Raoul Morgan—they're still looking for him. He was a Franklin Avenue drug dealer. He took a shot at me. I was chasing him and he took a shot at me. He got away. I spotted him across the street and he took another shot at me. After he shot, I chased him across Eastern Parkway, through a bunch of abandoned buildings. He ran right past his house, which is why we are able to identify him. His little nephew waved to him as he ran by. 'Hey, Uncle Raoul,' the kid yells. And I'm behind him. He went over a couple of fences and I lost him. To this day, I'm glad I never caught him.

"I didn't know this until afterwards when the detectives canvassed the area—he was waiting for me. I was chasing him and we kept going over fences, but I just couldn't make it over the last fucking fence. He ran into an apartment building, made it up to the second floor, and broke into an old woman's apartment and held her at gunpoint, waiting for me.

"He would have had me cold. If I would have kept on following him up to that apartment and gone into it he would have been behind the door waiting for me to come in. I'm glad I never caught up with him. I would have been dead.

"At first when someone pegs a shot at you, you don't even think. It's amazing, but you don't. You just react. After everything calms down, then you get a little shaky. A little nervous. Then you think, 'What could have happened?' And that's the worst time, because in the street, after the guy shoots at you, you want to beat him, you want to kill the fucking guy. But it happens very fast. Afterward, when you're doing the paperwork about a half hour later, you realize that this fuck sitting across from you could have killed you. Because now it's just you and him sitting across the table from each other. Then you start, you know, digging him. If you're so inclined, that's when you hit them in the head."

Henry was not usually inclined to beat up his prisoners. In fact, he seemed to get along with most of the people in his sector. Some cops, his partners included, even thought that Henry liked skells more than cops.

Sometimes he arrived at the scene of a robbery or a mugging to find cops beating a black suspect.

"That's enough," he would say.

"Screw off, Winter, he ain't your prisoner."

Then Henry would try the pragmatic approach. "If you beat the guy to death, he's not going to be anybody's prisoner." Sometimes the beatings even stopped.

In time Henry began handing out his own form of street justice. At first, instead of simply arresting young mugging suspects, Henry would drive the teenagers home. He realized that the kids would be back on the street the next day if he arrested them for petty theft, and he thought that they would get into bigger trouble if he personally talked to their parents.

But Henry was being naive. He was being "Long Island." Henry based his opinions on his childhood in the suburbs, not the ghetto. When Henry was a kid and a cop brought him home, he got a beating from the cop and his parents. Now, when he brought a ghetto kid home and stood in the tenement doorway, his badge shining and his blue uniform looking immaculate, Henry took the beating—an emotional one. If he said, "Your son robbed a person. He stole an old lady's pocketbook. Talk to your kid. Straighten him out," the kid's parents often screamed, "What the fuck are you bringing him home for? He's no good. You handle him. He's yours. He's in the street."

In the beginning, Henry even cried. Things bothered him back then. Finding dead infants in garbage pails bothered him. It bothered him to see elderly people dead too. Dead kids and elderly people bothered him most of all. And in order to keep some semblance of sanity, Henry Winter set up little emotional guidelines for himself. Any victim falling between the ages of sixteen and sixty was fair game, he decided. He wouldn't care about them. But he would allow himself to be bothered—and even cry—if he saw a victim of a crime younger than sixteen or older than sixty.

A cop from the 77th had to set up some sort of immunity system against tragedy and trauma, Henry decided, if he didn't want to wind up like Peter Heroin.

It seemed to Henry that no one in the ghetto had any respect for life. On July 4, 1981, there was a wild shootout on St. Johns Place. Two men and a woman died, their bodies lying in the street. A crowd of citizens formed, ignoring the dead draped in white sheets, and gathered around a brand-new Mustang parked near the shooting scene. The car had a bullet hole in the right front fender.

"Poor car," one man said.

"At first, I couldn't get over how little life meant to people in the precinct. Especially the kids. I would say to one of them, 'You killed that guy for ten dollars?' He'd say, 'Yeah but that was my ten dollars.' I couldn't understand that at first. But then I saw the way these people lived and I understood.

"Ten dollars is a fortune in the ghetto. Take someone living in an abandoned apartment—they use the stove for heat, don't have water. They've got to run downstairs and get water out of a fire hydrant, go back upstairs, warm the water, and put it in a tub to wash the kids. The bathroom doesn't work. They use another abandoned apartment on the next floor as the bathroom. Just going on the floor. The windows have been broken for two or three years, they're covered with cardboard. You walk into the place, it's freezing, and you find a kid that killed someone for ten dollars. To this kid ten dollars is a lot of money. It's like ten thousand dollars to us.

"When someone comes up to us and puts a gun in our face, we say 'Take the ten dollars.' But in the ghetto, the kids won't give up the money. And if they do give it up, even if they're unarmed and the muggers who ripped them off have nine-millimeter guns with fifteen shots in each, the kids'll give chase. They'll go after the robbers unarmed. Somehow they'll catch them for that lousy ten dollars. The kids don't want to press charges. They got their money back. They're happy."

Police Officer Henry Winter was determined to make a difference in the lives of the people he met. Steadily, he lost faith in the justice system. He got tired of seeing the drug dealer he had arrested on one corner one day, back on the streets waving to him from another corner the next day. Henry began to realize that a police officer could do more harm to a bad guy than any New York City court.

One day in 1982, he spotted a drug dealer on a corner in his sector. Henry would chase the dealer off the corner only to find him back there later in the day still peddling marijuana. He dropped the man's drugs down the sewer one time and arrested him another. These actions had the same effect on the dealer's curbside business—none.

So one day Henry grabbed the dealer off the street and led him back to the station house into the muster room and sat him down at a table.

"Empty your pockets," Henry said.

The dealer was not carrying drugs. But he did throw a wad of crumpled one- and five-dollar bills on the table. Henry studied them for a while—the bankroll came to $170—and then came up with a terrific idea.

"This would make a nice fire," he said.

Henry piled the bills into a small heap and lit a match to them. The dealer began to scream, drawing a small crowd of police officers into the room. As his fellow cops shrieked their approval, he burned all the money, reducing the cash to a pile of cinders. For added dramatic effect, Henry then blew the ashes into the drug dealer's lap. The cops cheered, all of them failing to take action on what amounted to the robbery of a drug dealer by a uniformed police officer in their own station house.

The dealer gritted his teeth. Henry sat back and laughed.

"You can't do this," the dealer finally announced.

"Fuck you," Henry said. "You fucking prove it's money. To me it's burnt paper. Now get the hell out of this station house, asshole. And if I ever see you on the streets again, we're going to come in here and have another little bonfire. We may roast marshmallows next time."

The dealer left the precinct without saying another word, never to be seen in Police Officer Henry Winter's sector again.

Flushed with success after this small, albeit temporary, victory over a Bedford-Stuyvesant drug dealer, Henry was soon taking the law into his hands regularly. He became judge, jury, and hangman—forcing frightened dealers to flush their drugs and money down precinct toilet bowls. He felt good about himself as a police officer. He was making the bad guys suffer.

That same year Henry had some trouble with a seventeen-year-old mugger named Brown who made his living robbing elderly women of their handbags on Utica Avenue, keeping the money, and selling the pocketbooks on Eastern Parkway to passing motorists who stopped for traffic lights.

Responding to a call of "burglary in progress," Henry once caught Brown trying to jimmy the lock on a woman's door with a screwdriver. Henry handcuffed Brown and knocked on the door. He asked the woman if she wanted to press charges.

"No," she replied. "Just get him out of here."

Henry was incensed at the woman's lack of civic pride.

"Come on," he said. "You've got to press charges. Look at your door. He damaged your door."

"No, no. I don't want to get involved."

The woman's response was typical, a refrain heard by police officers throughout the ghetto. But Henry would have none of it. He'd take care of Brown himself.

He told his partner Al Cimino that he wanted to "take a meal." Then he dropped Cimino off at the station house, saying he would take the burglar home.

Instead, Henry drove his prisoner to the far side of Brooklyn, all the way out to Canarsie, ordering him out of the car on an isolated pier.

"Now give me your sneakers," Henry said.

"What?"

"The sneakers. Your felony shoes, kid. Give me the sneakers."

The suspect handed over his sneakers and Henry departed, leaving Brown to walk back home barefoot. Henry laughed as he drove back to the precinct, throwing the sneakers out of the car. He was extremely satisfied with himself. He was making a difference.

Three months later in December, Henry caught Brown on Nostrand Avenue trying to rob an old lady of her handbag. This time Henry didn't even bother to ask the woman to do her civic duty. He simply loaded Brown into his car and told another officer, "Cover for me. If any jobs come over the radio for my sector, just pick them up and pretend to be me. I'll be back in a little while."

In the back of the car, Brown said, "Ah, shit. I just bought these sneakers."

Once again Henry swung by the station house, dropping off his partner. Cimino, who was into physical fitness, liked nothing better than to be left back at the station where he was free to lift hundreds of pounds of dead weight in the gym.

"No more games, kid," Henry said, turning to his prisoner

once his partner was out of earshot. "I'm going to tan your hide. Either that or you're going to jail."

"Beat me," Brown pleaded. "Give me a beating. But don't take me to jail."

"Fuck this beating shit. Nothing is going to stop you from coming out here again."

So Henry drove out of Bedford-Stuyvesant. Past Canarsie. Out of Brooklyn. Past Queens. Out of New York City. Past Valley Stream and onto the Southern State Parkway.

"Where am I going?" Brown demanded.

"Shut up," Henry said, his patrol car flying east through Long Island at 80 miles an hour at three o'clock in the morning.

"I'm getting out."

"Go ahead. You want to jump? Go ahead, jump. I don't care."

Henry continued east, passing a state trooper's barracks, then turned south toward Jones Beach. He drove straight to the beach and parked his car at Parking Field Nine, ordering Brown out of the car.

"Remember the last time I made you walk back from Canarsie with no sneakers?"

Brown was aghast. "Oh man, you aren't going to make me walk all the way back home without sneakers?"

"No. You are one hundred percent right. This time, take *everything* off."

The suspect undressed and Henry departed, checking his rearview mirror in time to see Brown emerge from the parking field in T-shirt, underpants, and a pair of black socks. Heading back to the precinct, about forty miles away from the parking field, Henry threw the man's sneakers, pants, shirt, and jacket along the way.

"Jesus," Henry said much later that night after hooking

up with his muscle-bound partner again. "This car is a gas hog. How did the needle get to E so fast?"

Brown made it back to the precinct to file a complaint against a cop nicknamed "Blondie" the next day, but he later moved out of the neighborhood. An investigation into the Jones Beach affair was dropped. No one believed the kid's story anyway. No cop was crazy enough to drive a two-bit mugger an hour out of town in the middle of the night just to teach him a lesson. Not even in the 77th Precinct.

Steadily, Henry developed friendships with street people. He could talk their language. And if Henry couldn't talk their language, he simply made one up.

He was patrolling his sector one day when Whitey Gilbert, a detective working as a field training officer with a group of rookies, suddenly came on the air. Gilbert was a straight arrow cop who operated by the letter of the law whenever he was breaking in a crop of rookies. The same guy who said, "The fucker went that way," when he was with other veterans, now told rookies, "The suspect alighted in this direction."

On this day, Gilbert was in a tough predicament. He had responded to a neighborhood dispute only to discover a group of blacks from Guinea arguing in their native tongue—French. No one in the group spoke any English except the cops, who spoke no French.

"Seven-Seven, Charley," Gilbert said, putting out a call for help over the radio. "Does any unit out there know French?"

Tony Magno, a police officer who speaks a lot of Brooklyn and a little English, nudged Henry and grabbed the radio, smiling.

"Oui," Tony said.

They decided during the ride to the scene of the dispute that Henry would handle any and all foreign languages. When he arrived, Henry waved Gilbert off and headed into the heart of the fray, the rookies standing back in absolute awe.

"Polly vou you woo woo. Frar a shocka une dos trees, polly voo kess que say arrestee."

The people stopped arguing and looked at Winter, blinking, astounded by what they had just heard. The cop was talking absolute gibberish. They screamed back at him in rapid-fire French.

Undaunted, Henry held up his hand, demanding to be heard.

"Le grande la loo, woo woo, we papa."

Again the Africans stopped arguing. Taking his cue, Henry turned to the unsuspecting rookies and began his interpretation.

"The time and place of occurrence," he began, "was ten hundred hours at this address." An obliging rookie took copious notes and Henry returned to the argument, interjecting even more gibberish and confusion into the proceedings.

"This guy says this women stole his money," Henry concluded, making up a story to go with his make-believe French. "She denies taking the money. They just agreed to settle it in court."

Gilbert filled out a complaint report, handing it to his interpreter, who then explained the meaning of the paperwork to the Africans.

"Wee, wee, poly see, you woo woo, en courto," he said.

Henry shut the door and the cops left.

"Thank you so much," Gilbert told Winter and Magno. "I owe you a beer. I couldn't have done it without you."

"Ah, it was nothing," Henry said. "You just have to speak the language."

"Oui," Tony added.

By now, Henry was approaching legendary status as the 77th Precinct's resident prankster. But there were contradictions too. Certainly he was not a cop to be fooled with. Sure, Henry had once used his flashlight to cold-cock a Jamaican woman holding a baby during a dispute when the woman called him a "blood clot," but he also had a soft side— particularly when it came to kids. He routinely handed out twenty-dollar bills to kids hanging out at the precinct house for washing his truck. None of them were even tall enough to reach the hood of Henry's truck. He could not find fault with ghetto kids, only their parents. It wasn't a kid's fault that he was growing up in a slum, Henry decided.

In the week before Christmas in 1983 Henry was called to an apartment near the corner of Washington Avenue and Lincoln Place. A mother had left her seven-year-old daughter Toya alone with a teenaged boy, the child's cousin. The cousin, fourteen, had raped the girl. Henry and his partner arrested the cousin and took Toya to the hospital, where they spent most of the night. The child wouldn't talk to anyone but Henry.

He called the district attorney's office and a prosecutor arrived at the hospital with two anatomically correct dolls. Henry took his shield off and began playing with the dolls, gaining the child's confidence. Finally Toya used the dolls to reenact the rape scene for him.

Later that night Henry Winter, father of two small daughters, left the hospital and drove home to a fitful night's sleep. Still haunted by what he had seen and heard, he went out to a store the next morning and bought Toya several presents, including a Cabbage Patch Kid doll. Betsy gave Henry two dresses that no longer fit his own girls. He then drove to the hospital, giving Toya the doll, dresses, a coloring book, and crayons. He returned to the hospital again the next day, dropping off more toys and a twenty dollar bill.

"Now when you get better, you go out and buy yourself a real Christmas present. You buy whatever you want."

Then he got busy. It was Christmas time in the ghetto. Muggers were robbing shoppers. Teenagers were shooting each other over presents, killing each other over sheepskin coats and new sneakers. New Year's Day was no better. Winos and junkies were stabbing each other over $2 bottles of cheer and bags of junk.

It seemed to Henry that a man could know no deeper gloom in life than to be working in a ghetto during the holiday season. To raise his spirits, he loaded up his truck with presents—hand-me down clothes from his own wife and kids—and drove down to an area frequented by neighborhood hookers, Lincoln Terrace Park. Henry knew that a lot of the prostitutes would have kids. He stayed parked there for an hour, handing out clothes. The prostitutes were thankful, and even offered Henry free use of their own wares in exchange for his gifts.

"No thanks. But Merry Christmas anyway."

Six months later, Henry spotted Toya playing outside her home. The child was wearing one of the dresses he had given her, but the gift was now dirty, tattered and torn. He talked to the girl briefly, long enough to hear Toya say that her mother had sold her Cabbage Patch doll after she got out of the hospital and spent Henry's twenty dollars on drugs. Henry went to look for the mother, but never found her. That was a good thing, Henry decided, because if he had caught up with Toya's mother, the precinct's homicide list would probably have grown by one.

In time Henry forgot about Toya and her mother, but a little piece of him died with the memory.

One day Henry responded to a robbery in a brownstone on Virginia Place. An elderly couple had been beaten and robbed of their gold and antique jewelry by their grandson, a mildly retarded twenty-five-year-old man named Charlie Isaacson. The couple gave the police officer a picture of their grandson and Henry set out to find the robber.

Henry spotted Charlie on a nearby street corner and placed him in his car. But after questioning the man for five minutes Henry could see that the robber was a little slow. Charlie confessed that he had taken the jewelry (valued at close to eight thousand dollars) to a local pawn shop.

"I got this much back," Charlie said, handing over twenty-five dollars.

Henry was furious—not with the retarded robber but with the pawnbroker. Accompanied by Charlie, he burst into the pawn shop a few minutes later.

"Did you just take some jewelry from this guy?" he demanded.

The pawnbroker answered, "No."

Henry kicked down a partition and found the jewelry on a table. The pawnbroker was frightened and handed over the jewelry, never even bothering to ask for his own twenty-five dollars back. Henry returned the jewelry to Charlie's grandparents along with twenty-five dollars interest. Rather than take Charlie to jail, he accompanied him to Kings County Hospital, where he was admitted and treated for six months in the psychiatric ward.

Over the years Henry and Charlie became great friends. Henry gave Charlie his home phone number, and even brought him home for dinner. He taught Charlie how to talk to girls, advising him not to tell them he had money right away. And whenever Charlie smoked marijuana, he called Henry's house. "Mrs. Winter, could you please tell Mr. Winter that I'm high?"

Charlie still stole from his grandparents from time to time, but whenever Henry heard the call on the radio "Virginia Place," he would handle the job.

"Okay Charlie, what did we get for the jewels this time?"

Charlie became Henry's project. Here was one person in the ghetto of Bedford-Stuyvesant that he could really help.

During his stay in the 77th Precinct, Henry met thousands of people and made hundreds of friends. But to this day only one Bedford-Stuyvesant resident still calls him at home. He calls regularly and always asks the policeman's wife the same thing.

"Mrs. Winter, is Mr. Winter still in town? Is he allowed to talk yet? I saw what happened on the television, you know. Is my friend Mr. Winter all right? Can I do anything for him?"

The caller is a retarded man named Charlie, who still occasionally clips a dollar bill or two off his grandmother's dresser.

6

"Will you just shoot me?"

Brian Francis O'Regan was living the American Dream in reverse.

Like another Valley Stream cop, Henry Winter, O'Regan left his suburban home each day to go to work in a slum. But unlike Henry Winter, Brian never came to grips with this great conflict in his life.

Brian was seven years older than Henry, and he also had graduated from Valley Stream Central High School. Unlike Henry, he hadn't avoided the temptation of the military and Vietnam. He felt an obligation. Brian joined the Marines after high school.

He got as close to the Far East as the Dover Air Force Base in Delaware, but that was close enough. Brian spent part of his six-year enlistment keeping inventory of dead soldiers. He carried a clipboard and a mechanical pen, and he watched life flow past him in little black bags with zippers. One. Two. One hundred. Two hundred. One thousand. Two thousand . . .

Later, Brian was assigned another job, keeping living Marines squared away while he worked as a military policeman. They were both jobs, and Brian could handle them. He had been instilled with esprit de corps. But in 1973, as the guns in Vietnam became a distant echo lost in the clamor of the escalating troop withdrawal, Brian O'Regan came home to Valley Stream, moving back into his parent's house on East Dover Street.

Brian came from the working class. His mother Dorothy arrived in the suburbs from Flushing, by way of St. Albans, Queens. As a child she had often worked alongside her father, a truck farmer, unloading crates of fruit and vegetables onto the docks. Brian's father fixed oil burners for a living and tinkered with engines as a hobby. Mr. O'Regan had created a stir on his block once when he built a Ford with two front ends, a vehicle which surely brought panic to the neighborhood's one-way streets. Another time, Brian's father turned heads on Merrick Road when he rode down the middle of the street standing on a motorcycle.

Essentially, the O'Regans were sensible people. When St. Albans got too crowded they moved further east, winding up in Valley Stream. If you wanted to enjoy life, the O'Regans agreed, you had to have a good job and be willing to work hard. So when Brian came home from the war and told his father he wanted to become a New York City cop, Brian's father deemed his twenty-eight-year-old son's career choice a wise one, worthy of an O'Regan.

"One thing about the Police Department," Brian's father used to tell him. "They never lay anybody off."

Originally Brian dreamed of joining an outfit called the Emergency Services Unit—a division of gung-ho officers who are widely regarded as the department's cops of last resort. Emergency Services cops ride in trucks and wear flak jackets. They carry shotguns, battering rams, and, when the situation demands them, machine guns. In a sense, ESU cops are to the New York City Police Department what marines are to the armed forces. Whenever either group arrives at an incident, there is likely to be some sort of ass kicking.

ESU cops earn their paychecks storming into buildings, kicking down doors, and rescuing hostages. They surround bank robbers, focus infrared gunsights on snipers during riots, pull people from burning buildings, climb bridges to talk would-be suicide victims out of jumping, dig city workers out of street cave-ins, and use steel saws to cut accident victims out of cars. An Emergency Services cop was the kind of hero Brian O'Regan wanted to be.

He graduated from the police academy on May 29, 1973, raring to go, ready to arrest the whole city, as cops like to say. But without a friend in high places, sometimes called a "hook," to guide his career, Brian had to settle for the luck of the draw. Fate led him to a locker in the 77th Precinct.

Other rookies groaned when Brian told them of his assignment. "Oh boy, you got a ghetto job." Brian shrugged off the warnings. He had a gun and shield. The shield read: City of New York. To Brian that meant you went where the bosses sent you.

"Pride and glory," he would later say. "That's what I liked."

Although assigned as a lowly patrolman in a ghetto precinct, Brian soon started acting like a member of the Emergency Services Unit. By day he leaped from one roof to another in a single bound. He dodged bullets on the street and twisted steel doors off their hinges. At night he returned to the suburbs, his body scraped and his mind raw from what he had seen. Family members suggested that Brian get himself transferred to a better environment.

"Your precinct has more murders than any other precinct in the city," his older brother Greg once noted. "Don't you worry about that?"

"No," Brian answered, truthfully.

Still, his father offered to call an inspector he knew and work something out. But Brian would have none of it. He figured a cop had to work his way up into the Emergency Services Unit.

"I'm new," Brian told his family. "I need some more time there."

In July 1975, when the city started laying off cops, Brian O'Regan joined another 2,863 officers who were ordered to turn in their guns and shields. He left the department on the same day as another policeman working in Rockaway, Queens—Henry Winter. Like Henry, Brian started sending out résumés. A bachelor, O'Regan had no anchor to Valley Stream other than his parents, and they were still young enough to look after each other.

One day he got a letter from the Broward County Sheriff's Department in Fort Lauderdale, Florida. They were hiring. Brian packed up his belongings and drove south, joining the Broward County Sheriff's Department as a deputy sheriff.

He was amazed by what he found in Florida. For openers, there was his patrol car—Broward County deputies took their cars home at night. There was also the uniform—a combination of brown pants and a short-sleeved white shirt trimmed with green and gold. The latest in south Florida cop wear included a Smokey the Bear hat, complete with a little gold braid. Where once Brian had worn a dull, oblong silver shield over his heart, he now wore a brilliant gold star. Relatives visiting Brian in Florida discovered a cop in starched white shirt and creased pants driving a car with a steam-cleaned engine. The car shone so brightly that Brian's nieces joked about borrowing their uncle's wire-rimmed sunglasses just to look at it.

"He always had a smile on his face," said his niece Kathleen. "He'd say, 'How do I look? How do I look in my uniform?' "

Brian had a reputation as a model deputy who never lost his head. And when a Miami ghetto erupted in a race riot one summer night in 1979, local police enlisted the help of Brian O'Regan, a Broward County deputy with experience in Black Brooklyn, to help quell the disturbance.

"They wanted me in Miami for one reason," he later said. "You can't push me. I don't explode."

In late 1980, he was still working hard in Florida, collecting thank-you letters from citizens he had aided and hearing talk from supervisors about a promotion to detective, when he got bad news from home. His father had died of a heart attack.

Brian flew back to New York, and took a cab straight from the airport to the Moore Funeral Home in Valley Stream. Looking tanned and refreshed, Brian created a mild scene as soon as he entered the sitting room. All his relatives were in the back of the funeral parlor, sitting on folding chairs and chatting. Brian was incensed. No one was sitting near his father's casket.

"Why are you all back here?" Brian said, an edge to his voice. "You've left him all alone up there. You should all be up front with him."

Brian stormed to the front of the room, and spent several

minutes kneeling over his father's casket. Then he plunked himself down in a folding chair near the body, and sat sentry over his dead father for the remainder of the wake.

After the funeral, Brian announced to the family that he was moving back home so he could look after his widowed mother. The New York City Police Department was hiring back the officers it had laid off in 1975, he explained. His family urged him to stay in Florida, insisting that they could look after Dorothy O'Regan.

Apparently disturbed by the way the family cared for his father's body, Brian decided to stay. He turned his back on the Florida sunshine and refocused his attention on the gray decay of the city.

"I never saw anybody take anything in Florida," Brian said years later. "No one even tried to hand us money when we stopped them. We were beyond that sort of thing. It just wasn't done. I still have a letter from Florida, saying I could come back there and work anytime I wanted. The letter isn't worth shit now. It might as well be written on toilet paper."

On January 13, 1981, following a two week stay at the police academy, Brian O'Regan got his old badge back—NYPD shield number 1145—to go along with his old assignment—the 77th Precinct. He put on a frayed blue uniform and climbed into a dirty squad car and reacquainted himself with the squalor of the ghetto. Polished brass buttons, steam cleaned engines, and Florida sunshine were part of another lifetime.

At some point during his first tour, Brian drove onto the Atlantic Avenue viaduct, getting his first overview of Black Brooklyn in more than six years. A gloomy cloud of depression filled Brian's radio car. As far as he could see, there were tenements, housing projects, and abandoned buildings.

"What the fuck am I doing back here?" he thought. "I got to be crazy."

Brian wasn't crazy. But he was pretty sure that another patrolman in his precinct, Henry Winter, was certifiably nuts. The two cops met soon after Brian arrived in the precinct, and at first, Brian wanted nothing to do with Winter, who lived across the street from his uncle back in Valley Stream. Like everyone else in the station house, Brian had heard that Henry was a rat.

Henry had a way of grating on other cops, Brian decided. At first he made other cops, including Brian, nervous. No one who worked with Henry was ever sure what he was going to do next. Among other things, he liked to take his pants off and jump on tables. But Henry did know how to talk to girls. And that was a talent that a bachelor like Brian envied.

"Henry Winter has personality," Brian later said. "Did you ever know a guy that you really hated, and everyday he comes up to you and pats you on the back and says, 'How you doing, buddy boy?' Pretty soon you don't hate the guy anymore. You may even like him. That was Henry Winter. I liked Henry. In a way, I still do. 'Buddy boy' was his favorite word. If you want to see Seventy-seventh Precinct cops jump out of their graves just go up to them now and say, 'Hey, buddy boy.' "

Brian soon realized there were strange things going on between the cops and the robbers out on the streets of Bedford-Stuyvesant. A lot of the cops Brian worked with were bad guys. Shortly after returning to the precinct, he arrived at a smoke shop, a grocery store that sells marijuana over the counter, in answer to a radio report of three men with guns. He got to the scene in time to see a team of other cops smash through a storefront window in hot pursuit of three completely imaginary suspects. Once inside, they rummaged through the shelves and floorboards looking for drugs and money.

"Somebody said, 'Did you drop the dime?'" Brian later remembered. "I didn't understand. I just looked at him."

On another occasion he and another veteran cop were called to a smoke shop on a late tour. As Brian watched, the veteran and a patron started arguing. Suddenly, the cop picked the customer up and hurled him through the storefront window. Then the patrolman stepped through the broken window and picked the man up off the sidewalk by the scruff of the neck.

"You're under arrest," the cop said.

"What for?"

"Breaking and exiting," the cop decided, pointing at the window.

Brian also knew the lesson of Francis Shepperd, a black cop from the 77th Precinct. Shepperd barged into a numbers spot in full uniform and robbed the place at gunpoint. He then returned to his radio car and handed over half the haul to his new partner, saying, "Here's yours." Anthony Longatano was petrified, certain the department was staging some kind of integrity test. He left the money on the seat beside him and turned his partner in. Shepperd was arrested and fired.

"I'm going to take a lot of white boys from the midnight tour with me," Shepperd was heard to say. But nothing ever came of it. Longatano was left behind in the 77th Precinct. Later, Brian watched the cops he worked with on the midnight tour scrawl the word "rat" on Longatano's locker. One of the few cops in the precinct that the department could trust not to act like a criminal, Longatano was taken off patrol and assigned to a seat in front of a typewriter.

Brian had been in the precinct for a short time when he

responded to a radio run of a burglary in progress at a Nostrand Avenue dress shop. The store's plate glass window was smashed by the fleeing burglars. Brian pulled up to the scene with another squad car from the 71st Precinct, and the cops entered the store. One officer walked over to the register and pushed a button. The cash drawer slid open. The cop dug his hand into the drawer and came up holding a fistful of dollars. Brian couldn't believe what he saw.

"What do you want?" the cop asked.

"I don't do that," Brian insisted. "I do not do that. I don't want any of it."

Although shocked by the sight of another cop robbing a store, he chose to overlook the incident. He was not a corrupt cop, at least not yet, and he wasn't a rat either. He still believed in something called esprit de corps.

No matter what he saw other cops doing, Brian decided he would never turn one of them in to the Internal Affairs Division. He would not crack the Blue Wall of Silence. Rats did that. And rats were bad for morale.

"I just can't turn," Brian said later. "The Blue Wall. You don't tell. I couldn't tell. I'd eat the gun first."

Steadily, life in the 77th began to bother Brian. There seemed to be one horror after another as he turned each corner. He responded to a call about a dispute one evening and found a woman sitting on the bed in her apartment next to an open window. From the look of the bed sheets, it was obvious that she had just given birth. But there was no baby in the room. And there was no baby in the apartment. Brian shined his flashlight out the bedroom window and saw a tiny mound on the ground below. He realized it was a baby.

Brian went downstairs and stood over the dead infant, crying. "I stood there and stared at it and I kept thinking,

"It's so little, it's so little. Before long you build up a wall. Now I wish I could care about something, like if somebody jumped out a window. After awhile, anything could have happened in that precinct and I didn't care. I did not care. You can love something and you can hate something. I just didn't care."

Brian kept arresting people, though. He delivered a half-dozen babies and made nine gun collars in a single month. He accumulated department commendations by the handful. But then his depression deepened. He started giving his gun collars away to other cops. His overtime dropped. His outside interests waned.

Brian became less interested in arresting bad guys and more interested in getting back at them. He couldn't stand putting people in jail anymore because he couldn't bear the sight of them waving from street corners the very next day.

A drug dealer named Mitch who operated a business on the corner of Lincoln Place made a mockery of Brian and the law. He arrested Mitch regularly, sometimes catching the dealer with guns and cocaine. But Mitch was always back on the street the next day, smiling broadly and waving at the cop who had just arrested him.

"How come you can have combat fatigue in the service but you can't have it on the job?" Brian would soon ask. "They say that in the ghetto, it's a war on crime. At least in a war you can kill a guy and feel good. He's not around anymore. But out here you arrest people and the next day they're out on the street, waving to you. So, really, what did you accomplish?"

In early 1983, the newspapers and television stations carried a story about two cops from the 77th Precinct who had been accused of robbing a Nostrand Avenue smoke shop. Brian's younger brother Kevin, a high school classmate of

Henry Winter, phoned to ask Brian what was going on in his precinct. The answer disturbed his younger brother.

Brian said, "I don't know, but sometimes you just work too long in a precinct, and things can happen."

At about this time, William Gallagher, the precinct's union delegate, was looking for a new partner. Considered to be a braggart and a bully by other cops, Gallagher liked to call himself a hero. In fact, he had the medals to back up his boasts. After coming on the job in March 1969, Gallagher amassed twenty-nine commendations for Excellent Police Duty, five citations for Meritorious Police Duty, and one Exceptional Merit Award.

But when other cops in the precinct looked at William Gallagher they saw a thief, not a hero—a bloated man with a swollen sense of self-importance. He avoided arrest by keeping an ear open to rumors emanating from his union, fancying himself an infallible thief.

Gallagher looked at Brian O'Regan and saw a potential disciple, someone to mold and shape, belittle and ravage. In time, Brian would become the perfect partner for a cop like William Gallagher, which is no partner at all. Sometimes the two men rode in their car for hours, but Gallagher never deemed it necessary to speak to the man he worked with.

"Gallagher was cement," Brian would say later. "He was macho. He wanted me because I'm easy, because I'm a follower."

Just as the union delegate had earlier exposed his midnight shift fill-in partner Henry Winter to the dark and deliberate acts of bribe-taking and suspect-robbing, Gallagher now initiated Brian O'Regan into thievery. During one of their first nights together on a midnight tour, he led Brian into an all-night smoke shop, saying as he entered, "I want to do this place."

At first, Brian had no idea what his partner was talking about. But then he saw. And Brian O'Regan was never the same cop again.

Using one hand to hold a gun on the storekeeper, whom he was threatening to arrest for selling marijuana, Gallagher located a cash-filled tray under the counter. He grabbed three hundred dollars and then returned to the radio car with his prisoner, taking him for a short ride around the block and lecturing the man on the perils of dealing drugs in his sector.

"You want to play, you got to pay," the police union rep said before freeing his victim.

Later Brian watched his partner count the stolen money out and split it into two equal piles. Then Gallagher held out $150 to his new partner. Brian froze. Gallagher kept his hand out. Brian didn't want to embarrass a cop he idolized. He didn't want a confrontation with a hero. So finally, he just squeezed his hand around the money and shoved it into his pocket.

Much later Brian said, "I felt like I was one of the boys."

Within days after accepting the money, Brian was lost to the New York City Police Department. He brought a new single-mindedness to his work. Like Henry Winter, Brian had become the law. Guys like Mitch from Lincoln Place were no longer a problem. If Brian caught Mitch with drugs now, he would just steal them and walk away. And unlike other cops in the precinct, Brian wasn't simply robbing people to get their money. He was using the act of robbery as a vehicle for punishment.

"I did it for the glory," he said later. "It was all done as a way of getting back at the people you couldn't hurt. No one becomes a cop to steal."

By mid-1984, Brian and Henry had adjoining lockers. And sometimes Brian would see Henry counting out large sums of money after a tour. The word on the street was that

Henry was crashing through windows into drug locations and stealing money. Brian was conducting similar raids on his own tours.

"I used to see him standing there counting hundreds of dollars," O'Regan said. "Henry would turn to me and say, 'Not a bad night.'"

Shortly after hooking up with Gallagher, Brian met a twenty-one-year-old rookie policewoman in the 77th Precinct named Cathy. In Brian's eyes, she made a police uniform come to life. A petite Polish girl with wavy hair, soft blue eyes, and a high forehead, Cathy was equally impressed with Brian. They met on an arrest, during which Brian subdued a prisoner without benefit of a nightstick.

"I like the way you handled yourself out there," the rookie said later.

"Really?" said Brian, blushing.

Soon they were dating. And then they were doing more than dating. Brian was talking about his dreams, filling the night air on walks through Park Slope with talk of children and a home. To his surprise, Cathy listened.

But he had some advice for her too. The veteran told the rookie, "Get out of this precinct as soon as you can. Get out of this precinct before it changes you."

She took his advice, and transferred out, getting a job in a Manhattan command. The relationship continued to flourish even as Brian continued to rob people. Soon he was showing up for work in a tattered, stained uniform. He grew fat and unhappy, his mind and body taking on the consistency of jelly.

"I had no pride," Brian said of his deteriorating personal appearance.

Over the months and years, Brian O'Regan lost more and more of his resolve. The same cop who dreamed of joining the Emergency Services Unit now drove around with a sledgehammer in his trunk. He bought special steel-tipped shoes so he could kick down doors more easily. He even thought about sending away for a portable rope ladder. "I wanted excitement. Some kind of adventure."

Soon Brian put his military training to work, surprising fellow thieves with his knowledge of tactical maneuvers and theories of attack. He became known as a tactician, spending hours scouting out fortified positions for weaknesses, taking an inventory of lookouts, bodyguards, and potential gunmen. Henry Winter, among others, was in awe of O'Regan's organizational ability.

"Other cops robbed people," Henry said. "Brian conducted operations. He missed his calling."

Brian later agreed. "I would have done great in narcotics."

No robbery was beneath Brian, who had a reputation for spending both sides of a dollar. Tony Magno, who rarely got his hands dirty while conducting illegal drug raids, was amazed at O'Regan's staying power. Although he was nervous on the streets when discussing an upcoming burglary, saying things like, "No bullshit, guys. This time just in and out. Please." Brian was always the last one to leave a drug raid. He would get down on his hands and knees to search floorboards for secret compartments. He stood on chairs to poke holes in ceilings and punched his fists through false walls. It was not beneath O'Regan to lay on the floor and search behind broken toilets. "See," he once yelled, pulling a bag of drugs from underneath a feces-filled bathtub in an abandoned apartment, "I told you the shit was here." By the end of a tour, Brian's hair was often littered with Sheetrock dust and his uniform covered with grime and filth. He never seemed to notice.

"You just couldn't stop what was happening," Brian said. "It was like we had a fever or something."

But by this point even Brian knew he had more than a

simple illness. He knew he had psychological problems, perhaps triggered by some physical ailment. He went to see a physician on Ocean Parkway in Brooklyn, only to be told there was nothing physically wrong with him. The doctor suggested that Brian see a psychiatrist. Soon.

Instead, he began taking antidepressant pills. One night Brian mentioned in confidence to Gallagher that he was thinking of getting some help. The next day, cops were pointing at Brian with one hand and twirling a finger near their heads. "Woo, woo," they said. Brian had a new nickname in the precinct—the other cops called him Spaceman. Officer Spaceman stopped looking for help. "If you tell someone you have psychological problems, they think you're crazy."

"Brian kept saying that he wanted to get off the job, that he wanted to get out on a medical disability. We used to talk about it. He'd say, 'Henry, I got to get out while I still can.' So I said, 'No problem. I'll just shoot you.' We decided to stage an accidental shooting. Brian loved the idea. Guys in the Marines did stuff like that to get out of Vietnam. He kept asking, 'When are we going to do it? When are we going to do it? And so one night we decided to do it.

"We drove down to a building on Portal Street, on the borderline between the Seven-One and the Seven-Seven. We were working together on a late tour. So he says, 'What do you think? Should we do it?' I didn't want to, but Brian said, 'Aw, come on.' He was carrying a .22-caliber pistol that looked like some kind of cowboy gun. A big gun with a long barrel. He kept saying, 'Aw, come on, let's do it.' And I kept telling him, 'Nah. We can't do this.' But Brian was persistent. I finally agreed to shoot him.

"At first he wanted to be shot in the leg. But I told him, "No, no. You can't do it in the leg, Brian. You got arteries all over the place there. You could bleed to death. Do it someplace else. Just take a finger off. Shoot the trigger finger off and you'll never be able to qualify with the other hand. They'll have to give you a medical disability.' Brian thought about it for a minute and said, 'No, I don't want to lose a finger.' Then we started passing the gun back and forth on the street, saying, 'You do it,' 'No, you do it.' We went on like that for awhile. Then I just said, 'Brian, I can't fucking shoot you.' He said, 'Come on. Will you just shoot me? We'll set it up like we chased some skell into the building and shots were fired.' I said, 'No, no, here, you take the gun, you shoot yourself.'

"Brian took the gun in his right hand and aimed it at his left. I stopped him and said, 'No. Do it the other way around. Take the gun in your left hand and shoot yourself in the right hand. Who gives a shit about your left hand? You shoot right-handed. Shoot the right hand." Brian looked at me and said, 'Okay. I just wasn't thinking there for a moment.'

"So now Brian's got the gun in his left hand and he's pointing it at the palm of his right hand. And I said, 'No, don't do it like that. The bullet will just go right through your hand and you won't do any damage that way. Close your hand, make a fist and then shoot into the fist.' I was trying to psych Brian out. Nobody would shoot through a closed fist. But I said, 'Go ahead, if you shoot into your fist you'll take your finger, your knuckle, and everything.' He goes, 'You think so? You think this is the way?' 'Believe me.' He held the hand open again. 'Not like that?' I tell him, 'Not like that Brian. It goes right through if you do it like that. How many times have you seen guys shot in the hand like that, it goes through and nothing?' He says, 'Yeah, yeah, you're right about that.' Finally I said, 'Make a fist and shoot yourself through the fist.'

"He stood there for a second pointing the cowboy gun at the fist but he couldn't do it. 'No way Hank. I ain't doing that.' I said, 'That's right. You shoot yourself in the fist and there goes the whole fucking hand.' Brian put his gun away and we drove back to the precinct. Brian couldn't shoot himself.

"Later Brian and I used to sit in the car in the Seventy-seventhth Precinct asking each other, 'What the fuck are we doing here?' He should have been in Broward County in Florida and I should have been in Colorado. Now we were both sitting in the middle of a slum with a banged-up patrol car and frayed uniforms. We felt like two idiots. But really, that's it with life, isn't it? You make a choice somewhere along the way and then you live and die with it. There's no turning back."

7

"I was exhausted. I couldn't hit another person."

Tony Magno grew up in an Italian section of Brooklyn and as a kid he loved two blue uniforms. One uniform belonged to the New York City Police Department, the other to the Brooklyn Dodgers.

At first Tony dreamed of wearing Dodger Blue. He played sewer-to-sewer stick ball on 71st Street between 19th and 20th Avenues, pretending to be his favorite Dodger, Carl Furillo. He idolized Furillo as a baseball player because he was Italian and his middle name was Anthony. But Tony liked all the Dodgers, even Jackie Robinson, and he told his Italian friends that anybody who played for the Dodgers was socially acceptable, even if he was black.

"Jackie Robinson isn't black anymore," he said. "He's

blue. It's the same with the cops. Once a guy puts on the uniform, he's a cop just like Jackie Robinson is just a Dodger."

He hung out with a small, loosely-defined, relatively harmless group of Italian kids from the neighborhood who laughingly referred to themselves as "The Seventy-first Street Faggoteers." They rarely got into fights and carried metal combs and a ready supply of Vitalis instead of weapons, but they did wear motorcycle jackets, garrison belts, white Keds sneakers, tight jeans, and white T-shirts. Mostly the Faggoteers played baseball, but in time they gave up the game for girls.

When Raymond Giamanco bought a 1958 Chevy convertible, the gang expanded its horizons, traveling into the nearby neighborhoods of Bay Ridge and Bath Beach to meet new girls in new Italian neighborhoods. Tony nicknamed the car the "pushmobile."

"Half the time when we took the car out we wound up pushing it back home," Magno later remembered. "We were always running out of gas and having breakdowns."

By the early 1960s, Tony had set aside his stickball bat for a pair of wooden drumsticks. He sat in his living room, beating on a pair of telephone books, keeping time to Benny Goodman and other Big Band sounds on his father's stereo. After wearing out the yellow pages, he started on the furniture. His father rescued the family sofa when his son turned fourteen, buying him a set of Gretsch black diamond pearl drums which he set up in the basement. Soon all the neighborhood rock and rollers were hanging out in Tony's cellar, dreaming about playing in nightclubs and deposing the Beatles.

Unable to read music and unwilling to read textbooks, Tony was regarded as a mediocre musician and an uninterested high school student. He had to attend night school for a full year after his senior year in order to qualify for a high school diploma. When he eventually graduated, in 1965, Tony took a job as a stock boy at May's department store on 14th Street in Manhattan, where he was known as a soft touch who would sometimes switch the price tags on clothes.

At this stage in his life, Tony had little understanding of geography or history. He knew, for example, that there were run-down black neighborhoods in Brooklyn but he had never really seen a slum. And the one time he tried to make a killing through thievery—stealing a yellow parchment from the basement of his drum teacher's home—he embarrassed himself.

"I thought I really had something big—the original copy of Lincoln's Gettysburg Address. When I tried to sell it, they laughed me off the block."

In early 1966, when he was seventeen, Tony decided to join the Army, asking his father to co-sign his enlistment papers. Ernest Magno, a World War II veteran who saw action in North Africa and Italy, refused, telling his son, "I ain't signing your death certificate. I did enough fighting for both of us." Tony dropped the idea of becoming a war hero.

In July of that year a guitar-playing friend invited Tony on a boat ride with two girls, one of them a shy blonde from the neighborhood named Marianne. The foursome headed out into Jamaica Bay, listening to the radio for hours while basking in the sun. Midway through the trip, Marianne decided that she was extremely impressed with Tony the drummer. She liked the way he looked in tight black chinos, and the way his starched white and yellow shirt hung off his string-bean frame. He seemed to be a cross between Fabian and Elvis. So when the boat docked, Marianne sprinted away with Tony Magno's ID bracelet.

"I was pretty sure he'd call me anyway," she explained. "But I wanted to make sure."

Within weeks the couple was dating seriously and by early 1967 they were talking about getting married. But there was one small problem. Tony couldn't offer Marianne any long-term security, and she wasn't the type to marry a department store clerk, even if he was fairly adept at switching price tags and looked like Fabian.

Tony knew that he wasn't going to make it as a rock-and-roll star either. His band—they called themselves the Paragons—had flopped at its one nightclub audition, stumbling through versions of "Hang on Sloopy," "In the Midnight Hour" and "House of the Rising Sun." To make matters worse, several customers came to the club hoping to see the real Paragons.

"They claimed false advertising," Tony said. "They came in to see the Paragons and saw what amounted to the Slobs instead. We never got to play another club after that."

A week or so later, Marianne told her boyfriend that he couldn't marry her until he got some sort of normal job.

She suggested that he study for an upcoming civil service exam and follow up on his dream to join the police force, now that the Dodgers had moved west. The couple got copies of old tests and studied for long hours in the evenings, sitting on the girl's couch and whispering sweet nothings like "perpetrators," and "homicides," into each other's ears.

Nineteen-year-old Tony Magno was contacted by the Police Department in mid-1967 and offered a job as a police trainee, a job that carried a military exemption. He was ecstatic—he was going to be a cop once he turned twenty-one. Marianne couldn't have been happier that she was going to be a cop's bride. They were married on January 5, 1969, ten days before Tony was sworn in as a police officer. Because he was still in the academy, he was only given two days off. They honeymooned in Manhattan, taking a room at the Sheraton Motor Inn for the weekend.

"It was a nice way to start a marriage," Marianne thought. "We worked and struggled together, and we got somewhere. So we appreciated the little that we had. We were very happy with very little."

Tony was appointed to the New York City Police Department on January 15, 1969. They took away his police trainee uniform and gave him a silver shield and a .38-caliber service revolver. He joined a group of recruits on a trip to Smith-Gray Uniform Tailors in Manhattan where he plunked down $200 for two uniforms. After working for a week during a snow emergency in the 17th Precinct, Tony Magno was assigned to his first command, the 77th Precinct in Bedford-Stuyvesant, Brooklyn.

"The first corruption I ever did, I was a police trainee. I was too young to actually come on the job but they had started this new unit. Police trainees. We had a stupid little uniform. Gray pants and a gray shirt with a little blue tie. We had a hat too, but we didn't have to wear it. It was one of those fold-over World War II hats. They sent us out into a borough command office and we either did paperwork or answered phones. I got sent to the old Eight-Oh, which is now part of the Seven-Seven. One night I'm on the switchboard with a fill-in lieutenant from the old Thirteenth Division. Somebody needed a tow truck, so I called one. But after the job was completed, the driver came into the station house, handed me fifty dollars and said, 'Thanks.' I just stood there with my mouth open. I was making one hundred and twenty-nine dollars every two weeks at that point, and I didn't know what to do with the fifty dollars. I was scared shitless.

"So I told the fill-in lieutenant, 'The tow truck driver came in and walked out leaving me money. Do you get half? I don't know what to do.' He looked at me and said, 'Kid, this was your contract. You got the money. You keep the money.' I didn't know what to do so I put the money in my pocket and that was that. I didn't even think about corruption. I didn't even know what the word 'corruption' meant.

"The only other thing that I knew was wrong was guys sleeping on the job. Even guys that were radio dispatchers used to sleep. They set up beach chairs behind the radio receiver boxes, and guys that worked right in the radio room would go in there and sleep. At three o'clock in the morning one guy could handle the job, so they took turns. I remember when the sergeants came off patrol, if things were quiet, they'd go upstairs to the dormitory too. Everybody slept. The lieutenant on the desk slept. There were times I was the only guy alive in the station house on a twelve-to-eight shift. There were no lights on except the desk light and the switchboard light. The only way a person could tell it was a station was the two little green lights out in front that said 'Police.'

"Before we graduated, I had told everybody in the academy that I knew where I was going. I had a hook. I was going to the Six-Two out in Bensonhurst, my old neighborhood. It was all arranged. My uncle, who worked in a bakery, knew some inspector in Brooklyn South. The inspector used to come in for coffee and free pastries in the morning and one day my uncle tells him, 'Look, my nephew is in the academy. Do you think we can get him out here?' The inspector said, 'No problem. I'll just make a phone call.' So it was set. I was going to the Six-Two. My uncle said, 'This guy is a Scotch drinker. When this is all over, you might have to buy him a case of Scotch.' No problem. My father would have bought the Scotch. All the other guys were worried about where they were being sent. Not me.

"But then, when they called us up to the podium, I looked at the paper and saw the number Seven-Seven next to my name. I couldn't believe it. 'Holy shit,' I thought. I went from the Eight-Oh to the Seven-Seven, from working on the switchboard to working on the fucking street on the same blocks that run through the Eight-Oh.

"It was the same shit. Black area, the whole fucking bit. I came from a completely white neighborhood and I didn't even know that fucking area of Brooklyn existed. I didn't even know there were black people, that many anyway, in Brooklyn. The guys sure got on me good. 'Oh, you got the Seven-Seven, huh, Magno? Well you must have one hell of a hook to get that assignment. Who's your hook with the department anyway, Malcolm X?' I never even called my uncle. I just said, 'Aw, fuck it,' and went to work in the Seven-Seven."

As a member of the New York City Police Department, Police Officer Anthony Carl Magno, shield number 259, had only one major failing. He didn't like to arrest people.

Having spent close to two years in a slum station house as a police trainee, Magno had already decided that he didn't have to arrest people to be a successful cop. He had watched veteran cops skate through their tours, drinking beer, cooping, and eating free meals while handing over the few arrests they made to the more ambitious younger cops who hoped to parlay their staggering arrest and overtime totals into a gold detective's shield.

Tony wasn't interested in a gold shield. He liked the intimacy of a patrol car. It was the guys in the precinct locker room that Tony really cared about, not the criminals in the street.

And so he arrived at the 77th Precinct in February 1969, determined to assist on as many arrests as he could but never to get stuck with one of his own.

"I can't take court," Tony explained to his partners over the next seventeen years. "I don't like that part of the job. Going to court makes me feel like a prisoner."

Although he would have been happy to give all his arrests away to other cops, he finally had to arrest somebody. The arrest was given to him by two of the precinct's most legendary cops, David Greenburg and Robert Hantz.

Known as "Batman and Robin" on the streets of Bedford-Stuyvesant, Greenburg and Hantz were alternately regarded as heroes and rogues by other members of the department. They certainly put the 77th Precinct on the map, collaborating with author L. H. Whittemore on a bestselling book about their exploits entitled *The Super Cops: The True Story of the Cops called Batman and Robin*. They were the most active cops in the precinct, so Batman and Robin rarely wasted their time with two-bit thieves and burglary suspects.

Six months after he arrived at the Seven-Seven, Batman and Robin insisted on giving Tony his first collar. He escorted a drug suspect back to the station house where, under duress, Tony filled out the paper work. He later accompanied his prisoner to court, where the defendant asked to make a brief statement at the close of his arraignment.

"I just want to tell the court that this officer did not arrest me," the defendant said pointing to Magno. "It was two other officers that got me. This officer only showed up later."

As the defendant spoke, Magno melted into the bench. The judge asked the arresting officer for an interpretation.

"Not me," Tony said, committing perjury on the first arrest of his career. "I wouldn't do that."

"Next case," said the judge, banging his gavel.

Tony left the courtroom determined never to make another arrest unless it was absolutely necessary. He spent the rest of his career chasing bad guys, cornering suspects, taking their guns away, smacking them around, placing them in handcuffs and then handing them over to some other cops who handled the arrest, the paperwork and the court appearances. Having successfully avoided the one aspect of a policeman's duties that made him feel like a criminal—his day in court—Tony operated as one happy and contented cop.

However, he was not happy, even in the broadest sense, with his assignment to a ghetto precinct. No matter how he tried, he could not get used to poverty. He did not like the acrid smell of the ghetto, the taste that came into his mouth when he stepped into a urine-filled elevator, or the smell of poverty on his clothes. He did not understand this sort of destitution, a squalid existence where people were willing to sit down at the dinner table with roaches and put up with having their kids bitten by rats in the dark. He was a staunch conservative who believed that all of the world's problems came under a single heading he called "that liberalism bullshit." Tony scorned the very people he was sworn to protect. He escaped them in the precinct locker room.

"I wasn't brought up this way. I tell you I went into buildings in that precinct and I gagged. I had to put my hand over my mouth just to breathe. After a while, they say, you get accustomed to it, but I never did. I wasn't used to certain things about the way those people lived. When you see people living in shit it takes something away from you. It steals something from you. I saw kids in diapers that hadn't been changed for two or three days and it hardened me. I'd walk into apartments with the linoleum half ripped up off the floor, and grease in the kitchen with hundreds of roaches just swarming around. We had to keep moving in those apartments, stamping our feet. We didn't lean on the walls because we didn't want to take the roaches back to the precinct or get them on our uniforms and take them home.

"I remember going on one job where there was a middle-aged woman with rips in her housecoat sitting at a table eating in the middle of this skelly apartment with roaches crawling around on the table. And she was flicking them away from her plate like they were pets, like it was nothing. It makes you cringe. It makes you cry. But what can you do? We had to go into these apartments and breathe in these places.

"One time I went into an apartment and a big woman was lying on the bed, having a baby. She's heavy into labor. She can't wait for the ambulance. The place is disgusting. Her other kids are running around. I wouldn't go into the delivery room if my own wife was having a baby, but I'm here now. And I helped the lady deliver the baby. I wanted to puke but I didn't. I put my hand over my mouth and helped her. There wasn't time for how I was feeling. We just delivered the baby and got the hell out of there. But what did we deliver the baby to? What kind of life is that kid going to have?

"To make matters worse, the people gave us shit. In the old days, when I first got to the precinct, it seemed like more people had respect for you. Even though they looked like shit, if we raised our voices, they knew they couldn't fuck with us. Now, they yell at us as soon as we walk through the door. 'Who the fuck called you? Who needs you?' Eventually you start asking yourself the same questions. I did. It got so I didn't give a shit what was going on in some places. But I wouldn't leave the precinct either. I was married to the job and the guys. Once I got in the precinct and got comfortable, I never wanted to leave. I loved it there. I loved the guys. It was like a second home to me."

If it's true that one day can change your life, Tony Magno's life was forever changed by what he saw and did in the 77th Precinct on one humid summer evening when the whole city went dark, Wednesday, July 13, 1977.

Tony, the cop who rarely left the sanctuary of his home, was sitting on his living-room couch after finishing a day tour and dinner when the lights went out at 9:34 P.M. Like several million other New Yorkers, he figured that he had blown a fuse. But on the way to the basement, he heard people yelling in the streets. No one in Brooklyn had power. The fourth-largest city in the world was plunged into darkness on a humid ninety-five-degree night.

At first, the blackout was just inconvenient. Tony set up his house, lighting candles, loading fresh batteries in radios and flashlights. His neighbors gathered on stoops, quietly swapping ghost stories. The neighborhood kids all agreed that the blackout was a novelty, a reason to stay up late. But as Tony listened to the radio and heard the call for all city police officers to head into their precincts, he became concerned. Thousands of people throughout Black Brooklyn were rioting and looting, gutting shops and burning down buildings.

He decided that he had to go into work and fight the ghetto looters, leaving his own family unguarded. It seemed to be a clear choice. He was a cop and on this night the city needed cops.

"You are not going in to work," Marianne advised him.

"I have to go in," he explained. "It's my job."

Assuring his family that they'd be all right, Tony called Zeke Zayas, another police officer who lived nearby, and the two agreed to accompany each other into work. Neither Zeke nor Tony was prepared for what they would see that night—a night of madness when it seemed that every Bedford-Stuyvesant resident had taken to the street, looting shops of everything from cars and bikes to aspirin and toilet paper.

In the next twenty-four hours police made 3,300 arrests and heard 45,000 phone complaints throughout the city. The fire department received 23,722 alarms and responded to 900 fires, 55 of them serious. One hundred cops were injured while trying to restore order. A dozen people were shot dead by armed shopkeepers, snipers, and frightened police officers. Looters in the Bronx broke down the metal door to an automobile showroom and drove away fifty cars. Roving bands in Harlem carried off stolen television sets and stereo equipment. In Queens, looters rushed away from broken stores carrying couches and beds. Airline pilots flying over Brooklyn reported that the borough was aglow with fire. Mayor Abe Beame later described the blackout as "a night of terror."

It was an evening perhaps best captured in one headline and one anecdote—both of them from the *Village Voice,* a week after light had been restored. The article, which included a photograph of several looters running down the streets with televisions and furniture on their backs, was entitled, "Here Comes the Neighborhood." Written by Denis Hamill and Michael Daly, it included the story of one young black man who rushed home to his mother in the middle of the blackout with a stolen air conditioner. Using a flashlight, she plugged the air conditioner into an electrical outlet and pressed the "On" switch. When the machine failed to start after several tries, she was furious and threw the air conditioner out the window. "It don't work," she screamed. "Go get another one."

"We got into the precinct without any trouble. As soon as we hit the shitty area—I hate to say it but it was the black area—we saw a lot of people all over the place. The streets were a mess. There was trash and garbage everywhere. The place looked like one big broken window. We got into the station house and went downstairs to get our helmets. I had never worn one before and I felt like an idiot with this stupid pot on my head. I was scared but excited too. I wanted to be out there.

"I remember one of the first calls was a ten-thirteen on Atlantic and Bedford—assist patrolman, shots fired. As soon as we pulled up I heard a shot, then one or two more. I thought, 'Oh, fuck. What did we get ourselves into here?' All the guys were ducking. Some of us had our helmets on backwards. No one knew where the shots were coming from. There must have been twenty cars there, and we all just got back in them and left. There was utter chaos. We didn't know what to do.

"Then we went out on patrol, if you can call it that, in two cars—one unmarked car followed by a patrol car. The unmarked car would pull up to a store and drive up on the sidewalk, pointing the headlights into the store so we could see what we were doing. The place was a shambles, it didn't even look like a store anymore on the inside. One group of guys would run into the store and start slamming the looters with their sticks. I figured, I ain't going in there and get hit by a stick. I stayed outside and put my deviant mind to work. They could only hit one person at a time inside the store, but I could get six people as they ran out of the store.

155

I stood by the door and waited. And I got every one of them as they came out. Whack, whack, whack. I couldn't hit the women in the face. They'd come out and say, 'Officer, please don't hit me.' I had my stick raised but I said, 'All right, I won't hit you.' But as soon as they ran past me, I hit them in the back of the head. I couldn't look them in the face. And it kept going on like that for hours and hours. I was Babe Ruth that night. No one got away from me.

"People fired at us later on that night too. We didn't know where the shots were coming from. It was crazy. The only light on the street was coming from a burning Thom McAn shoe store. People were still inside the burning store stealing shoes. That really got to me. Guys were taking a chance on burning up for a pair of shoes. I really let those looters have it with the stick. I hit this one guy right in the face and he didn't even look like a human anymore.

"One time on Nostrand Avenue we turned around and just starting firing back down the street toward a building. The shooting stopped. They were like rats out there. We'd walk into a store and the place would be crawling with them. They cleaned out the jewelry stores and the grocery stores. I mean everything. And I knew some of the people I was hitting. I was just about to bash this one lady and she yells, 'Tony, it's me.' I looked and it was the school crossing guard. I couldn't believe it. I told her, 'Just drop the shit and get the fuck out of here.' Even the people that I liked, my friends in the neighborhood, were out there looting. I lost all respect for the neighborhood after that night. There were some cops taking things too. Guys were loading up their trunks with stuff. I saw a lot of liquor being passed around the precinct that night."

"I was never so happy to see the sun come up in my life. My arms were falling off. I couldn't swing the nightstick any more. I was exhausted. I couldn't hit another person. But even after daylight people were still out there looting. We got called to a furniture warehouse on Grand Avenue, and people were running down the streets with couches and beds on their backs. They just wouldn't let the stuff go, either. We split their heads with the stick and they'd still hold onto the shit. It was like they already owned it. It scared me to see people like that. It made me think about the neighborhood a lot. Before the blackout, I just figured that we were working with the scum all the time, that there were still good people out there in the community. But after that night, after I saw everybody in the community looting, I just didn't give a shit about what happened on the street any more. I used to just drive through the precinct sometimes and wonder: How far will they go the next time the lights go out?

"It would have made a difference if I could have done something—if I could saved someone's store or something. But when it was all over I felt like a jerk. We went back to the precinct and drank beer. We stayed there and got drunk the whole morning. The cops that came in gave me shit. 'You gotta be some kind of jackass, Magno. You were home with your family and you came into this cesspool in the middle of the blackout?' And they were right. I should have stayed home. All I really did was crack some heads. We didn't arrest anybody. One of the guys told me, "Magno, you batted .900 out there tonight. I only saw you swing and miss once.' Eventually, a day or two later, I got home. But I didn't tell Marianne much about what happened. What was there to say? That I didn't trust people anymore?"

Over the years, Tony rarely took his job home with him. Although he did bring most of his partners home for early morning card games and beer drinking sessions, they rarely talked about work. It was not unusual, Marianne noted, to wake up at 7 A.M. in order to send the kids off to school and discover a half dozen of her husband's friends sitting around her dining room table, drinking beer and arguing. Other cops soon decided that Tony had the perfect wife— she could put up with cops.

Actually, there was only one thing that Marianne hated about being a cop's wife. She could put up with her husband's hours and his drinking buddies. She could put up with his frustration and his brooding silence. But she could not put up with being alone in the house—knowing that her husband was out there working in the city's most dangerous precinct— and seeing a police car stopped on her block.

"If someone ever calls up and says I've been shot, don't believe them," Tony used to tell Marianne. "They don't call you when your husband gets shot. They send a patrol car out to get you. They come to the house."

So whenever Marianne looked out the window and saw a police car stopped on her block, she would freeze, imagining the worst.

"If I saw a car coming down the block slow, I'd get very scared," Marianne said. "I'd think, 'Oh God. Something happened to Anthony.' Thank God they never stopped though. If they had, I wouldn't have been able to make it to the door. It's funny, isn't it? My husband is a cop out working in a car on someone's block and the sight of another cop on my block could send me over the edge."

Tony went through a lot of partners in a lot of cars. He walked into many dangerous situations where bad guys were armed with big guns, but he rarely fired his own and never had to shoot anyone. He got medals too and occasionally made the newspapers, once arresting two men with a loaded gun who had raped and murdered a post office worker on her way home from work. Tony took a gun from one of the men, catching him on a stairwell leading to a tenement roof where the body of the woman was later found.

"I consider this one of the most brutal homicides I have encountered in my police experience," wrote Deputy Inspector William J. O'Sullivan, the commanding officer of the 77th Precinct, in recommending Tony and three other officers for an award of Exceptional Merit on May 9, 1979. "The two perpetrators had taken the victim, whom they did not know, from the lobby of her building by force. During the two hours they held her, she was systematically raped, tortured, and subjected to the vilest abuse until she died. The medical examiner told the officers he had never seen a human body in the condition of the deceased. In this incident, the police officers used initiative and extremely good judgment in their investigation of what might have been passed off as a routine prowler run. They conducted an investigation and arrested two vicious perpetrators, who might have succeeded in escaping less professional officers."

Tony was given a medal and honored by the precinct's community council with a plaque. And for once, he didn't even mind going to court.

Firmly entrenched as a prince of the locker room by 1982, Tony started thinking about semi-retirement—getting off the streets and taking a cushy inside job at the 77th Precinct. Young cops already referred to him as "the next Johnny Massar," and he wasn't insulted by the comparison to the precinct's hard-drinking veteran.

When his partner of six years, Johnny Miller, transferred out of the ghetto to a Staten Island command near his home, Tony took the breakup like a death in the family. On the night they got word of the transfers, Magno and Miller drove through their sector with tears in their eyes, at a loss for words to explain how they felt about each other. At one point during their final tour, the cops were called to a street disturbance. In the heat of their last action, the partners snapped. They struck out at several ill-fated residents who made the mistake of looking at them cross-eyed. Giving someone a beating made both cops feel better.

After Johnny left, Tony started to drop hints around the station house that he'd be willing to work inside all the time, but eventually he got over it and decided to put a few more years in on patrol. As a senior man, Tony was given his choice of new partners. Tony decided that his new partner would have to be an active cop, a veteran who knew the streets and was willing to make arrests and go to court. Tony wanted someone he could trust to back him up in the hairiest of situations and who wouldn't mind him having a beer in their squad car. Finally, he made his choice. He hooked up with a blonde, blue-eyed cop who had a reputation for being a loner and a prankster.

Tony Magno chose Henry Winter.

"First time I saw him he was just like another cop. But I had heard of Henry Winter. The rumor back then, in 1980, was, 'Watch this guy. Did you hear about him? He came over here with a cloud over his head.' I asked the guys, 'What do you mean?' And they said, 'We don't know about this guy. He don't fuck around with the guys. He don't drink. He came over here after his brother-in-law did his thing in the Seven-Five. He's bounced around a few precincts. We're not sure about him. We got a feeling he might have something to do with Internal Affairs.'

"Henry was in another squad then and I didn't work with him. But then stuff started coming back on him. Everybody knew that Henry had a clear head on the streets but was a bit of a flaky-type guy, and he started saying and doing things that were off the wall—jumping on desks with his pants down, burning a drug dealer's money. I don't know how it got around, but everybody knew Henry was doing something weird out there even though he was working with a super-straight guy. He was sneaky about it, doing whatever it was on the side. Eventually he had a falling-out with his partner. The guy just turned around one day and said, 'We ain't partners no more.'

"Then Henry came into my squad and started driving the sergeant, Bill Dougherty, for awhile. They got along good. The sergeant still liked to get involved in making arrests, and Henry liked to make collars, so they gelled. But Sergeant Dougherty was on the lieutenant's list, so of course he made lieutenant and left Henry hanging loose. My partner had left to train rookies. So now I had nobody, Henry had nobody.

"Henry knew I had time on the job and I knew he was all right, real flaky and shit. So I thought, 'What the fuck? Let's hook up.' I asked Henry one day in the latter part of 1983, 'What are you going to do, want to work together or what?' So we did. A couple guys approached me and said, 'Aw, don't hook up with him.' I heard shit like that for no good reason. They just said, 'He's not like you.'

"At this point, I was involved in minor stuff, the type of corruption that was standard operating procedure. No drugs. I'd drink beer in the car. Maybe I'd take some money hanging around in the open at a burglary. I might take a can of tuna fish out of a store along with batteries for my flashlight and cigarettes. But that was it. Everybody was doing that shit. I never came out of an apartment with a million fucking dollars.

"I just had to dance with somebody, and I decided to dance with Henry Winter."

8

"Yep. They got it all, lady."

Henry Winter and Tony Magno became partners in crime midway through their first tour together. The cops drove past the corner of Lincoln Place and Franklin Avenue, an area in the precinct with a reputation for being a drug flea market. Tony spotted a black teenager talking with a group of older men near a stoop. He recognized them as neighborhood cocaine dealers, and saw one of the men slip what looked like a tinfoil package into the teenager's hand.

Smiling, the man turned around to face the street and saw the radio car with the police officers staring at him. The man acted very suspiciously, Henry and Tony later agreed. He ran down the block.

Sitting in the "runner's position"—the front seat on the

162

passenger's side—Henry kicked open his door and bolted after the man. Tony drove ahead of his partner, shutting off the suspect's escape route. As Henry chased him down an alley, the suspect began dropping one-dollar bills. Henry kept chasing the dealer until the money jumped from one-dollar bills to twenty dollar bills. Then he stopped and picked the money up off the sidewalk.

The suspect ran straight into Tony's arms at the end of the alley. Tony threw his prisoner up against the car and frisked him for money and drugs, waiting for his partner to arrive on the scene. A crowd gathered as Tony finished the scavenger hunt, cheering the action.

"Let him go," Henry said, his pockets already stuffed with money. "He's got nothing on him. We can't hold him."

Tony let him go, saying, "We're doing you a favor. We're going to let you go this time."

The cops returned to their car and drove off. They parked a short distance away and Henry pulled out the money—just over four hundred dollars.

"How did you get it?" Tony asked.

"I'm running after the guy," Henry explained with a coy smile "and he starts dropping it. I backtracked and picked it all up."

Tony made a face and restarted the car. He was afraid the drop was some kind of integrity test. Pondering the situation, he drove around for a few minutes before finally pulling over again.

"Well?" Henry asked. "What do you want to do?"

"Let me count it," said Tony, assuming the role of mathematician.

He counted the cash out into two piles and then looked up.

"Well?" Henry repeated. "What do you want to do?"

Tony held out his hands, weighing both the dollar amount and his decision.

"Ah, fuck it," he said, shoving his cut into his pants with one hand and passing Henry his share of the rip-off with the other. "We're partners, ain't we?"

Most of the cops in the station house believed that the 77th Precinct's newest partners were an ill-fitting couple. In theory, Henry and Tony were in total disagreement on everything from dress and music to politics and sports.

Tony was a dry cleaner's dream. Ever the sharp city dresser, he wore thin black Bally shoes, a sleek black leather coat, finely creased slacks and starched cotton shirts. Henry, the suburban outdoorsman, picked his clothes out of an L. L. Bean catalogue. He wore brightly colored Reebok sneakers, corduroy jackets, dungarees, and flannel shirts.

A check of the AM radio in their squad car confirmed that they were men of different tastes, if not worlds. Tony kept one button preset to an oldies station, while Henry kept another set for a station playing country and western music. On day tours, the partners listened to oldies, with Tony eventually teaching his partner the finer points of doo-wop. On midnight tours they listened to country music, with Henry helping Willie Nelson explain why Tony shouldn't let his babies grow up to be cowboys.

Sporting events presented another problem in Sector Ida-John. Tony lived for the Mets and Giants. Henry died with the Yankees and the Jets. Election nights usually brought more disagreements. Tony would hoist a can of Budweiser to salute victorious Republican candidates, but Henry honked the horn in deference to Democratic winners.

And so it was that Henry Winter and Tony Magno spent much of their time together. They argued, honked horns, sang doo-wops, mimicked Dolly Parton, and laughed. They began to enjoy the time of their police careers. They became the perfect partners. You might even say that they loved each other.

"Tony and I were completely opposite, so whatever he talked about was interesting to me, and whatever I talked about was interesting to him. I could put an experience on Tony, and he could put one on me. It just worked out perfect.

"Tony stayed with the guys after the tour to drink beer and bullshit, but I was on my way home five minutes before our tour ended. Tony didn't make collars, I did. We had nothing in common whatsoever. I talked about hunting and fishing; he talked about other guys on the job and what was happening in the precinct. We always talked.

"It's funny. If you have something in common with someone, you usually become competitive. You can really get on each other's nerves. But we were like magnets. Our differences drew us closer together.

"One thing we agreed on was the car. Tony and I really took pride in it. We started with an old car and then got a new one. We kept it cleaned and waxed. If something went wrong, even if a bulb went out, we'd spend the money ourselves to fix it. Once we were out on a three-day swing and came back to find the car's whole front end demolished. It was destroyed. We didn't get it back for six weeks. Meanwhile we were driving around a shitbox car that was falling apart. Finally we got our car back. We saw them pull it in just as we finished an eight-to-four tour one afternoon. We went over, looked at it and said, 'All right. It's in good shape.' Then we went home. We came in the next day and the car was totaled out again. The guy driving it was some tall Jewish cop—a rookie no less. We called him everything underneath the sun. Tony was really pissed. He screamed at the guy, 'Hey, you can't even drive. You're not a cop, you're a fucking little whore.'

"We were in total agreement on the car. And there was another thing we agreed on too. After a while, neither one of us saw anything wrong with ripping off drug dealers while we were in uniform."

As with most criminals, Henry and Tony started out small. Shortly after they teamed up, they were sitting on a corner in their sector watching a group of suspicious-looking men parade into a smoke shop on Brooklyn Avenue. They decided to get a closer look at what was going on inside. Tony drove to a corner pay phone and Henry dialed 911—the police emergency number. Disguising his voice to sound like a Jamaican black, Henry reported seeing a man with a gun in the smoke shop.

"The mon inside, he have a gun. For sure the mon shoot someone."

He then returned to the car to wait for the call. "Ida-John, Central," Henry said. "We'll handle that job."

With guns drawn, Henry and Tony rushed into the building. Several men fled out through an unguarded rear exit. Inside, Tony found a marijuana-filled cigar box. The cops were disappointed—they wanted money, not drugs. So they led the counter man into the bathroom and forced him to flush the drugs down the toilet.

Within months of that first operation, Henry and Tony were conducting similar raids on numbers parlors in their sector. They would rush into buildings, screaming, their guns drawn, chasing gamblers out into the street through rear exits. Once everyone had left, Henry and Tony would scoop up any money left behind, and leave.

In addition to hitting numbers parlors, they took money

whenever they had the opportunity. They once stepped over a dead man's body, discovered in his apartment on the last day of the month, to seek out and steal his rent money.

The cops hit their collective low as thieves on a winter day in 1984. Responding to a radio call of a burglary in progress, they arrived at a Park Place apartment to find a woman standing in the hallway, shaking. She had come home to find her door ajar and jewelry missing from her bedroom bureau.

"I ran out of the apartment," she said. "I was scared the burglar might still be in there. I think he got everything, but I'm not sure."

Henry was interested. "What do you mean you think he got everything?"

"Well I keep a lot of money in the closet, but I didn't dare open it. The money is in a tin box. Could you go in and check to see if it's still there?"

Henry and Tony entered the apartment, leaving the woman in the hallway with a neighbor. Tony guarded the door while Henry removed two hundred dollars from the tin box. Henry stuffed the money into his pocket and the cops returned to the hallway, filling out a burglary complaint report.

"Yep," Henry announced. "They got it all, lady."

Later they split up the cash in the patrol car. Henry felt bad about what he had just done. His conscience bothered him. This wasn't some street dealer or numbers runner they had just ripped off, this was a frightened woman who trusted them. The partners discussed the possibility of returning the money, but Tony didn't want to compound the mistake with a lie.

"Forget it," he decided. "What's done is done. We'll never do it again."

Feeling disgraced, they decided they wouldn't rob anybody

but really bad guys. They had to have some code of ethics, they agreed. They were not, Henry and Tony assured each other, complete degenerates. They were businessmen, and even the cruelest businessman had to operate by a set of principles.

But soon they had another problem. They were running out of bad guys. A lot of smoke shops in their sector had closed because the drug merchants had moved to neighborhoods where the cops weren't quite so active and so greedy. Several numbers parlors also shifted their bases of operation, relocating in sectors beyond the reach of Winter and Magno. Apparently shut out, Tony and Henry refocused their attention on the ghetto's burgeoning drug trade.

"We'll become like Robin Hoods," Tony announced one day. "We'll steal from the rich and keep it."

While on patrol one day in late 1984, Henry and Tony rounded a corner on Schenectady Avenue and spotted a man carrying a shoulder bag. He looked at the cops, did a double take, and then sprinted down the street. He entered a storefront that the police listed as "a known drug location" in their intelligence reports.

The cops got out of their car and chased the man into the building. Henry grabbed him in the back of the otherwise empty store and asked, "What are you doing here?"

"Nothing. Just hanging out."

"What are you hanging out here for? There's nobody here."

Then Henry noticed that the man no longer had his shoulder bag and he ordered, "Get out of here. Now."

The man obliged and, once he'd left, Tony found the bag hidden behind a large commercial refrigerator. He opened it and called Henry over.

"What is it?"

"Fucking money. A lot of money."

They returned to their car with the bag. As Henry drove away, Tony counted out more than $5,500. The cops took $2,500 apiece and returned to the station house where they vouchered the bag and remaining $500 as found property. The man they robbed confronted them in the precinct parking lot.

"Please give me the money back. They're gonna kill me when I tell them what happened. They won't believe me."

"We're vouchering the bag and the money," the officers answered. "Tell your boss to come down and prove the money is his. It'll be right here. See the desk officer and tell him where you got the money."

When they turned the bag in, the sergeant discovered an additional $1,500 in a compartment the officers overlooked. Henry and Tony looked at each other and said, "We blew it. How stupid can we be?"

The bag's owner realized he would have to answer some hard questions about the drug trade if he tried to reclaim his cash and he never bothered to set foot in the 77th Precinct.

Henry and Tony were ecstatic. The incident brought a renewed sense of purpose to their work as members of the New York City Police Department. No drug dealer was safe from them. They broke down doors and climbed fire escapes into fortified apartments, getting the drop on surprised dealers.

Within a year after first teaming up, Henry and Tony were hooked on the excitement they felt whenever they harassed drug dealers.

"We always tried to leave the bad guys with a little something. If you go into a place and take everything, they're gonna bitch. They may even come down to the precinct and file a complaint against you. Of course a lot of guys did file complaints against us. They always identified us as 'Blondie and his partner.' Tony used to go crazy when he heard that. He'd scream, 'Keep your hat on when we're out in the streets. Being out here with you is like being with Fay Wray.'

"But if you catch guys and let them go with a little money and drugs they're not going to bitch. They're as happy as a pig in shit. They're thinking, 'I'm not going to jail. So I lost a little money. I'll make it up next week.' Plus they didn't know we were actually keeping the drugs and reselling them. They thought we vouchered the drugs after we let them go. That was easier for them to take than if we walked over to a toilet and flushed one thousand, fifteen hundred, two thousand dollars worth of cocaine away. They got pissed when we did that and said, 'You should have locked me up.'

"Did I feel guilty about what we were doing? Yeah. At that particular minute. When someone handed me money, I felt guilty. I think anybody would feel guilty then. But then all of a sudden we'd get a ten-thirty [shots fired] or something on the radio. And we'd go answer the job and forget about what we'd just done. Once I got through the day, I lived with my guilt. There were times I thought, 'What's going to happen? Holy shit, what am I doing? Taking a lousy couple of dollars. It's not worth it.' But it just seemed like, 'So what?' Who actually is going to come out here and look at us?

"Even though I was a bad guy, I had the feeling, 'Hey I'm bad on one side, but on this side I'm making up for it.' If people really needed us, we were there. We weren't taking anything from honest workers. I know it doesn't matter whether its an honest worker or a skell, it's still wrong. I know that. But we were taking money that was illegal to begin with. Drug money. It's weird but I never thought I was robbing those people. I was robbing a lowlife. A drug dealer. Someone who shouldn't be there to begin with. The law couldn't touch these guys. If we caught them they just went down and paid the fine. They could afford the fines. Hell, they were making money hand over foot. I know it sounds like a rationalization. But what we did worked. We ripped these guys off and they moved out. They should legalize that. Go in and rip all these guys off and they'll all disappear.

"At first Tony didn't like playing with drugs. He had no problems with money, none whatsoever. He just didn't want to have anything to do with dealing drugs. But after we started selling the drugs back on the street and getting more money, Tony just didn't even think about it anymore. He just did it.

"See, he was set in his ways. He had been on the job for fifteen years by the time I hooked up with him in 1983. He didn't give a shit what the bosses said. If we were going on our meal hour and they wanted to give us a job, we'd try to eat on the job. We'd say, 'Yeah Central, we'll take that job.' But we wouldn't go to it. We'd park somewhere, have our dinner, and after we ate, we'd go to the job.

"If we were goofing off, we'd sit on any job except an emergency call. If the call was a cardiac, we'd go. If we had a young kid suffering an asthma attack, we'd answer it right away. If there was a gun battle in the street, say at Plaza Street East and Underhill, we'd say, 'Maybe we better take a ride down there because maybe good people are involved.' But if we heard Lincoln and Franklin, a shit area, we'd just sit back and have our dinner. Let them shoot everybody the fuck up. Who the hell cares? We'll just go and pick up the bodies. Everybody else is gone. If two guys are having a gun fight, who do you take? You take the loser. He's sitting there with a bullet in him, so you get to lock him up.

"But really, it all depended on what mood we were in. If we were working a four-to-twelve shift, and Tony came in really early, like maybe around one o'clock in the afternoon, and he partied with the guys downstairs until I came in, then he'd be in a happy mood. He wouldn't care if the precinct turned upside down. We'd handle our jobs. But we wouldn't go crazy to back up another unit or take a job in someone else's sector. We'd do a job and shoot back to Macho's Bodega on Buffalo and St. Johns for a beer.

"We sat in the back on milk boxes, drinking bottles of beer and playing with the roaches, betting on the fastest ones. There were times that we'd have eight or nine cops in the back of the store, hooting and hollering, arguing about who was going to go out to the refrigerator to get the next round of beers. Anthony, a guy who hung out in the store, was an old-type numbers man who wrote everything down on a piece of paper. Everybody played their number with him and so did we. Tony and I hit a lot. He was good. We'd see Anthony on the way into work and he'd wave to us, 'I know, you hit today.' We got everything we ever needed from the bodega—cigarettes, batteries, sandwiches, and beer. All for free. The store owner and Anthony the numbers man both loved us. We were the right type of cops."

In a precinct that seemed to have gone mad, Henry and Tony were regarded as two of the most outrageous characters. Given the right set of circumstances—which was almost any circumstances at all—they could be counted on to commit the most unimaginable offenses. No one in the precinct could match their flair for handling a simple dispute.

One day early in 1984, Tony and Henry responded to a call about a husband-wife dispute in a tiny Park Place apartment. Tony arrived to quell the ruckus wearing shiny new shoes, which he had purchased earlier in the day. The husband, a wife beater, refused to leave the apartment. As Tony shoved the man out of the apartment, he stepped on Tony's new left shoe, landing on it in such a manner that he cut a tiny sliver of leather off the toe. Tony screamed, pointing at his shoe. The dispute stopped.

"I just paid forty fucking dollars for these shoes," Tony yelled, throwing the man around the apartment.

The shaken man pulled out twenty dollars and handed it to the cop. Tony's eyes went wide with a deranged look Henry had never seen before. He pocketed the money and then rifled the man's pockets for more.

"Is this all you got? Twenty dollars? Twenty dollars when I just paid forty dollars for these shoes? You're buying me a new pair of shoes." Tony said.

"Yes sir. But twenty dollars is all I got."

Magno turned on the heel of his good shoe and stormed out of the apartment, rushing back to the patrol car. Winter followed, amazed by his partner's anger. Henry waited until they had driven away from the scene before finally daring to speak.

"You know you just fucking robbed that guy?"

"Fuck him," Tony replied, his face still red with rage. "We're going back next week to get another twenty for the other shoe."

* * *

Henry rarely lost his cool. He did, however, once floor a fellow officer who refused to escort a teenaged shooting victim from the site of a gun battle to the hospital. The cop wanted to go visit his girlfriend instead, and Henry sent him off to see his girl with a shiner under his left eye. So on rare occasions Henry, to use a cop expression, "wigged out."

A few months after Tony cut his shoe, Henry entered an apartment to settle a dispute between a Jamaican woman and her landlord. Seeing a uniformed officer at her door, the woman made peace with her landlord, and aimed her sights at Henry, calling him a "blood clot" and suggesting that he engage in a sexual relationship with a goat. Henry took exception to this and raised his flashlight over her head, preparing to strike her. She stepped back into her apartment, grabbed her infant child off the floor, and returned to the fray.

"You blood clot cop. You can't hit me, I'm holding a baby."

Henry stepped forward and whacked the woman on the top of her skull with his flash light, rendering her unconscious immediately. He caught the baby as the woman crumbled, and then placed the child in its crib.

This time it was Tony who looked on mouth agape and stupefied.

"You crazy ass, you've got to be kidding me."

"I couldn't take her no more," Henry explained as they reached the street. "Come on. Let's get out of here."

A week later Tony and Henry returned to the same apartment building to settle another dispute between yet another tenant and the landlord. Henry spotted the Jamaican woman sitting on the stoop holding her baby as they pulled up in their patrol car.

"Hellooo, Officer Winter," she called. "How are you?"

"All right, and yourself? How's the baby?"

"Oh good, good."

Of course, there were members of the community who thrived on testing a police officer's mettle, particularly a cop like Henry Winter who wanted to get along with everyone, cop or thief. On a summer day in 1984, Henry entered an apartment building on Lincoln Place to handle a dispute on the second floor. As he entered the building, Henry met a Jamaican marijuana dealer named Panama Mike, who was selling drugs in the building's vestibule.

"You be gone by the time I come down stairs," Henry said.

He returned a few minutes later only to discover Panama Mike still selling nickel bags of marijuana through a mail slot in the door.

"Have some respect. What did I fucking tell you? I don't care what you do, but when I tell you to be gone, you get the hell out of here."

Panama Mike smiled and said, "Fuck you, Blondie. I'm going to kick your ass the next time you come around here."

"All right, you kick my ass next time I come around here."

Henry continued toward the door, heading for a metal garbage can near the entrance.

"Come on Blondie, me and you, right now."

As they reached the door, Henry grabbed the garbage can and swung it, splitting Panama Mike's nose open. He fell to the floor, and Henry picked him up and put him in the garbage can. Then he left the building.

"How did it go in there?" Tony asked.

"Good. I just left Oscar the Grouch sitting back there in a garbage can."

* * *

"Tony and I got medals for handling one dispute back in the summer of 1984. There was this new kid in the precinct, a guy we called Scoop Mahoney. He was walking a foot post one day and called in a ten—eighty-five—officer needs assistance. Scoop was yelling, 'Man with a knife, man with a machete.' So Tony and I decided to go see what Scoop wanted. There's Scoop on the corner with a guy with a big machete, swinging it like crazy. And every time Mahoney went near him, the guy took a swing at him. The guy was acting really flippy. Other people went after him and he'd swing at them too. Tony and I arrive on the scene and there's all these cops with guns drawn. I said, 'What's he calling in an eighty-five on this for? The guy's got a machete, he's swinging it at you, just drop him. Shoot him.' We're sitting in the car looking and looking, and finally Tony looks at me and I say 'All right.'

"So we get out of the car and now the place is loaded with cops. I don't have a night stick on me. I never liked carrying a stick. I figure if you really have to hit somebody, I mean hit them in the head with all your might, you're gonna kill them anyway, so why not use a gun? Mahoney comes running over to me and says, 'What do I do? I can't get the machete away from him.' I said, 'All right. Give me your stick.' So Tony starts talking to the guy, 'Hey, put down the knife. I'll fucking jack you up.' I tell Mahoney, 'Just get his attention for a second.' Mahoney does it and I walk behind the guy and pow. He goes out cold. I get the machete, I give the machete and the stick to Mahoney, then me and Tony get back in the car and pull away.

"It was Mahoney's collar. We met him back at the station house and he tells us, 'Look, I'm putting in for a medal and I'm putting you guys in for one too.' I says, 'No. No. You handle it.' He says, 'No, I'll put down that I did everything, but you were there, so I'm putting you in too.' And that's the way it went. We got some dipshit medals and Scoop later made detective."

On February 17, 1984, Henry and Tony made the city's daily newspapers for the first time as a team. Henry had narrowly escaped serious injury the night before, when a robbery suspect turned and fired a .357 magnum at him during a chase. The *New York Post* ran an account of the shootout at the top of page four under the headline, " 'I was lucky,' says cop who ducked bullet." The article was illustrated with a large photograph of Henry leading a blood-ied suspect away in handcuffs. It was a nice photograph, a graphic picture, the very same photograph that the *Post* later ran on page one to illustrate an even bigger story about Police Officers Henry Winter and Tony Magno.

"It was about one thirty in the morning. Tony and I were out on patrol, driving down Park Place when we reached the corner of Bedford Avenue. Two guys waved us over and said, 'We just got robbed,' and pointed to five or six guys across the street—like a wolf pack. I said, 'Anybody got guns?' and one kid says, 'Yeah. Two guns.' We drove up to the pack and they took off. I jumped out of the car—I was driving—and took after two guys. This fucked Tony up because now he had to come all the way around the car from the passenger's side to get into the driver's seat. I used to do this to him all the time, it drove him crazy. He used to scream, 'If you're driving, you stay with the car. I run when you drive.' But I always forgot. Sometimes I even forgot to put the car in park. I'd just jump out and start running with the car rolling down the block after me. I'd be chasing the bad guy and Tony would be chasing the car.

"So Tony is running circles around the car and I'm chasing this guy down the block. He got to the corner first and made a right turn down Park Place. I came around the corner and there he is standing in the combat position behind a car pointing the magnum at me. And the fuck fired the gun. The bullet hit the wall behind me and I dove behind it. I stayed there for a minute and then stuck my head out again in time to see the guy rounding the corner with a silver gun in his hand. I ran past the spot he fired at me from and found the magnum. He had two guns. We chased him to a building and then other cops responded to the scene. They found him hiding in the closet of an abandoned building and brought him up to the roof.

"I felt like beating the shit out of him. We tried to take care of him but there were too many people around. I smacked him around a few times but then the guys pulled me off. Everybody was uptight. Some parolee had just shot three cops in the South Bronx the night before, killing one of them. They had to call me off. I was going to kill him. I was going to throw him off the roof. He would have been gone.

"When he heard the shot, Tony broke off his chase and started looking for me. We were both scared. I caught up with him just before they found the guy. He says, 'You okay, shithead?' And then I remembered, we had just ordered chicken wings with hot sauce before all this shit broke, so I said, 'You know we just ordered our food.' So while all this shit's going on, Tony runs down to Nostrand Avenue and picks up our chicken wings with hot sauce. As they're transporting this guy to the station house, we're just sitting there eating our chicken wings and hot sauce in the car, trying to pretend that someone didn't just try and kill me."

9

"Buddy Boy, Buddy Bob."

In the beginning no one in the 77th Precinct was sure who could be trusted to steal.

Henry and Tony had worked together for six months before they learned that there were other bluefish cops out there, particularly on the midnight tours, running in schools, robbing almost each and every drug dealer they came in contact with.

Throughout most of their careers Tony and Henry worked around the clock. They would work a week on the 8 A.M.-to-4 P.M. tour, then spend another week on the 4 P.M.-to-12 A.M. shift, before finishing out the cycle with a tour on the midnight-to-8 A.M. detail. In the beginning, they stole only when the right moment presented itself, in broad daylight and the dark of night. They used their uniforms for camouflage and their badges as passkeys. Their guns provided security.

But the precinct's most prolific robbers were found on the midnight tour. Police Officers William Gallagher and Brian O'Regan and another half dozen cops lived for the night, when the darkness hid their misdeeds from prying eyes. By late 1984, with their daylight escapades already well known to the men on the midnight tour, Henry and Tony had been welcomed into the After Midnight gang—a group formerly known as Sergeant Stinson's Raiders. They were deemed fit company by Gallagher, a swaggering presence who used his ties to the police union to warn the cops of investigations.

Soon Henry and Gallagher were standing off to the side after roll call, plotting a series of moves that would ultimately land them in reinforced apartments where they were free to terrorize dealers at gunpoint, stealing drugs, money and guns. The cops made up nicknames for each other and talked on the radio in coded messages. Henry became Buddy Boy, Gallagher became Buddy Bee. Brian O'Regan was known as Space Man and the rest of the thieves fell under a single title: The Buddy Boys.

" 'Buddy Boy' was a word that we used among ourselves. 'Buddy Boy' was me. 'Buddy Bee' was Junior Gallagher. 'Buddy Bob' was the code word for what we did. It meant, 'Are we doing anything tonight? You agree to make a little money tonight?' We used the codes over the radio. If Junior was calling our car, he'd say, 'Buddy Boy, Buddy Bob.' That meant, 'Hey Henry, are we doing anything tonight?' If I called Junior it would be, 'Buddy Bee, Buddy Bob.' Pretty simple stuff. But no one listening to the radio could have figured out what the fuck we were talking about.

"Now, if we wanted to hit a place, we'd answer with a 'Hey, two-three-four,' 'Two-three-four' was the code name for a park on Bergen Street between Troy and Schenectady, behind the St. Johns Recreation Center across from a fire house, old Engine Company Two-Three-Four. That's where we got the name. We'd drive into the park and position our cars next to each other between two ball fields and a handball court. If there was anybody hanging out in the park, they'd take off as soon as we drove in. We could see out in all directions, so if the shoofly—some supervisor trying to check up on us—came into the park looking for us, we could see him coming. But nobody ever came. We could talk about whatever we wanted once we got to two-three-four.

"So we'd drive in there and discuss what we wanted to do. I'd say to Junior, 'What place you got in mind?' And he'd answer, 'Two-sixty-one Buffalo. I came in that way before work and scouted it out. I didn't see too many lookouts in front of the place.' And then we'd talk about how we were going to do it. Who's going in the front? Who's going to go in the back? Who went in the back last time? Who got dirty last time? Things like that. Then we'd say, 'All right. Let's do it.'

"We'd drive down the streets with our lights off. We'd give the lead car about a four- or five-second head start to get around the corner first. They'd go in the front or back way and we'd go in the other way. Sometimes we'd even park down the block and walk in, just to get the jump on the lookouts. If it was a heavy drug area, with a lot of lookouts, the scouts would start whistling back and forth as soon as they spotted us, yelling their own code words. We'd sneak up on places through backyards and alleys. It was almost like stalking a deer. Tracking through brush and making sure no one saw you doing anything. It was exciting. We created our own thrills.

"Sometimes it was easy and we didn't even need to show our guns. We'd just knock on the door, they'd open the door up and we'd walk in. They never stuck around to see what we wanted—they just ran, jumping out windows and climbing down fire escapes. We didn't care. We weren't there to arrest anybody. We were there to scoop up their money and drugs and then get the fuck out.

"But we always tried to make them think they were getting away. If a guy stayed and we came up with shit, we'd act all serious. I'd say, 'Whose collar is this?' and Brian would say, 'I got him.' Then someone else would say, 'Take him out in the hallway and put cuffs on him.' But as soon as Brian got the guy into the hallway, we'd call him back on some excuse and Brian would tell the guy, 'Now don't move. You stay right here. You're going to jail as soon as I get back out here.' Then Brian would come back into the room and we'd hear the guy scurrying down the hall, making his getaway. We'd laugh and say, 'Oh, the bad guy just got away.'

"We had this one idiot one time. Gallagher, Brian, me and Tony were on a job. We actually left the guy in the hallway, went back into the apartment, and shut the door. When we came back out five minutes later, the guy was still there. I look at Brian. He looks at me. We can't believe this guy. We go back inside, shut the door, and wait another five minutes. The guy is still standing there. So we closed the door and we ran away. We went out the fire escape because the fucking guy just would not leave. We made some noises in the apartment, and then left one by one, going down the fire escape thinking this was the dumbest fucker we'd ever seen. We had to run away from him! Then we got back in our cars and drove to the park to see who got what and divvy up the drugs and cash."

The Buddy Boys became more brazen with experience. Henry, having nearly broken his foot when he tried to kick down a metal door with sneakers, bought a pair of steel-tipped boots. Gallagher and O'Regan began carrying a sledge hammer, crowbar, and pinch bar in the trunk of their patrol car. They all packed screwdrivers in their attaché cases along with their paperwork.

Some of the cops became experts at kicking down doors and crashing through walls. No door could hold them. They split oak doors with one mighty swing of their hammers and used crowbars to pry metal doors off their hinges. If the cops wanted to get into a third-floor apartment, they would climb to the roof, tie a rope around an elevator housing and then rappel down the side of the building, crashing feet first into the apartment window. Some Buddy Boys also carried ash cans—small but powerful fireworks—which they would light and slip through mail slots, literally bombing people out of their apartments.

If the cops found themselves ill-equipped for a manuever, one of them would rush off to a firehouse to borrow axes and bolt cutters. The firemen, unaware of their role in the burglaries, scratched their heads and asked each other, "What the hell are these guys doing out there?"

One night the Buddy Boys arrived at a building on the corner of Eastern Parkway and Rogers Avenue, only to discover they had no means of getting to an adjoining roof. They had to place a man on the roof to keep the dealer they were after from escaping out his apartment window with his drugs and money.

"We need a ladder for this job," Gallagher decided.

"I saw a ladder at an excavation site on the way in to work today," Henry said.

So Tony and Gallagher sat in the apartment while Brian and Henry tore off in a patrol car, driving to the far end of the precinct where they found a wooden ladder at an excavation site. The cops wedged the ladder between the lights and the roof, ruining the car's paint job in the process, and then sped back to the scene, laughing as they raced through the city streets with an eight-foot ladder hanging off the top of their patrol car. Then they drove the car up on the sidewalk next to the building and put the ladder on top of the car. Henry and Gallagher climbed up the ladder, entering the dealer's apartment. Tony and Brian broke through his front door.

"He was very surprised to see us," Henry later remembered.

"Brian started talking about making his own equipment. He wanted to put together a scaffold that would fit into the back of his car. Then he talked about mailing away for things. He was going to get one of those rope ladders that you throw up, it hooks on, then you pull a string, it comes down, and you climb up. He was actually going to send away for this thing so we could rip places off. I told him, 'Come on. What are we going to do, start a business here? Do you want to get a van, too, and paint "H and B Removal" on the side?' Holy shit. That's what it was like. I mean, I'm not glad this happened to me, but it was getting pretty crazy on the midnight tours. Anything and everything went. You could do whatever you wanted to do and nobody could stop you. Getting a van wasn't out of the question. I think that if this was still going on we'd have a van by now. We would have all chipped in, got a van, and set it up with everything we needed—crowbars, helmets, axes, ropes, ladders, and acetylene torches. We could have parked it somewhere in the precinct before heading into work. Then we could have said on the radio, 'Buddy Bee, Buddy Bob. Get the Buddy-Boymobile.'

"There were a lot of times, hairy times, when we went up against big guns. Sometimes I came through the window, and I said to myself, 'What the fuck am I doing? This is ridiculous.' You're coming in through a window, it's a dark alley, you don't actually know who or what's in there. You just got a tip from one of your squealers, and here you are, four cops, going in with little thirty-eights, surrounding a building, kicking in windows off a fire escape. You don't know what the hell you're getting into. But we did it. There were a lot of times we went in and I could hear my heart coming through my chest. I was so dry I couldn't swallow. I was afraid to go in that window. But when the "Buddy Bob" came over the radio, the foot went in, I dove in that window, wound up on the bed next to a guy with a loaded gun, and came out with forty fucking dollars. I could have been killed. I just took ten years off my life. I got three new gray hairs. And for what? For the excitement of it all, that's what. We were lost in a frenzy.

"It was like we were insane or something. I mean one time we hit this bar on Schenectady Avenue on a late tour. It was Gallagher, O'Regan, Nicky Scaturico, and me. Brian and I jumped over a fence and came in the back way. Gallagher and Nicky came through the front. The idea was to scare them out the back way. Nicky and Junior banged on the front door, trying to sound like Emergency Services cops. So these guys opened the back door and we were right there. Surprise. All in uniform. We tossed everybody. While me

185

and Nicky were in the back searching through things, a line of customers formed. Brian started selling them coke through a slot in the door. And it was a good thing he did, too, because we came up with a small amount of money and a large amount of coke. So O'Regan made more money for us. He did it for about an hour. There was this one guy who came up to the door and wanted to sell his sweater. It was a nice, a brand-new sweater. But there was a long line so we couldn't open the door. That would have been bad for business. Brian tried to get the guy to slip the sweater under the door, but it wouldn't fit. And O'Regan, once he got money, he wouldn't give back change. One guy slipped Brian a fifty and wanted two twenty-dollar tins of coke and ten dollars change. Brian slipped the guy three twenty-dollar tins back. The guy started screaming, 'I don't want this, I want my change.' Brian slipped him another tin. But the guy was insistent, he kept getting louder and louder. And Brian would not give the guy any change. We were screaming now in our best Jamaican dialects, 'Geeve the mon his change.' Brian wouldn't do it. So we had to skate out the back door because the guy was raising too much of a riot."

By mid-1984, the Buddy Boys were in trouble. Not with the cops, but with drugs. They were confiscating hundreds of dollars worth of cocaine and marijuana as well as guns. Originally the cops had been content to flush the drugs down toilets. But being good businessmen, they soon realized that there was a profit to be made in drug dealing. They decided to fence most of their stolen drugs, guns, and electronic equipment through a middle-aged Jamaican drug dealer named Euston Roy Thomas who ran a grocery store and restaurant on Lincoln Place. Nicknamed "Roy," the dealer had ingratiated himself with the cops in the 77th years earlier when he stepped into an argument between a cop and a drug dealer, taking a bullet in the face. Roy still carried the bullet in the back of his head, a tiny mustache covering the entrance wound under his nose.

"Don't worry about me," Roy used to tell the cops. "I got a bullet in the head. If someone comes around here asking about my friends, I don't remember too good. You be amazed at what I remember to forget."

William Gallagher, who had been partners with the cop Roy tried to help out, never forgot the drug dealer. When it came time to fence drugs and guns, Roy was only too happy to accommodate his cop friends. He paid them fifty cents on the dollar for their coke and marijuana and a fair price on their guns, all of which he later resold on the street. No fool, Roy also gave the cops a payoff not to raid his own drug locations, explaining that he did not want to be in the business of buying back his own drugs.

By the winter of 1984, Henry and Roy had developed a certain sympathy. Henry often visited Roy's grocery store on Troy Avenue, asking how his business was going and talking about wives. Roy's Jamaican wife, Grace, was always trying to get her husband to hire her cousins from the islands for his business. Roy preferred kids from the neighborhood. Sometimes the couple's arguments were very loud and violent, and then Henry would arrive at the store and settle the dispute, reminding Grace that it was bad manners to point a loaded gun at one's own husband. Henry would then leave the building with two or three hundred dollars in his pocket and Roy's blessing.

"Buy yourself a cup of coffee," Roy would say.

Roy was well known to the precinct's homicide detectives. A lot of people died on the dealer's block. Although Roy's name figured prominently in discussions of drug-related homicides near the intersection of Troy and Lincoln Place, he was never arrested for murder. Henry knew Roy to be a tough guy but he didn't know him to be a killer. He thought of Roy as a friend, so much of one that when the police officer called his wife to wish her a happy New Year on December 31, 1984, he even put Roy on the phone with Betsy.

"Oh pretty lady," Roy said.

"Goodbye," Betsy said.

When Henry got home the next day, Betsy met him at the door.

"Who was that guy you had on the phone?"

"Oh, that's my friend Roy."

"You got some friends. I don't believe what you do in that precinct!"

Henry could not have known then that some investigators were already thinking the same thing. Homicide investigators assigned to the precinct's detective unit had arrived at Roy's store in January 1985 to inquire about a dead man found on the doorstep. A few days later Tony and Henry came in while detectives were questioning Roy, trying to determine whether he had seen or heard anything relating to the murder. The interrogation proved fruitless. "I got a bullet in my head. Sometimes I forget."

The detectives asked Henry and Tony for help, and Roy was only too happy to talk to them about the case, the detectives noted. One detective working the case, Steve Niglicki, went back to his supervisor, Lieutenant Burns, and reported the questionable relationship between the cops and the drug dealer. Burns filed a report with the Internal Affairs Division.

A set of wheels began to turn at One Police Plaza.

* * *

By this time Henry had many street friends in the precinct, and most of them paid through the nose for this relationship. One of them was an elderly black drug dealer named Herbie, who operated a drug business out of an apartment on St. Johns Place. The officers met him while raiding one of his properties, where they found one hundred crack-filled vials in the bottom of a bag in the kitchen. They also found eight hundred dollars on Herbie, which they placed on a counter in the kitchen.

"You're going to jail," Henry announced.

Obviously having dealt with cops from the 77th Precinct before, Herbie seemed unimpressed.

"Look," he said, "We can work out a deal."

The cops walked out of the kitchen, leaving Herbie alone with the crack vials. When they returned, he had stashed the drugs and there was a wad of money lying on the table. As the men continued to talk, Herbie suddenly opened a newspaper and flashed four hundred dollars at the cops. Tony and Henry exchanged glances and then grabbed the newspaper.

"Have a nice day," Herbie said as the cops left his apartment. "Come back real soon."

A few days later, Herbie put out word on the street that he wanted to see the cop called 'Blondie.' Henry drove to the apartment and the two men walked down the street, exchanging pleasantries. Then the cop and the drug dealer got down to business. Herbie explained that he was planning to expand his drug operation and wanted Henry's assurance that certain cops would protect it. He offered Henry two hundred dollars for this assurance, and Henry took the money.

"Be good," Herbie said as the cops drove away.

* * *

"We took the money to watch his place but then we got rotated off midnights back to day tours. Herbie got hit three times right after that. Boom. Boom. Boom. And he put out the word that he wanted to see Blondie again. So I went over to see him and he says, 'Look. I'm getting hit on the midnight tours. You're supposed to be watching me and telling me when I'm going to get hit. I need to get somebody on the midnight tours.' So I went back to the station house and told Gallagher about Herbie. I said, 'Billy, you know this guy on St. Johns, he paid us a couple times for watching him, but we can't do it anymore and he wants a friend on the midnight tour. If you want to speak to him, go ahead. Tell him Blondie sent you.' Gallagher went down there and Herbie set him up. At first he got eight hundred a month, but then it went to one thousand and on up to fifteen hundred dollars. Junior and Brian were splitting seventeen hundred a month from Herbie when this whole thing broke."

A third man who bribed Henry and Tony to protect his drug operation was a middle-aged black from Pacific Street named Benny Burwell. Originally Henry and Tony had no idea that Benny was dealing drugs. They believed he paid them fifty dollars a week to keep an eye on his brother's social club. But one day in February 1985, two young cops named Richard Figueroa and Michael Bryan cornered Tony and Henry on the street outside the station house.

"We know what's going on at Pacific and Ralph," Figueroa insisted. "And we want a piece of your pie."

Tony gave the young cops the same look that he gave the guy who stepped on his forty dollar shoes.

"Where the fuck do you guys get off asking for a piece of my pie?" he screamed. "I'm a senior man. I got seventeen years here. You want your action, you go out and get your own piece of pie. Who the hell are you to tell us what you want? This is my contract. You find your own."

But the younger cops were adamant about being cut in on the payoffs.

"Well, we want a piece of your pie," Figueroa insisted. "And if we don't get it, we're going to go harass the guys."

"Do whatever the fuck you want to do," Tony advised them before stalking off.

A few days later Benny called an emergency meeting with Magno and Winter. The shaken dealer explained that two young cops had come into his store and started pushing his customers around, demanding to be paid off. Benny's brother Frankie gave Tony and Henry eight hundred dollars cash, telling them, "Split it with those other two cops. I never want to see them again."

"Hey, we didn't have nothing to do with this," Tony said. "Yeah, okay," said Frankie. "Just take care of those guys and tell them to stay the hell out of here."

Tony went back to the precinct house and split up the money—robbing the cops in the process. He kept six hundred dollars to share with Henry and gave the younger cops two hundred dollars to split. After the initial payoff, Henry returned to Benny's store every other week. He would go in for cigarettes and come out with a brown paper bag filled with money. Tony became a reluctant paymaster, steadily giving the younger cops raises.

Four months later, Figueroa approached Magno in the locker room and told him, "Look, we don't need your Santa Claus no more. We want out. We got enough now." The brash younger cops offered no explanation for their change of heart. Tony was confused. Why would two dirty cops suddenly stop taking free and easy money? They couldn't have developed a conscience all of a sudden. Henry and

Tony thought the cops must have heard something that scared them straight.

"Something around here stinks," Tony decided. "I think we just stepped in shit."

"There were investigators tailing us by September 1985. They were easy to lose. We'd spot them and race down one way streets with our lights off. No Manhattan cop could keep up with us when we wanted to lose them. But we knew they were out there. There were too many reports on us by now. They would have been idiots not to be tailing us.

"One day we were going to a job and we saw the shoofly's car behind us. We go to another job, the shoofly follows us. He was constantly following us. So we went on one more job, and came out of the street the wrong way and there's the shoofly, parked on the corner of Park Place and Troy.

"So Tony said, 'Fuck this. Let's call in a man with a gun right on that corner store where he's parked. Let's see what he does. Let's see if he's gonna back us up or take off like a scared rabbit.' We went around the corner, getting in a position where we could still watch him, and called in the gun run from a corner pay phone. And then we watched. We were going to bust his chops, run up on him and say, 'Hey, if you're on the job and a gun run comes over, you back us up, asshole, no matter who you are.' But as soon as the gun run came over the radio, the guy took off like a bat out of hell. He didn't want to get involved in any kind of gun thing. He took off like his pants were on fire. We laughed our asses off over that one."

On a chilly October morning in 1985, William Gallagher called Henry at home. The precinct's union representative had heard some disturbing news from another union official,

Ray Lessinger, the Brooklyn North trustee with the Patrolmen's Benevolent Association.

"We got to talk, Buddy Boy. I got some information," Gallagher said.

"All right," Henry replied. "Tell me."

"Not on the ring-a-ding."

"All right, Billy. Where do you want to meet?"

"Meet me at Marine Park tonight. Five o'clock."

The men met outside the park, and then walked. It was a clear evening with a chilly darkness descending as they strolled along, hands behind their backs. For some reason, Henry had hunting on his mind. Deer season would be opening soon. He would pack up his truck and drive north into the Adirondacks to spend two weeks roaming the woods, trying to take home a prize buck or doe.

But William Gallagher didn't have time for small talk.

"Ray says they're running an operation to try and catch you and Tony. One of the guys that was doing undercover work on you got into trouble with drugs. He got bagged himself. But Ray says the thing is still hot. You might not make it to Christmas. Ray says if you make it to Christmas, chances are you'll be okay."

Gallagher went on to explain that the case was being handled by investigators assigned to Internal Affairs and possibly even the Special Prosecutor's Office. Junior also said that as far as he knew only Henry and Tony had been targeted in the probe.

"But look," Gallagher said, putting his hand on Henry's shoulder. "If anything goes wrong, just keep your mouth shut and we'll get you the best lawyer we can. We'll run rackets for you and everything. Money won't be a problem. We'll take care of you."

"Yeah." Henry's body shook with a chill that had nothing

to do with the cold. "No problem. You know me, Bill. If they come and ask me any questions, I don't know anything."

The two men shook hands.

"Don't worry about it. Ray says it's not that bad. He just wanted you to be aware of things."

"Tony and I chilled out after that. I went away hunting and told my friend Jimmy the garbage man what had happened. He said, 'Don't worry about it. Even if you do get jammed up, it isn't the end of the world.' But I was scared. I just wanted to make it through Christmas. I didn't want to go to jail at Christmas time. We stopped taking money from Benny. That was over. We weren't doing anything on the streets. I didn't know it, but Crystal Spivey, a black female cop we hung out with, had arrested Benny with major-weight cocaine. And they turned him. Isn't that great? Crystal Spivey busts the guy, they turn Benny to get me, and then they turn me so I can get Crystal. A neat little package.

"So we weren't into anything. Then all of a sudden we got a radio run one day in February to meet a complainant on the corner of Ralph and Pacific. We went looking but couldn't find a complainant. We do see Benny, and he says, 'Hey guys, how you been?' He didn't tell us he'd been collared, and Crystal never told us she arrested the guy. So now Benny is standing there on the corner saying, 'Hey, can I talk to you guys?' We put him in the car and drove away. We had no idea he was wired. We drove away and he told us, 'I'm looking to open a new place. It will be like the old times.' I think I said, 'Yeah. No problem.' This was Benny. We weren't scared of Benny. He handed Tony the money—about two hundred dollars. We dropped him off and drove away. Tony looked at me and said, 'I don't know. Something's not right. Benny was nervous. He was shaking.' We went back and forth for a couple of minutes and I saw a twinkle in Tony's eye and I'm sure he saw a twinkle in mine. I put my hand out and Tony put the money in my hand. I put it in my pocket and forgot about it. That was that.

"They had a truck there. We never saw it. They were running videotape on us. Benny was wired. I think we took money from Benny another four or five times after that. He was always wired. We always took the money. We probably got about fifteen hundred total. It wasn't a lot, but it was enough money to catch us. Enough money to catch us and make us turn in our friends. We did a little better than Judas, I guess. How much is thirty pieces of silver worth anyway?"

10

"I know there's somebody out there watching me."

Dennis P. Caufield, the superintendent of public works for the Long Island village of Valley Stream, was relaxing at home, his feet up, watching television in the den on the afternoon of Saturday, May 24, 1986. The former cop had rebuilt his life. His name was respected again. No one could strike a nail in Valley Stream without first getting Dennis Caufield's signature on a building permit.

And then, just before six o'clock, Dennis answered the doorbell and greeted his brother-in-law, Henry Winter, at the front door. Henry had bags under his eyes, Dennis noted.

Dennis had already heard the cover story about his brother-in-law's misadventure at sea, and he figured that Henry had been up all night fixing the propeller on his boat. But then

196

Dennis saw an odd look in Henry's eyes—a frightened expression that the former New York City police officer immediately recognized. On a night eight years earlier, Dennis had left work in the 75th Precinct to meet a group of police investigators in a prosecutor's office. He had come home after the meeting with the same look in his eyes.

"You want to talk?"

"Yeah," Henry replied, his eyes focused on the living room rug.

"Here?"

"No, please Dennis, not here," Henry said, now looking up, his eyes already moist.

"Let's go to the firehouse then. We can always talk there."

They climbed into Henry's truck and drove over to the Valley Stream firehouse, where they worked as volunteer firemen. They exchanged no words as they drove, an eerie silence filling the cab of the truck. Both men knew what was coming. They had never felt closer.

Dennis led Henry into the firehouse and down to the basement, where they entered a small room, closing the door behind them. They sat down on opposite sides of a pine table. And then Henry began to cry. Dennis reached across the table, touching the shoulder of his wife's younger brother.

"Oh God," Henry sobbed.

After a few moments, he composed himself and started talking. In time, he told his brother-in-law everything. He explained that he had been taken in by investigators the day before and confronted with videotaped evidence of his own misdeeds. He retold, in intricate detail, the story of a good cop who turned bad. He explained why he had stolen, how he had been caught, and what the investigators were now asking him to do.

Dennis listened and waited. He knew what was coming.

Any second now Henry was going to ask him for advice. Should he, a cop in trouble, wear a wire on the guys he worked with in the 77th Precinct and become an informant like his brother-in-law, or keep his mouth shut and slink off to jail?

"What should I do, Dennis?"

For years, Dennis Caufield had been asking himself the same question. He had even told Henry once, 'If I had to do it all over again, I never would have worn the wire. It's not worth it. You do that and you're not a cop anymore. You're not a hero. You're an informer. Cops never look at you the same after you send another cop to jail. You never look at yourself the same way either."

But now, faced with the chance to do it all over again and the opportunity to use Henry to correct what he perceived as a terrible wrong in his own life, Dennis could not ask his brother-in-law to do anything less than he had done.

"You know what I went through. But you don't want to go to jail, and believe me, they'll put you in jail. If they got that much tape on you, and they wasted that much time investigating you, you will go to jail. I'm not saying for how long, but you will go to jail. Do you want to go to jail and have your kids grow up when you're not around?"

"No."

"The shit you were doing," Dennis continued. "I'm not saying it was right, I'm not saying it was wrong. But it's better it happened this way. How would you feel if you were in a box? Somebody's going to get killed out there. It's better that you do what they want you to do and nobody gets hurt."

Henry had already made the decision to cooperate. Now he wanted to know how he would feel. He wanted to know how a man who betrays his friends lives with himself. He wanted to know how he could look at himself in the mirror, a razor at his throat, and never cut anything more delicate than his beard.

"You're shit for the rest of your life," Dennis said, his own eyes now misty. "It will eat at your gut. There will be times when you're going to flip out—break walls, punch windows. You'll have headaches and nightmares. You'll lose your friends and your self-respect. You'll cry and you'll fight with your family. There will be times when you'll want to eat the gun. And it never goes away. You do this and it never goes away."

The men commiserated for another half hour and then left the firehouse, Henry driving Dennis back home. They talked on the telephone again several times over the next few days, but the firehouse chat put Henry in the right way. He was ready to do whatever he had to do to stay out of jail. But as he drove home that night, back to his unsuspecting wife and children, Henry focused his attention on one freakish aspect of the conversation. It seemed to Henry that Dennis had been staring him straight in the eye and talking to himself.

On Monday morning, May 26, three days after being dragged into the special prosecutor's office and identifying a group of their fellow cops as thieves, crooks, bandits, and drug dealers, Henry and Tony returned to their first tour of duty in the 77th Precinct. Henry arrived looking refreshed, his face severely sunburned and his blonde hair slightly bleached. There was even a bounce to his step as he entered the muster room to answer a 7:05 A.M. roll call.

"Hey, Buddy Boys," he said to no one in particular. "What's doing?"

Tony seemed to be in another one of his moods. He was heard cursing foil wallpaper and telling a younger group of cops, "Go fuck yourselves."

All seemed to be normal in the abnormal precinct.

By the time Henry and Tony rolled out onto the streets, they had almost forgotten their new roles in the precinct. They had not yet been given recording devices to carry around. They drove out to their sector and parked the car. Then they talked, the dark, brooding weight of their fate finally settling in.

"The guys are too smart in this precinct," Tony decided. "I don't see how we're ever going to get away with this without anybody finding out."

Stopping to use the bathroom a few hours later, Henry and Tony walked into the station house and Tony was confronted by a young cop named John Tracy, a kid Magno regarded as his protégé, and his partner, Bill Hock.

"I got to talk to you," Tracy advised the veteran cop. "I heard something about an investigation in the Seven-Seven from my cousin who works in the special prosecutor's office."

Tony was stunned. His mouth went dry. Somehow he managed to look uninterested.

"Yeah? So what do you hear?"

Tracy told Magno that his cousin, a secretary in the special prosecutor's office, was at work on Friday when a group of cops from the Seven-Seven were brought in, one with blonde hair and blue eyes. He had been out fishing on a boat. He had a sunburn. Tracy's cousin had advised him that she thought there was a big investigation going on in his precinct.

"That sounds like your partner," Hock added.

"That sounds like bullshit. If something happened to Henry I would know about it."

"Do you think we should tell Gallagher about this?" Tracy asked, genuinely confused. "He might be able to find out more."

Tony was horrified. The investigation was blown even

before it started. Henry's blonde hair had gotten them in trouble again. Now they were going to jail.

"Don't tell Gallagher. You'll get your cousin jammed up."

Tony walked around the station house looking for Henry, moving on legs that felt like jelly. He had to go to the bathroom. The conversation with Tracy had given him an instant case of diarrhea.

"I came into the precinct and met Tony at the door. He pulled me aside and whispered, 'They know. Tracy knows everything. They caught us. Tracy has a cousin in Hynes's office and she told him they brought in a blonde, blue-eyed cop, possibly from the Seven-Seven.' The guy's got a sunburn and he's a fisherman. Sound familiar, Buddy Boy?' I said, 'Oh, motherfucker.' I know there's only a couple of blonde guys in the precinct. What's the odds of it not being me? Blonde hair, blue eyes, and I'm burnt like a lobster. Tony says, 'How the hell are we going to get out of this? He knows it's us, the investigation's blown. We're going to jail. Even though we said we would cooperate, they're going to think we blew the investigation.' Tony tells me to go see Tracy. We thought maybe he didn't believe his cousin. It's our only chance.

"So I get Tracy and we go sit down at a table in the muster room. My hands are under the table because I'm shaking. Then he told me the story his cousin told him. He looks straight at me. I'm red from sunburn. I can feel my ears falling off because the guy is talking about me. And I'm sitting there saying, 'No, it's not me.' He keeps asking, 'Well, who do you think it is?' And my mind is going, 'It's you, you stupid fuck, they got you.' But Tracy just wouldn't believe it. He had the right information and he wouldn't believe it. Finally, I said, 'Well, Tracy, you're not going to tell nobody about this. You shouldn't tell anybody because you don't know who to trust. If you tell Gallagher you could get your cousin in trouble.' The kid never opened his mouth about it. But I think Hock knew it was me the whole time though. How could he not? Nobody's that stupid.

"Tony was scared. I was scared. We went out to a phone and called the 'hello' number they gave us. We screamed, 'We told you this was going to happen. These guys are too slick for you. They hear everything ten minutes after it happens.' Eventually they calmed us down. They couldn't even fire Tracy's cousin for awhile. That would have given us away for sure. The thing that really saved us was a shooting. Two cops from the precinct got shot right after that. They put a prisoner in the back of the car without checking him for a gun. They had already taken one away from him. Who figures the guy for two guns? They put handcuffs on him, put him in the back seat and he pulled a gun from the small of his back and shot both cops. Then he jumped out of the car and two other cops shot him dead. The cops in the car both lived, but it was close. Everybody in the precinct was devastated. Tony and I had to go to the hospital with them. We were supposed to meet the investigators in a hotel near Kennedy airport that night. We called them up and told them about the shooting. They told us, 'We don't want to hear it.' We said, 'Hey, we got two of our fucking guys here that may go out of the picture.' They came back, 'We'll be here when you get here.' I hung up and told Tony, 'These fucking guys, they ain't nobody to fool with no more.' And they weren't."

By the afternoon of May 28, five days after they were brought in, Henry and Tony were literally rolling. Shortly after turning out, William Gallagher approached Henry and Tony as they sat in the park.

"José Villarini wants to make a withdrawal," he said.

"What do you mean, make a withdrawal?" Henry asked innocently.

"He wants to hit a place," Gallagher replied. "You know perfectly well what I mean."

"Okay," Henry decided. "Meet us later on."

Tony and Henry left the park and drove directly to a pay phone, calling the 'hello' number. The cops explained that they were about to make a withdrawal. An hour later, a field operative assigned to Internal Affairs met them in front of the Brooklyn Museum, handing Henry a loaded tape recorder. He squeezed the bulky recorder into his pocket and drove back into his sector. A short time later, Villarini and Gallagher pulled up while Henry and Tony were handling a job.

"So what do you want to do?" said Henry, beginning the first tape of Internal Affairs Investigation No. TF53s84.

"Make a withdrawal," Gallagher said.

Villarini, who would later be suspended from the force for refusing to take a drug test, and was indicted for conspiracy, grand larceny, and official misconduct once he left the job, explained that he wanted to hit two drug locations, one at 277 Eastern Parkway and another at 409 Lincoln Place. The four cops crashed into several apartments without finding any drugs. The Lincoln Place address was an apartment house with no less than twenty apartments.

"What apartment you wanna hit?" Henry asked.

"I don't know," Villarini replied.

"What do you mean you don't know? This is your place."

"Let's hit them all," Villarini suggested.

The cops groaned. Villarini was not a Buddy Boy. He was an amateur. As they left the building, Villarini grabbed a resident and frisked him, stealing a knife from the startled man's pocket. Henry's tape recorder picked up the cop's frustration.

"Hey," Villarini said. "If I had to do this for a living, I'd starve to fucking death."

They were given tape recorders. Tony's was an Olympus microrecorder, serial number 211417. The machine was one half inch thick and approximately four inches long. Henry got a Panasonic microrecorder, serial number 6BBRB09497—a thinner, shorter recorder that fit inside a pack of cigarettes. They also got brief instructions on how to operate the machines.

"This is the 'on' button, this is the recording button and this is the volume button. You press this button to make it record and this button to make it stop," an investigator explained. Henry got equally impressive advice on how to conduct an undercover operation. "Just go out and do what you would usually do," he was told.

The cops were supposed to record all their conversations in the precinct, with Henry's machine as the primary recorder and Tony's operating as the backup system. They would meet investigators on their way home from work, driving to prearranged drops. Tony usually met the plainclothes investigators at an intersection on Ocean Parkway near his home. Henry met his contact at the corner of Foster and Ralph Avenues in East Flatbush.

The cops turned over the ninety-minute tapes they used during their tour and briefed the investigators on the contents of the recordings. The Internal Affairs operatives would then reload the cops' recorders with fresh batteries and new tapes. A brief header—used for voice identification—was then recorded on each tape along with the time and date.

It was soon apparent to investigators that Tony was not

cooperating in the probe. Sometimes he went out on patrol and left the recorder in his locker. He often submitted blank tapes, explaining, "Henry got all the conversations."

"The recorder is too big," Magno said, his voice filled with paranoia, "I know they can see it bulging from my shirt and pants. It feels like I'm carrying a thousand pounds of bricks."

"You'll get used to the weight," the investigators told him.

On another street corner, another set of cops was complaining to Henry.

"Look, you're doing all the taping and your partner isn't doing anything."

"That's because Tony's recorder is too big," Henry insisted. "It's too bulky for him."

"Then switch recorders," the investigators said.

Henry and Tony switched recorders. Soon both men were turning in tapes full of crisp, clearly incriminating conversations. The investigators were happy. Magno and Winter were miserable.

"The recorder sucked, Tony and I both agreed on that. You could never forget that you had it on you. Not like your gun. Sometimes you forget that you have the gun on. In the beginning I was always shifting the recorder from one pocket to another, trying to find a place that was comfortable. I put it in my shirt pocket. I put it in my pants pocket. I taped it to my crotch. It never felt comfortable. I felt like everybody could see it. Guys would look at me and I'd be sure they were looking at the recorder. But they never saw it. They would have shot me if they found the recorder on me. I would have shot me too. It's an unwritten law with cops. If you catch another cop wearing a wire on you, he's a dead man.

"I went to a Singer sewing machine center and bought a strip of two-inch elastic. Then I sat in my living room one night watching television, and sewed a pocket inside of my bulletproof vest. Right near my heart. I had never sewn anything before in my life. But my life, when you think about it, depended on this. I sewed a secure little pocket. The recorder fit in there nice and snug. I also sewed elastic strips into the sides of my pants. I had a strip on either side. That way I could move the recorder. If I was driving and talking to somebody on my right, I'd put the recorder on my right side. If I was in the passenger seat I'd put the recorder on my left side. I even had a Velcro strap that went over the recorder to make sure it didn't fall out.

"One time it did fall out. I was running up a flight of stairs behind Robert Rathbun and the thing flew out of my sock. It clattered on the stairwell. Rathbun was about five steps ahead of me. I grabbed it and threw it in my pocket. He didn't hear anything. But there were other problems too. When you put the thing on 'record,' a little red light went on. One night, I was walking past a window and I saw the reflection of a little red glow coming out of my chest. That scared the shit out of me. I had to cover up the light with a piece of black electrical tape.

"This may sound strange—people may consider me a scumbag or something—but after awhile, if I got good conversation on the tape, I actually felt good. I did my job. I believed if you're gonna do something, go all out, do it right. That's the way I am. But after handing in the tape and thinking about what I recorded people saying, I felt like shit. I'd say to myself, 'Oh fuck. What did I just give these people? What did I just do? I'm sending these guys to jail.'"

* * *

During the first week of their undercover duty, Henry and Tony put out the word in the precinct that they were willing to fence whatever the other cops could steal. They were interested in everything from stereos and videotape equipment to guns and televisions.

Steadily, they picked up more and more conversation from corrupt cops. The transcripts of their ninety-minute tapes were a catalogue of precinct gossip. William Gallagher insisted another cop on his tour was stealing cars while on duty. Gallagher explained that the cop would park his tow truck in the precinct and then tow cars back to Long Island, breaking down the car overnight and reselling the parts. Brian O'Regan boasted of robbing a grocery store of $8,000 in cash and $3,400 in food stamps. The cops arrived at the store to answer a burglary call and then robbed the store's safe, O'Regan explained. A precinct detective implicated a black patrolman in the contract killing of a man and woman in a parked car in an adjoining precinct. The cop was said to have been paid $1,500 by his relative, a neighborhood drug dealer who ran a bodega on Saratoga Avenue.

Investigators found the early conversations interesting but unappetizing. They needed real evidence of criminal activity, not hearsay gossip, if they were going to bring the 77th Precinct's rogue cops to court.

Roy, the Jamaican cocaine dealer from Lincoln Place, called Henry into his store on June 5, explaining that he felt something was "wrong in the neighborhood." A few days earlier he had spotted two men with a camera parked in an unmarked car across the street from the store. The men were taking photographs of Roy and his customers. He figured they were cops. His street instincts told him he had been targeted for prosecution in some larger investigation. Henry listened, his tape recorder rolling.

"I know there's somebody out there watching me," said Roy, a strong believer in voodoo. "I'm in for trouble. Someone is going to give me trouble. And it's someone close. I just can't put my finger on it."

Roy then used his fingers to count out a cash payment to Henry, bribing the officer to utilize a police department computer to check the license plate number of his mysterious camera-toting guests. The payoff was the first of three that Roy would make to Henry over the next four months—recorded bribes that eventually led to Roy's indictment on three separate counts of bribery in the second degree. On the day of Roy's arraignment, his lawyer told a judge, "My client doesn't remember too much. He has a bullet in his head."

A few days later Henry and Tony realized that the investigators were using even background conversation from the tapes to gain indictments. Henry was standing outside the station house on June 9, discussing "hits" with William Gallagher, when Zeke Zayas spotted his partner, David Williams, throwing two garbage cans into the back of his car. "What the hell are you doing?" Zayas said, laughing. "Can you believe this guy? He's stealing our garbage cans." Gallagher and Winter laughed.

"I didn't even know the conversation was on the tape," Henry said later to an investigator. "You mean you can be arrested for shit like that?"

Williams was later suspended, indicted, and arrested on a charge of petty larceny—to wit, the theft of two garbage cans. Zayas, having failed to report the theft of the cans to his superiors, was later suspended, indicted, and arrested on a charge of official misconduct.

On June 17, the investigators came up with their first hard evidence. The evening started when William Gallagher put out "Buddy Boy, Buddy Bob," over the radio. Henry answered with a "Hey, two-three-four" and then drove to St. Johns Recreation Center across from Engine Company 234. Henry, Tony, Gallagher, and O'Regan then discussed ways to hit a building they suspected of being a crack house at 143 Albany Avenue. Earlier on that rainy evening Gallagher and O'Regan chased a man whom they suspected of being a drug dealer into a building and kicked down a door, searching the apartment for drugs. They came up empty on the first burglary, and were in the mood to make a major score.

Driving with their lights out, a steady drizzle masking their approach, the two patrol cars descended on the block. Henry and Tony gave their Buddy Boys a four- or five-second head start, then tiptoed past a sleeping sentry who had nodded out in the vestibule of 143 Albany Avenue. Gallagher and O'Regan entered an adjoining building that was abandoned and boarded up. Each pair continued to second-floor apartments. The door to the apartment in Henry's building was locked. Tony knocked and then heard the sound of a metallic click.

"There's a gun in there," Tony whispered. "I heard a gun."

"All right, but we gotta go in."

After throwing the gun across a narrow air shaft into the second-floor apartment in the abandoned building, the man opened the door. Henry and Tony searched the apartment but found nothing. Across the air shaft, O'Regan found a .357 magnum lying on a pile of trash in the second-floor apartment of the abandoned building. Henry and Brian stared at each other across the shaftway and shrugged. Then O'Regan shined his flashlight out the window and down into the open air shaft, spotting a dry bag on top of a pile of soaked garbage.

"Look," he said. "That's got to be it."

Tony lowered Henry into the shaft, first dropping a bedspring out the window to break his partner's fall. Henry retrieved the bag, which was filled with three hundred vials of crack. Moments later Gallagher discovered a potato chip bag stuffed in the window sill of the abandoned apartment. The second bag contained another one hundred vials of crack.

"Ah, we got more stuff here," Gallagher said.

The cops came away from the apartment with four thousand dollars worth of cocaine, and let the man go free, saying, "You're lucky we didn't find this in your apartment." They drove directly back to the park.

"Give me the gun," Henry said. "I can get rid of the gun."

Gallagher handed it over.

"I can get rid of the drugs too," Henry said, looking for evidence to go with his tape of the robbery.

"No," Gallagher said. "We'll get rid of the drugs through Roy."

On their way home that morning, Henry swung by Foster and Ralph to meet the investigators. He handed over the stolen gun, telling the operatives that he would need two hundred dollars to pay Gallagher and O'Regan for it. Then Henry told the cops about their four thousand dollar score, explaining that Gallagher had taken the drugs to Roy, who would buy them at half price.

"That stuff is going back on the street?" an investigator said. "You guys are supposed to get the drugs back. The drugs are evidence."

"Sorry, but you never told us that part of the deal."

After a short meeting, it was decided that Henry and Tony

would go into the business of fencing the stolen drugs. The Police Department would simply outbid Roy, offering seventy-five cents on the dollar to Roy's fifty cents. Henry was told to make up a story about an imaginary dealer, as was Tony. Henry invented a black dealer named Bobby, and Tony thought up a Hispanic named José. The mythical dealers put Roy out of business.

"Hey, why are we dealing with Roy?" Henry said to Gallagher the next day. "Roy gives us half price. I got a guy that lives out by me who gives a much better cut. If you give Roy four thousand dollars worth of coke and he gives us two thousand dollars to split four ways, he's making two thousand on us. For what? We're taking the chances. I'll get us three thousand next time."

"Do you trust him, Buddy Boy?" Gallagher asked.

"Oh yeah. He's very good. I've used him before."

"We hit another place the next night, June eighteenth. We put out 'Buddy Boy, Buddy Bob' over the radio, and met in the park. Gallagher had scouted out Two-sixty-one Buffalo Avenue. 'It looks good. We should pay them a visit.' So we did. We followed him down the block and ran into the building. We hit one apartment and found nothing. Then we spotted two guys in the hallway who looked pretty suspicious, like they were hiding from us or something. O'Regan went over to the other side of the building. I was talking to a lady who told me about how three guys upstairs had threatened to shoot her. And as I look out the window, I see a guy shimmying down the ledge. He swings through the window into the apartment on a telephone wire and I grab him. I can hear the cops upstairs, right above me, kicking in the apartment door, so I know I've got the guy we're looking for. He says, 'Hey, come on, we can work out a deal.' I said, 'Fuck you. Come on, you're coming back up there with me.' On the way upstairs, he told me where the stash was. 'Look, the stuff is kept inside, underneath the rug, underneath the floorboards, there's a trap door.' I bring him into the apartment and everyone is looking at me. They haven't found anything. I said, 'The stuff is underneath the rug.' The guy wasn't lying. I pulled the rug up, lifted a floor board, stuck my hand in, and came up with one hundred seven dollars in cash and eight hundred dollars worth of marijuana.

"So as we're walking out, the guy says, 'Hey look, you know, can you take care of me? Can you give me a couple of dollars?' O'Regan said, 'Yeah, give the kid a couple of dollars,' and he grabbed twenty dollars from me and handed it to the kid. Then the guy said, 'Can you give me some smoke too?' He was wearing army pants. O'Regan lifted up a flap on the kid's pants and put some herb in his pocket. Then the kid says, 'You can't just leave me here. They'll kick my ass. You gotta walk me out like you're locking me up. I won't come back.' So O'Regan cuffed him. And then he says, 'Look, you gotta slap me around a little and make it look real.' So we walked him downstairs and by that time a little crowd had formed. As we walked him outside, Brian yelled, 'Hey scumbag, get in the back of the car.' We smacked him in the back of the head a couple of times, threw him in the back, and O'Regan and Gallagher took off.

"Tony and I drove back to the park. Within ten minutes Gallagher and O'Regan pulled up laughing, 'Oh, he must have got away. We don't know where he went.' We split the money up and then Gallagher agreed to give me the marijuana to sell. 'We'll give your guy a shot. Let's see how fast he comes back with the money.' Later that night I turned the drugs into IAD."

* * *

On June 21, Gallagher paid Henry one thousand dollars for the crack they had seized in the Albany Avenue raid. Henry turned the money into Internal Affairs and passed Gallagher the four hundred dollars he had gotten from IAD for the marijuana they had stolen from Buffalo Avenue. That same day Brian told Henry he had spotted a new drug location on Classon Avenue. The following morning Brian called Henry to tell him they had hit the Classon Avenue address, stealing seventy dollars and fifty-six vials of crack. There was also the matter of having stolen two thousand dollars off a fire escape in another drug dealer's apartment. Brian asked Henry to deal the crack through his friend. Henry turned in the crack and a tape of his phone conversation with O'Regan to an investigator. A day later, the investigator told him, "That conversation you had with O'Regan on the phone was great. Good work. Keep it up."

A week or so later, Herbie Woods put out the word on the street that he wanted to see Blondie. Henry arrived at the man's home on St. Johns Place and got a one thousand dollar bribe to watch over Herbie's bustling drug business.

"Buy yourself a cup of coffee," Herbie said.

"Pretty fucking expensive cup of coffee," Tony answered, the tape still rolling.

A few days later one of the investigators took Tony aside at a meeting and said, "Your remark about the coffee was very unprofessional."

Shortly before midnight on July 1, O'Regan walked over to Henry's truck and placed an envelope containing seventy-two vials of crack in the glove compartment.

"You want it in here, Hank?"

"Yeah."

Gallagher had written the notation "52/10" and "19/5" on the outside of the package. He slid into the truck next to Henry and talked about the upcoming Statue of Liberty celebration, which would culminate with the relighting of the lady's famous torch on the Fourth of July.

"So what's here?" Henry asked.

"Fifty-two dimes, and nineteen nickels."

"What does that come too?"

"Six hundred and fifteen."

"So figure you're gonna get four hundred dollars."

"Okay," Gallagher said. "If you get four hundred dollars, then one hundred is yours right off the top."

"Why would you give me one hundred dollars when you can take it to Roy and get three hundred?"

"Because we're giving it to you to get rid of it."

"I'm doing it as a friend. Keep your money."

Gallagher reached across the seat and gave him a playful slap on the back of the neck.

"Listen scum," he said. "Just see how you do. It's a small package. See if he can handle it. He's your boy, you're dealing with him. He's not our man."

Twenty-five minutes later, Henry sat huddled over his Olympus recorder with Detective James O'Brien and Sergeant Bernadette Bennett, two investigators assigned to the Internal Affairs Division.

"Did you record any conversations during your tour of duty," O'Brien asked, the tape rolling again.

"Yes I did."

"And who were those conversations with?"

"I had conversations with Police Officer O'Regan and Police Officer Gallagher."

"Did you receive anything tonight?"

"Yes I did."

"What did you receive?"

"I received a quantity of crack from Police Officer O'Regan

and a piece of paper stating the quantity was fifty-two dimes and nineteen nickels."

"Where did this occur?"

"This occurred outside the precinct. I was in my truck leaving to go home and they came up. Police Officer O'Regan put the envelope in my glove compartment."

"Was Officer O'Regan in uniform at that time?"

"Yes he was."

"Have you inspected the package?"

"Yes I did."

"And what do you know it to be?"

"I know it to be crack," Henry said firmly.

On the morning of July 4, after taking two days off, Henry returned to the 77th Precinct station house, meeting Gallagher as he came into the muster room. Henry clicked his tape recorder on.

"Hello, Officer Gallagher. How are you?"

"What have you got for me?"

Henry pulled out a roll of hundred-dollar bills from his pocket. He snapped four bills off the roll, counting out loud as he laid the money into Gallagher's outstretched hand.

"One. Two. Three. Four. Four hundred dollars, Buddy Boy."

Gallagher handed Henry back one of the bills.

"No, I don't want it."

"Take it, take it," Gallagher demanded, stuffing the money into Henry's shirt pocket.

"You work, you stick your neck out, you get paid," O'Regan added.

Then Gallagher handed Henry another package, explaining that they had hit a drug location at 1224 Lincoln Place—a crack den run by their old friend Roy.

"You take this," Gallagher said. "We can't take it to Roy. Someone may have recognized us."

Later that night Henry met Gallagher outside a United Parcel Service warehouse in Queens, where he was moonlighting as a security guard. Gallagher had just spent an eight-hour tour strolling the Brooklyn docks, watching the largest fireworks display in the city's history. He complained that his feet were blistered.

"Waste of time," he remarked.

Henry opened the package of drugs Gallagher and O'Regan had given him earlier in the night.

"I haven't seen coke like this around in a long time," he said, his recorder rolling. The men counted out dozens of tins of cocaine and at least seventy-one vials of crack, approximately fourteen hundred dollars worth of stolen drugs.

"Figure on getting about nine hundred dollars."

"I trust you," Gallagher said, walking away.

"You trust me?" Henry Winter said. "I love you."

The prosecutors assigned to handle the 77th Precinct indictments were pleased. By mid-July, they figured they had enough evidence on Gallagher and O'Regan to send them off to jail for years, if not for life. But there were problems with the investigation. Special Prosecutor Charles J. Hynes and his chief aides told Henry and Tony that they wanted to catch some of the precinct's black cops as well as other crooked cops working elite details. It was decided that the investigators would split the cops up, moving Henry upstairs into the Anticrime detail and keeping Magno on patrol.

There were problems with Tony, the investigators had decided. He had a bad attitude. He seemed uninterested in their corruption probe. He still regularly turned in blank tapes. Compared to Henry, Magno wasn't pulling his own weight.

"I went on vacation for two weeks and came back at the end of July. Henry was in Anticrime, doing his thing. I guess he was doing pretty well. We used to have these meetings at Creedmoor Hospital—the nut house. It was crazy. We had to come in on our days off and meet secretly in the basement there. I didn't mind it at first when they split us up. It had become, well, like a job. But when they separated us, all of a sudden the right hand didn't know what the left hand was doing. Henry and I had to set up hand signals. If I looked at him and he was twirling his fingers, that meant he was rolling tape on the guy he was talking to. I stayed away when I saw that. We didn't want to trip over our own words somewhere down the line.

"Originally they wanted me to go into Anticrime with Henry. But I told them that the guys know I've always turned down Anticrime before and couldn't take it now. It wouldn't look right. So I stayed on patrol. I come back from vacation and I'm refreshed. I said, 'Fuck, if anything comes along, I'll tape it.' I was worried about entrapment. But nothing came along. I wasn't getting any incriminating conversations. I was going onto steady midnights in August and I knew the shit would fly then because I'd be back with Gallagher and O'Regan. The midnights were always wild. I put out feelers, telling the guys I would be going on steady midnights, and all of sudden there's an emergency. I get a phone call at home. They want to see me at Creedmoor. Right away.

"So I walk in and there's the captain, along with Marty Hershey, the top lawyer from Hynes's office. I sat down and they gave me donuts and coffee. All of a sudden, Marty

Hershey yells, 'All right. Let's stop the bullshit.' The calm in the room was gone. Hershey yells, 'Tony, we're fed up with your act.' Now I'm shitting. I don't know what they're talking about. I thought I was doing exactly what they wanted me to do. And then Hershey starts ripping into me, 'You're full of shit. You ain't doing nothing.' I said, 'What do you mean I ain't doing nothing? Look at all the things me and Henry did.' They said, 'Never mind what you and Henry did. We can use Henry's testimony without you.' I was really scared, 'What do you mean? It was me and him working together.' Hershey says, 'Yeah, but Henry held the recorder.'

"Then they got really serious. 'You're out. I've got a sealed indictment on you and I'm going to open it up this week.' I started to plead with him. I'm shaking. I'm scared. Hershey said, 'We're going to lock you up. We're going to prosecute you to the full letter of the law.' I didn't know what to say, nobody there backed me up. I don't know if they did it to light a spark plug in my ass or what, but he made a mistake because Hershey turned me the wrong fucking way.

"They gave me a week to straighten out. I was pissed. I went home and started to punch the walls. And I was sick. I went to the bathroom three and four times a night. As soon as I walked in the precinct now I had to head for the toilet. I couldn't take the pressure. I got stuff on the tapes. I was giving them their property. And all I could think of was what that fucking Marty Hershey had said. 'We're going to lock you up.' I didn't know where to turn. I didn't know who to talk to anymore. I used to meet the IAD guys after a tour crying like a fucking baby at times. I used to punch the back seats of the cars and curse them. I drove them crazy. 'You fucking motherfuckers,' I cursed. 'Lock me up right now. Nobody gives a fuck about me. Take me to Central Booking right now. Fuck you, fuck them, fuck everybody.'

I even talked to the bosses like that. I didn't care who I was talking to. And then one day they sent Lieutenant Andy Panico out to see me. I told him, 'Listen, don't give me no fucking bullshit, Andy. I'll take you outside this car and I'll beat your fucking brains in right here in the fucking street.' I went crazy. He says, 'Don't talk like that. Look, you gotta still think of your wife.' 'Don't give me that bullshit about my wife. I don't want to hear that anymore. That Jew mother-fucker was going to lock me up.' I got racial and everything. I said whatever I could think of. This went on for about two weeks. I was going loony. I just couldn't get it out of my head. Nobody came on my side when Hershey came after me. Nobody."

Henry continued to shine in his undercover role throughout July and August. There were still rumors about him, but Robert Rathbun, the portly cop working with him, felt reasonably certain that his new partner wasn't wired. He sat in a park one day eating hot dogs with Henry, bragging about his greatest rip-off.

"We stole sixty-seven pounds of marijuana once. The whole car stunk of pot. We had to unload it fast. We sold it for forty-five hundred dollars."

"You got beat," Henry said.

Having been dumped in the 77th after screwing up on a narcotics detail, Rathbun began robbing drug locations with Henry. On July 11, he and Henry went on patrol in an unmarked car. Rathbun explained he was taking his kids on a camping trip in the morning and wanted to get some "sneaker money."

"How are those Reeboks you got on?" he asked.

A few minutes later, Rathbun and Winter pulled up to an apartment building at 1260 Pacific Street. The officers had no intention of hitting the place until the building's landlord told them, "There's guys dealing marijuana upstairs. Why don't you throw them out?" The cops proceeded directly upstairs to a second-floor apartment and Henry knocked on the door.

"Yeah, who is it?"

"It's me," Henry said, disguising his voice to sound like a Jamaican. "Open up."

A man opened the door and the cops, wearing plain clothes, rushed into the room, their guns drawn. Henry and Rathbun had just located a marijuana stash when they heard a knock at the door. Henry looked out the peephole and saw that a line of customers had formed in the hallway.

"Give me a nice tray," said a man pushing five dollars through the door's gutted out peephole. Henry sold two or three bags of pot before Rathbun relieved him. Pulling up a chair, the chubby cop collected money and dispensed parcels of marijuana through the door until he ran out of customers.

"Hey, I ain't got no money," said a young female customer. "How about doing the right thing?"

"Not today, honey," Rathbun replied. "Try back tomorrow."

While searching the apartment for more drugs, Rathbun discovered an old arrest warrant hidden in some trash. He held it up and said, "Hey, there's a warrant out for you guys. If we lock you up now, you're going to jail and you ain't coming out." He opened a window and walked out of the room. The dealers scrambled out the window to freedom.

Rathbun had sold about thirty bags of marijuana and he decided that he had enough money to go away on vacation. Henry drove his partner to the Kings Plaza shopping mall. Moments later he emerged from a shoe store wearing a brand new pair of black Reeboks.

"A nice fucking shoe," he commented.

Later that night Henry turned over his tapes and the remaining bags of stolen marijuana to investigators. He also explained how the cops had opened up the apartment for business, selling drugs to customers through a peephole. The investigators laughed. "You're kidding."

"No, we really did it. We opened the place up for business."

Soon all the men were standing on the corner laughing.

A few days later, Gallagher and O'Regan tried to reopen the apartment for business, but they were wearing uniforms and parked in front of the building, scaring off potential customers. They left after making only a few dollars.

On July 30, Henry's recorder picked up another illegal raid. Henry joined O'Regan, Rathbun, and a young police officer named James Day on a break-in at the Soul Food Restaurant. O'Regan uncovered a .25-caliber automatic in the trash, turning it over to Henry to sell. The cops also discovered a bag of drugs in a velvet Crown Royal bag. The cops left the restaurant and drove back to the park to count their score.

"Okay, who's got the bag?" Henry asked.

"Not me," O'Regan answered.

"Not me," said Rathbun, "I never touched the bag."

"I thought you had them," Day added.

Finally, the cops realized that the drugs had been left back at the restaurant.

"What are we?" Henry said, his recorder rolling. "A bunch of Keystone Cops?"

Tony Magno had become the model undercover cop. He showed up night after night, turning in miles of tape with dozens of incriminating conversations and thousands of dollars in stolen money, drugs, and guns. Gallagher and O'Regan had handed over packets of stolen heroin on August 10 and were hitting a new drug location every night they worked together. They regularly bragged about their scores to Tony.

"I found a new place on Bedford Avenue I wanted to do," O'Regan told him. "I said to Junior, 'I wanna do this place, but we're gonna need the hammer.' So I went back to the precinct and got the sledgehammer. I dropped Junior off in the back yard. I broke the fence down for him and he walked right through. I went back to the car and waited for him to get in position. So Junior goes over the air, 'Radio Check, Central,' giving me the signal he's ready. So I pull in front of the place, go upstairs with the fucking hammer and start rapping on the door. I hit it twice and it popped open."

"Surprise, surprise," Gallagher said.

"Boom. Boom. Hello," from O'Regan.

"Shocked the shit out of him," Gallagher continued.

"The guy and his girl both jumped out the window," O'Regan added.

"So what do you have for me?" Tony asked, holding a package of drugs in his hands.

"Roughly, the whole package is worth about two grand," Gallagher said.

"Two grand?"

"Yeah, it comes to about seven hundred in crack and about twelve, thirteen hundred in that other stuff."

"Smoke?"

"Yeah."

"Okay," Tony said. "Let me see what my guy will give us for it."

"We trust you," Gallagher replied.

On August 23, Tony paid Gallagher $1800 for the drugs, and he handed back $600 as a commission for handling the package.

"Why six hundred?"

"We were going to give you five hundred," Gallagher explained. "But I told Brian, 'If we give him five that leaves us thirteen.' He gets real superstitious on me. He says, 'Oh no. You know I don't want thirteen.' "

The Panasonic recorder picked up both cops laughing.

On August 25, Tony Magno got in more trouble. Investigators listening to the recording he had made the previous night were shocked to hear him insulting them at the end of the tape.

"It's five twenty-two and I don't know what else to fucking do. You read me, motherfuckers? I don't know what else you want me to do. I'm getting fucked up and you won't leave me alone."

A few moments later Magno returned to his tape recorder, continuing with his brazen outburst.

"Time is now five thirty, August twenty-fourth. End of past conversation. First part of conversation was Police Officer William Murphy who gave me information about Officer Monroe. Second part was with Officer Al Cortez who I dropped off at some broad's house on Schenectady Avenue. Now going to shut the fucking tape off. If my meet is there, I'll be there. If not, fuck you."

Tony continued to cruise along a block on Ocean Parkway looking for his drop. He returned to his tape recorder a few minutes later.

"Time is now five fifty. I've just made five passes at Avenue C and Ocean Parkway in the service road and I can not find my meet. I'm going to call my wife. And if there is a problem at home, I'm going the fuck home whether you like it or fucking not. If I have to bust my balls to get information, somebody should be here to fucking meet me. This is fucking bullshit."

A few minutes later Tony spotted Detective Patricia Perkins of the Internal Affairs Division in an unmarked car near his drop point. He handed over the tape and drove home, waiting for the explosion he knew was sure to follow.

"One day I was supposed to meet this detective out on Ocean Parkway and Avenue C. She went to Coney Island Avenue instead. I had been drinking some beers back at the station house, so I'm driving around in circles, looking for her, getting madder and madder. Then I started talking into the tape recorder. I put a lot of stuff on it. Finally I met her and gave her the tape. I was ranting and raving. They apologized and I left.

"Then they heard the tape. They called another emergency meeting at Creedmoor. This time they called Henry in too, even though he was on vacation. He met me on the street and said, 'What the fuck did you say? They want to call off the investigation.' I got scared for Henry. I didn't want him to go to jail because of what I was doing. They led me into the room and Captain Joseph DeMartini was there. I knew right away what he wanted. He said, 'I want you to hear something.' I didn't want him to play the tape in front of everybody, so I said, 'Look Captain, can I talk to you outside?' 'Sit down and listen.' They played the tape. Hershey was there too. I had said something about him on the tape too. He looked at me and says, 'Tony, I didn't know you were like that.' And DeMartini, in the middle of the tape says, 'Who's talking now? Who's the real Tony Magno? Is it the person talking to us here now or is it the person on the fucking tape? You got to remember something. My people are supervisors. They don't need your aggravation. They're not thrilled doing this stuff.' I says, 'Look Captain, it won't happen again, I apologize.' He was pissed. They all hated my attitude. But I didn't want to fuck Henry up, and I was worried. I said, 'Look, it will never happen again.' It never did happen again either. When I tell somebody something, I usually keep my word.

"I still couldn't believe what I was doing though. Sometimes in the locker room we talked about cops who wore wires. I always said, 'I'd kill any motherfucker that ever wore a wire on me.' I was never one for talking about Serpico or reading *Prince of the City*. I didn't even watch the movies. It just wasn't me. I couldn't believe I had become like that. Call me a hypocrite or whatever, but sometimes even after I dropped off those tapes I would go back and meet the guys at a bar. Here I had just sank them and now I'm drinking with them in Gallagher's bar. Then I felt like a cop. The only time I didn't feel like a cop was when I put that recorder on. I wasn't a cop at that point. I was shit. I was a cop for them. But once I switched that recorder off, I was back to myself again. It was Jekyll and Hyde. I'd be fucking around, goofing off with the guys. But if Gallagher and O'Regan came over in the middle of a conversation, I'd look around to make sure nobody was looking and click, click, start rolling tape on them. Then I'd turn the tape in and drive back to meet Gallagher at his father's bar for free beers. I'd be throwing darts and drinking beer with the same guys I was helping to get indicted. It didn't faze me one way or the other. I never even thought about it then. I felt great. I was a cop."

Henry rarely had any problems with the investigators. Some of them even brought him hot coffee and buttered rolls while they debriefed him on the previous day's escapades.

"I only had one problem with an IAD guy. And it was more embarrassing than anything else. A lot of the guys who are in Internal Affairs are God-Squad types—born-again Christians. I guess if you talk to God a lot, you really don't feel that bad about having a job where all you do is screw other cops for a living. So one night they send this guy out to see me—Thomas Bellino. We were going through the stuff and all of a sudden he asks me, 'Henry, do you ever think about God?' And I said, 'Sure, we all do.' The guy's eyes light up. He hands me a Bible and some literature that says I'm a sinner. Then he asks, 'Do you want to pray with me?' I couldn't believe it. The guy got down on his knees and started praying on the sidewalk in the middle of the night. I looked around, you know, because I thought someone was going to think we were some kind of nuts. This is the middle of Brooklyn we're talking about here. Finally I said, 'Ah, Tom, could you get up off your knees please? I don't really think I want to do that right now.' I called the 'hello' number later and said, 'Do me a favor, guys. Don't send me Bellino anymore.'

By September, Tony had gained incriminating evidence against a group of younger cops, and Henry had made new friends in the anticrime detail. The special prosecutor had enough evidence to seek criminal indictments against at least fifteen cops in the 77th Precinct. Another twenty-five would have to face departmental trials as a result of what they told Henry and Tony.

At this point, the investigators decided to expand their operation. They planned to use Henry's relationship with Roy to set up a sting against the cops assigned to guard airports. They even mapped out an operation that involved sending Henry to Jamaica with Roy on a drug-running sting. The drugs would be brought back into the country through Kennedy Airport with Henry paying off cops along the way. There was talk of involving federal agents as well.

"If you went down there, you'd have to go without a

gun," the investigators told Henry. "Do you trust Roy that much?"

"Sure, and Roy trusts me that much. He's been trying to get me down to the islands for years."

The investigators put the idea on hold, refocusing their attention on Crystal Spivey, twenty-nine, a black female cop in the precinct who had lost her gun on two occasions. They had information that Spivey, the daughter of a highly respected sergeant, was dating a known drug dealer and they were certain she was using cocaine herself. Hynes was intent on cracking the precinct's race barrier and getting black cops to incriminate themselves in his investigation. Spivey could become the bridge between Henry and the precinct's black cops, everyone agreed. She seemed to color all cops in the same light—blue.

"Crystal approached me in July. She was going out with a guy named Understanding, who lived on St. Johns and worked as one of Roy's coke dealers. She told me that's where she got her drugs. She said Understanding wanted her to protect his operation. I couldn't understand why she came to me, a white guy. There were plenty of black guys in the precinct who were into this shit. But apparently Understanding had talked to Roy and he said, 'Talk to Blondie.' So Crystal came to me and asked, 'How should I do it? What should I ask for? Do I ask for five hundred dollars a week?' I laughed, 'Benny was giving us fifty dollars a week and you want five-hundred.'

"I went over to her house to talk to her about it, and I was wired. She told me Understanding was her man and he was giving her an eighth of a gram of coke each week. We went through the whole thing. That's how I got started with Crystal. I told her what to ask for and what she would have to do. But I knew the guy was bullshitting her. He worked for Roy. He couldn't come up with that kind of money."

"All Crystal talked about was making money. First she wanted to get off the job and go into the record business with her boyfriend. Then she wanted to buy a card shop. Then she wanted to buy a condo. Finally the SPO [special prosecutor's office] decided to set up a sting. They said, 'She wants money. Let's see if she'll transport drugs.' I told her, 'Listen, I have a drug operation. A guy I used to work with back in the Twenty-fifth Precinct, I still deal with him. We run drugs from one location to another. You don't have to get out of the car. All you have to do is rent your gun and shield for the day. I would do it myself, but it looks strange with a black and a white guy in the car. I generally like to use black women to do it.' And she said, 'All right. I'll let you know.' A couple of days go by, and then she came back and went for the bait.

"We set it up for the morning of September fourth, my day off. I called Crystal at home and woke her up. I was wired with two recorders. They also wired my truck and fixed the radio so it couldn't be turned up. They gave me one of the big recorders this time—they call them Nagras. They're reel-to-reel jobs, a two-and-a-half-pound unit. And once you turn them on, you can't shut them off. The night before I went out and bought a loose-fitting sweatshirt. I drove out to the Canarsie Pier, they put me in a van and wired me up, taping the unit to my back. I used my small recorder as a backup unit. Then I went to pick Crystal up.

"We drove to the Brooklyn Navy Yard, where we picked up my man "Moe"—an undercover cop named Eugene Poulson. He was also wired. Crystal thought he was a drug dealer. We were followed by guys in nondescript IAD cars just in case anything happened. Crystal tells the guy, 'Nice to meet you.' Moe asks, 'Did Blondie tell you what's going on?' 'Yeah.' But Moe takes her through the whole thing anyway just to get it on tape again. 'We're going to pick some coke up. Then we're going to drive it to the Canarsie Pier and meet a guy. We give him the coke and our deal ends. You'll be paid five hundred dollars then.' Crystal gets in Moe's car and drives over to Park Slope to meet the guy with the drugs—another black undercover cop posing as a dealer. Moe and Crystal took the coke—five ounces—to the Canarsie Pier where they met another black undercover cop. We had two vans parked on the pier and videotaped the whole transaction. Moe takes Crystal back to the car and she says, 'That wasn't bad. We just got rid of the coke. Would you like to do it again?' 'Yes, yes, yes, yes!' Then Moe gives her the money. The camera picked it up beautiful. Crystal says, 'Thank you,' and gets out of the car. Then she comes over to my car and Moe takes off. She gets in and I said, 'Well, how do you like him?' She says, 'Oh, he's all right.' So I just drove her home. I went back to the pier and they took the wires off me. It was easy. They had her dead to rights on an A-two felony. Major weight. Major time. We opened a new door with Crystal. You could almost hear the whole precinct crashing down as we replayed those tapes."

11

*"If I was a rat, do you think this
precinct would still be here?"*

A few days after Crystal Spivey agreed to rent out her gun
and shield for five hundred dollars, riding shotgun on a ship-
ment of cocaine through Brooklyn, Henry Winter arrived
for work in the 77th Precinct and found the word "Rat"
scrawled across the face of his locker in black Magic Marker.
He ignored the crude memorandum. A day later someone
added a new entry: "You're gonna die."

A new wave of rumors washed over the station house.
By the second week of September, the precinct was flooded
with innuendo and finger pointing. It seemed that everybody
believed Henry was wearing a wire and cooperating in some
sort of corruption probe. Cops working with him in the
Anticrime detail suddenly stopped talking to him. They

walked out of the locker room as soon as he entered. No one wanted to ride with him in a car anymore. Steadily, his work in the investigation began to suffer. Where he once had turned over tapes glutted with tales of police corruption, he now turned in bland conversations.

Although no one could prove he was a rat, everyone knew something was up. Cops began to close ranks, whispering among themselves, avoiding each other. A mood of paranoia and edgy suspicion reigned in the 77th Precinct locker room.

"I don't believe it," Brian O'Regan told another cop, who told him Henry was probably wearing a wire. "Not Hank."

A few days earlier, another cop pulled William Gallagher aside and gave him a friendly word of advice, "Cops on the midnight tour are going to jail." Gallagher acted insulted. "Anybody who steals out there is crazy," he said.

For months investigators had tried unsuccessfully to plug leaks. But Officer Tracy's cousin insisted that there was a blonde cop cooperating with prosecutors in a search for crooked cops. Special Prosecutor Charles Hynes compounded his problems with a mistake in judgement. He asked a former New York City detective working as a city marshal to help him out in a corruption probe of Brooklyn's 77th Precinct. The city marshal turned down the job offer, then warned a friend in the precinct, David Williams, that Hynes was planning to lock up dozens of cops. Williams passed the information on to Tony Magno, who recorded the embarrassing conversation.

Even the Police Commissioner himself, Benjamin Ward, a man with a propensity for making public blunders, helped leak news of an investigation. Ward was an unpopular administrator who was nicknamed "Bubba" by the department's rank and file cops. When he was a deputy commissioner in 1972, he apologized to a group of Muslims after a cop was

shot to death in a Harlem mosque. In 1984, Ward's first
year as police commissioner, he faced charges of indulging
in a tryst at Rikers Island prison with a woman who wasn't
his wife. Ward was also accused of getting drunk at a police
union convention and urinating from his helicopter, a craft
without a toilet, on the way home. Ward admitted the extra-
marital affair and apologized for his public drunkenness at
a press conference. The new police commissioner had also
disappeared during the so-called Palm Sunday Massacre, re-
portedly drinking his way through the weekend as the city's
best detectives tried to solve the mystery of ten murdered
bodies found in a Brooklyn apartment, the city's worst single-
day slaughter. Somehow, the city's first black police commissioner managed to keep his job.

"The guy is always talking about accountability," Brian
O'Regan later said. "When is the police commissioner going
to hold himself accountable for his own actions?"

On July 23, Ward tipped union officials to the investigation
when he at first refused to sit on the dais at a press conference
with Frank Piro, a police officer assigned to the 77th Precinct
who had survived a shooting. Realizing that Piro was a target
of Hynes's investigation, he told union officials, "Get him
out of here. I don't want to be seen with him."

The startled union officials began asking Piro questions.
"Are you in some kind of trouble out there in your precinct?"
"Not that I know of," Piro replied. After he threatened to
leave the building, Ward was advised by a deputy commissioner that his actions were being monitored closely and
that to leave now would be a grave mistake, tantamount
to screaming on a bullhorn, "We're going after cops in the
Seven-Seven." Ward finally sat down with Piro, one of the
two cops who were shot in their patrol car by a handcuffed
prisoner on May 27, the second day of the investigation.

"We all started asking ourselves questions," said Jimmy Higgins, a police union delegate who attended the press conference. "Why doesn't the police commissioner want his picture taken with a hero cop? It didn't take much to put one and one together and come up with an investigation."

And so it was that rumors and leaks forced a premature end to the most widespread police corruption probe in years. The end, when it came, arrived swiftly.

On Monday September 15, a black police officer named Michael Titus walked through a set of metal doors leading into the 77th Precinct and continued directly down into the locker room. The younger brother of a detective assigned to the precinct's homicide squad, Titus had left the 77th Precinct earlier in the year to take an undercover assignment with a Queens narcotics detail.

Titus was scared. He knew he had good information. Devastating information. He knew the names of more than a dozen cops targeted in the probe and that Henry Winter was wearing a wire. Titus also knew the name of the agency conducting the investigation and that Winter had turned after being confronted with videotaped evidence of bribe-taking.

Fearing that someone in the precinct might implicate him in a conversation with either Henry or Tony, Titus returned to the Seven-Seven to warn other cops of the investigation and to find out if he was involved in the inquiry. He immediately sought out Crystal Spivey, telling her all he knew about the investigation.

"Not Hank," Crystal said.

Details of their conversation spread through the station house over night, burning from one locker to the next like a gasoline fire. Luckily, Henry had the day off. On Tuesday night, Tony arrived at the precinct to begin a midnight tour.

He had just put his tape recorder in his pocket when Bill Hock approached him.

"Hey," Hock began, his voice unsteady. "Titus was in here talking to Spivey the other day, and he heard there's going to be a couple of guys arrested. He said some guys were wearing wires."

Tony acted interested.

"Yeah, who?"

"Your partner."

Tony slammed his locker shut and turned to face the younger man.

"Anybody else?"

Hock stammered, his eyes focused on the floor. "I don't want to say," he mumbled.

"Anybody else?"

"Yeah," Hock said. "You."

Tony let out a deep breath. "It ain't me," he said angrily, walking away. "I got nothing to do with nothing."

Tony left the locker room and headed out in his car to Sector Ida-John. He sensed that the investigation was nearing an unnatural conclusion. A lot of cops had always been suspicious of Henry, but no one had ever before dared to accuse him, one of the precinct's most popular cops, of being a rat. Tony got in touch with Henry.

"Crystal knows what's going on. I think they all know. She's gonna want to talk to you when you get in here. Just play it smart when you talk to her."

Shortly before six o'clock on Wednesday, September 17, Henry drove his blue Ford truck into the precinct parking lot. He found Crystal's car and parked in front of it. If she wanted to go home when she got off duty at midnight, she'd have to ask him to move his truck. Henry went out to work for five hours and returned to his truck shortly before midnight, lying in wait, an Olympus microrecorder strapped to his crotch. He turned on the machine, which was loaded with new tape and fresh batteries, when he saw Crystal approach his truck at 11:54 P.M.

"The thing we're supposed to do with Moe tomorrow is off," he began, referring to a second bogus drug run he had set up with Spivey.

"You're getting chicken, man," Crystal said as she climbed into the truck's cab.

"No, I'm not."

"What are you talking about? I didn't change the plan when I heard this shit about you."

"Moe is not available."

"What's going on?" Crystal demanded.

"You tell me."

"The word is that the precinct is fucking going up in smoke. I heard that you, your ex-partner, and several other people are going down. A lot of people. A lot of names."

"I'm always under investigation. IAD is always looking at me."

"I hear it's coming from higher up than that, babe. We're talking about the district attorney's office and probably the special prosecutor. They got you on film for something. Film. They have you on video doing something. Did you know anything about that, Hank?"

"They got me on video?"

"Doing some shit in the precinct. Yeah, babe. Yeah. Taking money on a video? How could that be a rumor? What I'm telling you is on the grapevine. How? I don't know. But it's beyond IAD. That's what the word is. And also that you're a rat. And stay away."

"Oh really?" Henry said, his voice dripping with sarcasm. "That again, huh?"

"Yep. And that you, you know, are looking to give mother-fuckers up."

"You don't have to worry about that."

"I thought, well, let me talk to Hank. I wouldn't just dismiss this."

Crystal reached across the seat and ran her hand over Henry's chest, searching him for a wire. She patted his back with the palm of her hand and ran her fingers along the side of his pants. She did not check Henry's crotch.

"You want me to strip down?" he said, laughing. "I am no rat. You don't have to worry about that."

"Well, this is what the word is."

Henry was anxious. He wanted Crystal out of the truck. He wanted to get out of the precinct immediately.

"All right," he said. "Let me check this out. Who did you hear this from? Titus?"

"Yeah. He seems to think the only reason they haven't moved on you and Magno is because they're going after a lot of guys. A lot of the midnight motherfuckers. And that's a lot of people. And I have ridden with all of them."

"Is Titus getting it from a reliable source?"

"Yeah. He came here to tell the boys this is coming and to keep his name out of it."

"He said they had me on film?"

"That was the most clear thing. That and that you are a rat. A bona fide rat. I said, 'That doesn't seem like Hank, but . . .' "

The investigation was over. Henry could sense it. This would be his last tape recording in the 77th Precinct.

"You don't have to worry about Hank," Henry said. "I mean anybody that wants to toss me for a wire, can toss me. They can do anything they want. I don't wear a wire."

"Maybe they turned somebody on the street to get you. That's the fucking thing I wanted to talk to you about. Could some street dog have set you up, Hank? Cause that's the word. They got you and Tony on videotape. They caught you red-handed. And because of that, now you're turning around. Now is that true?"

"No. That's not true."

"Well check it out, Hank. The word is that you're a rat. I wouldn't expect that of you, Hank. I wouldn't expect you to dog me like that."

"No," Henry insisted, hesitating to catch his breath. "I mean if I was a rat, do you think this precinct would still be here?"

Henry paused again, pretending to be hurt.

"Why Blondie? Why me?"

"I heard this in June and I still talked to you about other shit. I had a certain level of trust. I hope that my trust isn't betrayed."

"It's there, don't worry about it."

"I wouldn't give anybody up," Crystal said, her voice bubbling with indignation. "I wouldn't do it. I go to hell with what the fuck I know about people. I don't play that shit at all. And Titus told me, 'The word is, Crystal, that you're really cool. That you wouldn't give anybody up.' Titus doesn't want to get jammed up. He said, 'That's why I'm here now. This is fucking real and it's going to be happening soon.'"

The two cops sat silent for a moment. Crystal had Henry dead to rights, he knew that. He wondered how far she would push him on the issue. But suddenly Spivey changed the subject.

"Well, this investigation is just for precinct stuff," Crystal said, shocking Henry with her boldness. "Moe isn't from the precinct, right? So as far as our business outside the precinct, we can probably continue. I mean, whatever shit you have to do, I hope this doesn't have nothing to do with our thing. I'm hoping you aren't setting me up for no bullshit."

"No," Henry assured her. "This has nothing to do with Moe. What I do with Moe has nothing to do with the precinct. We don't even come into this precinct. That's all off-duty stuff."

Crystal yawned.

"You have to be an adult," she advised Henry. "I can separate what's going on here between the precinct and what we're doing off duty. If you feel the water is too fucking hot, then we'll chill. We can still do our thing. I have no fear about that. But you can handle your program a little slicker than that, Hank."

"All right," Henry decided. "Let me let you go." I thank you very much for the information."

"So call me in the morning, please. Let's set something up with Moe."

"You got it."

"I need some fucking money, Hank. I've got some goals, babe."

"What are your goals, Crystal?"

"I want to buy a co-op," said the police sergeant's daughter. "I need five grand in a few months, that's what's happening."

"Why don't you talk to Moe?"

"The motherfucker didn't talk to me yet. The vibes I got from him was that he was real cool. Is the guy that ridiculous or what? He can't be this fucking devious. God wouldn't let me be involved with this motherfucker if he was that fucking devious."

"Moe is good people," Henry concluded, starting up the truck.

"Where you going?"

"Oh, Jesus," Henry said, his hands shaking on the steering wheel. "I forgot I was still working. I was going home."

The last noise investigators would hear from Henry Winter's Olympus tape recorder would be the sound of two cops laughing.

Henry went into the precinct and called the 'hello' number, his index finger fumbling over the buttons as he dialed. Detective James O'Brien answered the phone call in Internal Affairs headquarters.

"Crystal knows everything," Henry said, the words gushing out. "She knows I'm on film. She knows we were caught. She knows I'm wired."

"Calm down. Calm down. Relax. It will be all right. Is she still working?"

"No, she went home," Henry said.

"All right. That's good she went home. How are you?"

"I'm all right. But she knows everything. I mean what the fuck is going on here? Somebody leaked it. Somebody leaked it out."

The detective told Henry to finish out his tour, and that he would meet him later in the morning to retrieve the tape. Henry got off the phone and stared at the clock. When he looked up a moment or two later, he saw Roy Thomas standing in the middle of the station house.

"Roy is not the type of guy who comes walking into a police precinct unless he's in handcuffs. Cops go to Roy— Roy doesn't go to cops. He came right over and said that he heard something on the street, that the next two cops to hit Twelve twenty-six Lincoln Place were going to be killed. The address was a known drug location. They sold drugs out of the basement of the building. All of us had hit the place a lot. Gallagher and O'Regan had just hit it. I knew this was a legit threat. For Roy to risk everything and let people see him come into the precinct, people in the street, other drug dealers—well, I knew this was serious. The Jamaicans on the street decided that we'd gone too far. We're going to have some dead cops out there.

"So I went upstairs to the detectives. I told them Roy was downstairs and that he had information that some cops were going to be hit. They just looked at me and they couldn't believe that Roy came in. All I told them was that Roy was downstairs and that he had information. I went over and said, 'Roy, talk to these guys. Tell them everything you got.' He didn't tell them shit. He started in with his act, 'I got a bullet in my head, I don't remember too good.'

"I went back upstairs and hung out until the end of my tour—two in the morning. My head was spinning. I got Crystal telling me she knows everything, but still wants to run coke. I got Roy telling me two cops are going to be killed. Is it me and Tony that are going to be killed? Crystal knows. Titus knows. All the black guys know. Roy's black. What's going on? Am I dead today or what?"

Henry met Detective O'Brien later that night across the street from Prospect Park, in the Park Slope section of Brooklyn.

"They know the whole story," Henry began. "It's over."

"How do you know?"

"Here," he said, pushing his tape recorder toward the detective. "Listen to the tape."

Henry and the detective sat huddled over the recorder, dissecting Spivey's words. The investigators had never played any of Henry's tapes in front of him before.

"Holy shit," O'Brien decided. "We'll let you know what's going on tomorrow."

Henry slept fitfully. He heard tape recorded conversations in his sleep again. In the morning, he drove back to the station to start an early tour. At about ten o'clock his belt beeper sounded and he called the 'hello' number. An investigator told Henry to call Crystal Spivey and tell her they were going on another drug run. Immediately.

"We're going to take her," the investigators said. "Drive to the corner of Utica and Winthrop. There's a diner there. Get out of the car and we'll take her."

Henry woke Spivey out of bed and told her that he had set up another run with Moe. Then he picked her up at her home in Crown Heights and they continued on to the diner.

"You want something to eat?" Henry asked.

"Yeah, get me a hamburger."

Henry went into the diner and watched as a gang of undercover cops descended on his truck and Spivey. After they drove her away, he returned to his car and drove back to Internal Affairs headquarters on Poplar Street in Brooklyn Heights. He never again set foot in the 77th Precinct.

"Anybody want a hamburger?" Henry asked.

Crystal Spivey was rushed back to the special prosecutor's office and confronted with the videotape of her taking five hundred dollars from an undercover cop named Moe. Shaken by what she saw, Crystal initially agreed to cooperate in the investigation. She left the office with a microrecorder of her own.

Later in the day, an Internal Affairs investigator returned Henry's portable police radio to the 77th Precinct. Using bolt cutters to crack open his locker, he emptied Henry's belongings into a paper bag, leaving behind only a single brass collar pin with the number 77. On the way out, the investigator stopped by the front desk to make a notation in the precinct log book next to the names Henry Winter and Tony Magno.

"Transferred to IAD," the cop wrote.

Even as one investigator was returning Winter's portable radio to the station house—rather like throwing a lighted stick of dynamite into a crowded room—another investigator called Tony at home, telling him to report for work at IAD headquarters on Friday. Tony, ever the cop's cop, didn't want to believe he could never return to the station house he loved so much.

"I don't wanna come to IAD," he said, sobbing into the phone. "I don't wanna work there. I wanna stay on patrol with the guys. Just take the recorder away."

"No, that's it. Come on in."

Tony hung up. For the first time in the investigation, he felt like an informer.

"I was trying to keep reality away," he remembered about the phone call. "I knew it was going to come someday, but I always figured I would have another month, another year with the guys. And then the guys were gone."

Brian O'Regan drove to Winter's white frame home in Valley Stream on Saturday, September 20. He didn't see Henry's car in the driveway so he continued on to a flea market, studying a set of eyelet-edged sheets for extra holes. He called his girlfriend Cathy and asked if ten dollars was a fair price for the sheets. She told Brian it was a good deal. He hurried back to the sale but the sheets had already been sold.

"I never had any kind of luck in life," he said later.

O'Regan swung by Henry's house again and spotted Betsy Winter, a woman he recognized from photographs hanging in Henry's locker, entering the house.

"She looked like she had been through a war," he remembered. "I said, 'I'm Brian.' She said, 'He's not here and I gotta go.'" As Brian started to leave, Henry pulled up in the truck with his father-in-law. Both men were getting ready to go to a wedding reception. "I said 'Hank, how are you doing?' He said, 'Hey, buddy boy.' He has a big smile on his face and he says, 'I'll see you later.' He said he'd call me but I knew he didn't have the number."

Later that night, Brian drove to Gallagher's house near Marine Park. He walked into the house and found Gallagher sitting in his living room, sobbing. He had never seen his partner cry before.

"He was always concrete," Brian recalled. "Now he looked almost broken."

"I told my wife everything," Gallagher said.

"Everything?"

"Yeah. We could be in big trouble."

On Monday morning, Crystal Spivey walked into the Office of the Special State Prosecutor with a lawyer, who explained that his client would cooperate in retracing the leaks in exchange for probation. Hynes insisted that Spivey serve some jail time. The cop and her lawyer left, Spivey still carrying her tape recorder.

The following day, Hynes and John Guido went to lunch, taking an investigation folder along with them. The men agreed that they could not risk the chance that Spivey would tell all the other officers about the investigation. They returned to the office and sat around the oblong desk in the big room where Henry and Tony had first identified their fellow cops as thieves, robbers, and drug users. The investigators had nicknamed the office on the twenty-third floor the "War Room." There were dozens of photographs tacked to a bulletin board—mug shots of cops. Henry was there on that Tuesday morning. He watched while Guido pulled thirteen names from his investigation folder.

After thirty years, Guido was retiring from his position as Chief of Inspectional Services on October 15. This was the last major case for a cop who liked to say he came to Internal Affairs in 1972, A.S.: After Serpico.

"Take them," Chief Guido said. "Take them."

Henry was asked to leave the room. Moments later, cops and lawyers buzzed around Hynes's office, running to phones and making copies of documents.

"It's going down now," Captain Joseph DeMartini told Henry.

"What's going down?" he said, his hands shaking as he chain-smoked another cigarette. "Talk to me."

"Come on. Let's go back to IAD."

As the cops headed out of Manhattan, they heard the first news flash on the radio. Thirteen cops from the 77th Precinct were suspended for conduct unbecoming an officer. Hynes hadn't even had time to present the cases to a grand jury. The names of the suspended cops followed the initial headline. DeMartini and Winter stared at each other in disbelief.

"How the fuck did the names get released so fast?" Henry wondered.

Captain DeMartini asked the car's driver to pull the car over to a pay phone at the foot of the Brooklyn Bridge.

"Call your wife and tell her to get out of the house," he said.

"What?" Henry's voice shook.

"Just to be safe."

The cops surrounded Henry while he stood at the corner pay phone. He called his wife and told her to wait for him at her mother's house. But Betsy Winter did not leave her home. She greeted Henry with a snarl when he came in an hour later.

"I'm not running," she said. "Nobody is making me run from my own home. We're not going to get hurt because they'll get hurt first."

Shortly before sundown Henry took his two little girls, Meghan, six, and Elizabeth, ten, for a walk around the block. He explained to them that he would probably be in the newspapers soon.

"I was bad as a police officer and now I'm trying to make things better for us as a family," he explained. "I was taking money and drugs and selling it back to the department to catch other police officers. I ratted on them."

Meghan's eyes grew wide with bewilderment. Her daddy had broken one of the family's cardinal rules.

"Daddy, you told me never to rat on my sister," she said. "You always say, 'Don't be a rat on your sister. She gets in enough trouble on her own.' But you are ratting."

Henry tried to explain why he had ratted. He only had to mention the word "jail" once before Elizabeth hugged him.

"Daddy," she said. "Are you still a cop?"

"Yeah. I'm still a cop."

"Well, you'll always be a good cop," she decided. "I love you very much."

Henry walked home crying. He felt destroyed as a cop, but he was very proud of his daughters. The entire Winter family slept in one bed that night, hugging their father's tears away.

* * *

The Police Department never made official notifications of the suspensions. Brian O'Regan was sitting in his apartment when a friend phoned and told him to turn on the television. He watched his name flash across the screen. Gallagher heard the news on the radio. Rathbun was standing with a prisoner in Central Booking when he called his wife and learned he had been suspended. Another cop was just being seated with his girlfriend in a restaurant when he saw his name roll up the television screen at the bar. Brian called his sergeant, Robert Jervas, to break the news.

"I had to tell him five times. He wouldn't believe it."

One by one, the suspended cops came in to the 77th Precinct that night, turning in their guns and shields. Brian entered through a side door, avoiding the glare of television lights. He was escorted down to his locker by a cop assigned to Internal Affairs, who rummaged through his belongings, taking his police identification, gas card, and daily memo book.

"I guess they were afraid we were going to blow our brains out," O'Regan said. "I asked the guy, 'What kind of job do you have?' And he says, 'It's just a detail.'"

As his locker was emptied, Brian paused to write the word "Suspended" next to the date, September 23, in his memo book. Then he walked out of the precinct, driving back to a Catholic church in Rockaway. Despite the time of night— it was well after 8 P.M. by now—Brian coaxed a priest into hearing his confession. He then cleansed his soul of all the sins he had committed while working as a uniformed officer in the 77th Precinct.

"I thought the priest was going to fall over and take a heart attack. But he didn't even bat an eye. He just said, 'I've heard worse. Get a good lawyer and be prepared for what might happen.'"

In the morning, Brian and several of the other suspended

officers drove to their union headquarters, where they discussed the suspensions with lawyers. Gallagher, the once-brazen union delegate who had taught both Henry and Brian how to steal, cried six times during the meeting. Brian was amazed by the change in him.

"I couldn't believe it. He was always cement. I was a follower. He was infallible."

On the street outside the union office, Brian found Robert Rathbun sitting in his car weeping. Brian tried to console him. "Maybe they ain't got us that bad. Shit, Bobby, at least you got family."

Rathbun pulled a snapshot from his wallet. Brian saw the face of a smiling boy looking back at him.

"See this?" Rathbun said. "How can I ever tell him about this?"

By the time he reached his girlfriend Cathy's apartment in Park Slope later that day, Brian still hadn't cried. But then he met Cathy at the door and saw the redness in her eyes. "Have you been crying, Cathy?" She nodded. He walked past her and continued upstairs into the bedroom. He closed the door and sat on the bed crying.

Later Brian returned to his own Rockaway apartment, meeting his landlord outside the building. "That was me on the news, you know," Brian said. The landlord nodded.

"If you want, I'll move."

"Absolutely not."

Over the next few weeks, as a special grand jury prepared a first round of indictments against thirteen police officers, Brian avoided his family. He missed a dinner date at his older brother Greg's Long Island home and only returned to his mother's Valley Stream home at night, the darkness covering his identity. He also started attending church regularly, taking communion.

"I know when I die I'm going to heaven," he later said.

After one of his visits to church, Brian felt in such a state of grace that he even dared to call Henry Winter at home, leaving a short message on his old friend's tape recorder.

"Hey Hank," Brian said, his voice dropping to a whisper. "This is Brian. I don't hold any animosity toward you at all. What is done, is done. If you want to talk, let's meet and talk. Believe me, that's all it is. We won't even talk about anything that's going on. We'll just talk."

Henry came home and played the message over and over again. Then he began to cry. He could not chance a meeting with any of the Buddy Boys.

A few days later, William Gallagher called Henry's home, leaving a message of his own on the recorder. Speaking in a voice that shimmied like a car with a bad transmission, Gallagher said, "Hank, this is Billy. Billy Gallagher. You know my number. Call me and let me know what's going on."

Henry only noticed one thing about the message when he played it back later. Junior Gallagher was scared. Henry erased the message, choosing to remember Gallagher as the precinct tough guy.

Henry and Tony spent most of October reviewing tapes, correcting transcripts, and testifying before a special grand jury. Hynes told Henry to go out and buy new clothes to wear to court, explaining that he couldn't testify against cops in dungarees and flannel shirts. So one night in early October Henry and Betsy went shopping, buying tapered shirts, silk ties, tailored pants, and fine sports jackets for a cop who had only one suit hanging in his closet—the one he had worn on the day he married Betsy Bassett. Henry tried to pretend that he was having fun, but she saw through his mask. They paid for the clothes and headed home.

The next day Henry was sitting on the witness stand when he reached into his pocket and found a note that read, 'Have a nice day, Love B.' He smiled. His wife had never written him a love note before. An hour later, after telling a particularly harrowing story, Henry saw a look of disgust on several faces in the grand jury box. He reached into his jacket pocket and found another note. This one read, 'Don't worry about it. I love you. B.'

Over the next few weeks, Henry found dozens of love notes hidden in his new clothes. It seemed to him that every time he began to doubt his own life, asking why he had agreed to testify against other cops, he found the answer hidden in his jacket pocket.

"I did this for my family," Henry later said. "I had no choice."

On November 4, Brian O'Regan called a friend to say he and twelve other cops had been told to surrender for arrest and arraignment on November 6. The first set of indictments had come down in what the newspapers were calling "The Shame of the 77th Precinct." O'Regan and the other cops were told to report to Internal Affairs headquarters at 7:30 in the morning along with their lawyers. They would be arrested, given the *Miranda* warning, pose for mug shots, and have their fingerprints taken. Brian said he planned to wear dark sunglasses, a hooded sweatshirt, and a baseball cap. For the first time in his life, he was scared to go to Central Booking.

"It's funny how you can be good your whole life, for so long, and then . . . ," he said later.

* * *

Henry arrived at Internal Affairs headquarters on the morning of November 6 shortly after dawn, walking into the brick building through a steady drizzle. He sat at a desk near Tony, sipping coffee and eating a doughnut. He chatted nervously. Tony sat in silence. Words were no help to Tony. This had been an investigation of words. He was sick of listening to them on tape and reading them in transcripts. On this day—especially this day—Tony wanted to hide behind a wall of silence.

"They're bringing them out now," someone said at 8:30 A.M.

Henry got up out of his chair and walked over to the third-floor window. He looked down into the street and saw the cops he once worked with manacled, their hands behind their backs in handcuffs. With the exception of William Gallagher, almost all of the defendants wore jackets and ties. Crystal Spivey had tied her hair back with a pink ribbon. Robert Rathbun hid his tears behind sunglasses. They all cursed the newspaper photographers and television cameramen.

Henry walked back over to Tony, who was pacing near his desk. The cops could hear the metallic clicks of the cuffs that bound the hands of their friends.

"They're in handcuffs, Tony," Henry said gently.

Tony began to swear. He reached for a cigarette and said, "There's no need for that. The motherfuckers. They told us they wouldn't do that to them."

Henry and Tony stood at the window watching the cops head off to Central Booking in separate cars. Henry stood in the window for several minutes, watching silently, tears running down his face. A sergeant walked up behind him and put a hand on his shoulder.

"What are you doing this for? Come on. Get out of here."

Henry left the window and returned to a seat near his partner. He sat there several moments, trying to remember what the cops had looked like.

"You know, I didn't see Brian out there," he said, standing up, his voice filled with worry. "Where's Brian?"

12

> ## "Good morning. I missed my appointment."

On the evening of Wednesday, November 5, Brian O'Regan walked into the Ram's Horn Diner in Rockaway. He wore the night rain in his hair and a four-day growth of beard on his face. His delicate blue eyes were framed with dark circles. He searched out the restaurant, as only a cop can, with a single look.

Brian slid into a back booth, smelling of perspiration. He had called a newspaper reporter earlier in the evening, setting up the meeting. He said he wanted to talk. Brian O'Regan sounded scared. It was raining out and it seemed an especially terrible night to be scared and alone. So the reporter agreed to meet O'Regan at 10 P.M. in a diner near the cop's apartment in the Rockaways.

"Just come out," O'Regan said. "Just come out and we'll talk."

Originally the reporter balked at meeting the cop. His wife was pregnant, expecting their second child any day. The reporter mentioned that Brian had to be up early in the morning anyway. He had a date with an arrest.

"I won't sleep tonight," Brian said on the phone.

Although Brian should have been concerned with time—in nine hours he was scheduled to be arrested for his role in the 77th Precinct corruption scandal—he wore no watch. He looked out the window, rain spattering against the pane. A waiter came over and the cop ordered coffee, the first of six cups he would consume over the next four hours. Brian watched the waiter walk away before turning to the reporter.

"How many years do you think I'll get?" he whispered, the words hissing out of his mouth like steam from a boiling kettle.

There was no answer.

"Why didn't somebody come down and just say, 'Knock it off'? Why didn't the guys from Internal Affairs come down and say, 'If you do that again you're fired.' Why not transfer us? Why jail?"

Brian looked like a soldier suffering from combat fatigue. He jumped when a waiter dropped a spoon. He wore a brown United Parcel Service jacket over a blue T-shirt which read: "77th Precinct. The Alamo. Under Siege." The white words were printed over a drawing of the real Alamo.

"Now I'm under siege."

O'Regan said he had been sitting home the last few weeks worrying about jail. He had not been back to the precinct since turning in his gun and shield on September 23. "I don't want to see the precinct anymore. The precinct is hell.

Why would you want to go to hell? I know when I die, I'm going to heaven."

There was music in the background. Someone in the kitchen turned the volume up on a radio. Glenn Frey sang a song that was used in an episode of *Miami Vice*. "You be-long to the cit-ee. You be-long to the night."

Brian noticed the song and shrugged, ordering his second cup of coffee. "And the city goes round and round," he said. He tapped his right index finger on the table and looked up, eyeing the room suspiciously. "I look at people in the street now and get scared. I'm afraid someone is going to say, 'There's the guy. He's the one.' "

He tried to shift the tenor of the conversation, telling a story about giving a summons to a beautiful girl and how he was frightened of her beauty, unable to even look her in the face as he wrote the ticket.

"The sarge came up to me and asked, 'Why are you giving her a ticket?' I said, 'Sarge, I don't even dare look at her.' "

Brian tried to laugh. But the humor was lost somewhere between the thought and the sound. "I told my lawyer everything. He told me to take a plea, and I might get two or three years. He wanted $15,000 up front. I don't think he trusted me. How am I gonna do on the stand? I can't lie. I can't lie. I don't know how this will all end."

But he knew how it all started.

There was a burglary in a dress shop on Nostrand Avenue. Another cop dipped his hand into the cash register and pulled out a fistful of dollars. O'Regan sipped his coffee and ran a hand over his lips. "I will never forget that," he said.

Brian went back to his coffee and then glanced out the window. Rain pounded the streets.

"There were days I didn't care. I didn't care about nothing. I went to three doctors and they said I needed psychiatric help. They gave me antidepressant pills. But I never faced the facts. I had problems and I never faced the facts. Does a man talk about his weaknesses?"

He continued talking, rubbing the stubble of his beard. He was asked a bigger question: Why had police officers felt compelled to break the very laws they were sworn to uphold and obey?

"My partner keeps saying, 'We never hurt nobody.' And that's true. No one would have cared. If drugs are stolen in the ghetto does anybody really care? I don't even think the drug dealers cared. It was all done as a way of getting back at the people you couldn't hurt. We never hurt Joe Good Guy. For me, I did it for the glory. It wasn't money. It was like you were finally getting back at the slaps in the face you took."

Brian was now on his third cup of coffee. It was approaching midnight. He was beyond the point in life where a man worries about sleep. Or can sleep.

"Sometimes I used to get a feeling—a deep, deep feeling of guilt. But then it would go away. I'd get back on patrol and it would go away. I never stole before I got there. And we never stole when we weren't working there in uniform. I just didn't care. I'm dead and I don't even know it."

The corruption was widespread, Brian insisted. The truth about police officers in New York City would raise the collective hair on the back of the public's neck. Cops weren't just stealing in the Seven-Seven. They were robbing people in each of the city's seventy-five precinct houses.

"We are no different than the politicians."

It seemed to Brian that everyone in public office was a thief. Koch, the city's mayor—a man who will go down in the history of New York City politics as Mayor Nero—had brought a bunker mentality to City Hall by November, 1986. He had even stopped writing books. Koch sat back and watched a wave of white paper—federal and state indict-ments—roll over his city. Queens Borough President Donald Manes had committed suicide rather than appear in court on corruption charges. Stanley Friedman, the Bronx Demo-cratic chairman, would be led away in handcuffs. A Brooklyn Democratic leader, a senior Bronx congressman, and the Bronx borough president would all see their names typed on indictments. In this environment of graft, greed, and may-oral disinterest, Brian O'Regan said he saw no reason not to steal.

"Every cop is going to be petrified for two years after this. But then it's going to happen again. This won't stop kids from stealing. Did the Knapp Commission change us? How can you change human nature?"

O'Regan switched the conversation to broken dreams. His coffee cup was empty. He motioned for the waiter.

"All I wanted was a house, a wife, and a child. What was it Crystal Spivey said? That she did this because she wanted a co-op? That's all I wanted. I have a girlfriend. It's all over for her. She's twenty-five. I'm forty-one and going to jail."

O'Regan's eyes were misty. He looked out the window and spotted a passing patrol car from the 100th Precinct.

"That bothers me—seeing a police car. I want to be in that car. I would go to jail for a hundred years if I could go back in a patrol car when I got out."

By now it was two o'clock in the morning. Brian stood up, saying he had to get going, that he wanted to see his girlfriend before his arrest. The reporter, who had brought a friend to the meeting, could see that he was still restless. The reporter and his friend offered to stay with him until his arraignment.

"No. I got to see my girl."

O'Regan dug his hands into his pocket and came up with a roll of tokens. He offered the reporter two tokens to get back over the bridge from Rockaway into Brooklyn. The reporter told Brian he would be better off keeping the tokens, that he would need them to get to court in the morning.

"I have plenty. I'll have no problem getting there."

The cop and the reporter walked outside, standing in the rain next to Brian's car, a gray 1984 Subaru. Brian wiped his forehead with his sleeve and smiled. It was the smile of a man with a terrible secret.

He walked to the back of his car and opened the trunk, pointing inside to a green plastic bag.

"I got my whole uniform in here. You want any of it?"

"No," the reporter replied. "You keep it. Who knows? You may still need it."

O'Regan shrugged and slammed the trunk closed. Then he walked to the front of the car, opened the driver's door and leaned across the seat to pick up a small package wrapped in aluminum foil. "Then take this," offering the package over the hood of the car. "It's a piece of my girlfriend's birthday cake. She just turned twenty-five."

The reporter took the cake. Brian came around and offered his hand. It was a small hand, not the kind of hand you imagine a cop having. The reporter shook it. He was looking forward to writing Brian O'Regan's story. He said it was a story he wanted told.

"Thanks for coming out. It meant a lot to me just to be able to get out of the house and talk about this stuff."

Brian got into his car. The reporter waved and then jogged across the parking lot through the rain to his own car. It was a miserable night, the reporter decided. He closed his eyes as the car warmed up and thought about his conversation with the cop. The reporter had asked a lot of questions, and some of Brian's answers had been frightening. But only one of his statements would haunt the reporter over the next few days and months.

"You tell me why I did this," Brian had said.

Brian drove directly back to his Rockaway apartment and walked into the bathroom. He became sick, vomiting in the toilet. He washed his face and then went over to the phone, calling his girlfriend in Park Slope.

"I got sick after talking to the reporter. It must have been all that coffee. Bad coffee."

Brian did not go to see Cathy. Instead, he drove out to his mother's house in Valley Stream. There was so little time, he had decided by now, and so much work to be done.

He slipped into the house quietly, went to his bedroom, and began packing. He filled a cardboard box with a three-page will he had had notarized even before he met the reporter, a pair of spit polished police shoes, an identification card from the Broward County Sheriff's Department, his bank book, several greeting cards from his family, including a ten-year-old card from his grandmother that still had a $10 bill stuffed inside, and photographs of his family at Christmas. Brian neatly sealed the box with tape and wrote the numerals "7" and "7" in Magic Marker on the side.

He had placed a typewritten note in the box.

"I am sorry for the past happening. I love you all. Don't fight. Be happy."

At 4:30 A.M. Brian's mother awoke. She had heard movement in the house. She walked into her son's room wearing a flannel nightgown and asked if he wanted to talk.

"I don't have time," Brian said gently. "I can't. I have to appear."

Brian continued past his mother down to the basement, retrieving his dead father's electric razor from a box. He stood before a mirror, shaving the stubble from his sallow face. Hours earlier, before going to meet the reporter, he had said on the phone, "I look bad. I don't want you to think I'm a skell."

After shaving, Brian walked out of his red brick home into the darkness. Dorothy O'Regan followed as far as the back doorstep, and called out to him as he climbed into his car, "Brian, you're very upset. Drive carefully."

Brian had purposely left the cardboard box behind, laying it at the foot of his bed.

The cop drove down his tree-lined street and through the sleepy hollow of Valley Stream. He continued on until he reached the ramps leading to the Southern State Parkway. A left turn would have put the Subaru in the westbound lanes of traffic, taking him to Brooklyn. Brian pulled the steering wheel to the right and headed east, looking for a motel room.

He drove directly to Lindenhurst, checking into the Pine Motor Lodge on Route 109, approximately thirty-two miles away from Brooklyn where the other twelve indicted cops were getting ready to surrender. Brian had never stayed at the motel before. It was the kind of establishment where guests are treated like customers, and the clerks ask questions like, "Short stay or overnight?" Brian stood next to a Donkey Kong machine as he filled out a registration card with the name Daniel Durke. At 6:20 A.M. Brian paid thirty-five dollars and was given the key to Room 1. He entered the room and pulled a laminated Honor Legion plaque from a shopping bag, propping it up on a fluorescent light fixture over the bed. He switched on the television and sat down at the desk, beginning to write on a pad of Broward County Sheriff's Department stationery.

"Good morning. I missed my appointment."

The reporter slept late. He arrived for work in midtown Manhattan at 10 A.M., carrying Brian O'Regan's confession in a notebook. The wire service was already reporting that one of the indicted cops had failed to show up for his arraignment.

"Is this your guy?" an editor asked, pointing to the story. "Brian O'Regan?"

The reporter read the wire copy and felt ill. He returned to his desk and called the police, speaking to a detective in Internal Affairs. The reporter told the detective he had spent four hours with O'Regan in a Queens diner the night before and that the cop seemed scared and depressed.

"Don't worry," the cop said. "From what we understand this guy isn't suicidal."

"I think you're wrong. I didn't think so last night, but now I think Brian could kill himself. If he was a mailman or a mechanic it would be different. Those guys just run. But cops in trouble don't run. Cops have consciences. I don't think Brian can cope with being a criminal."

"Give us the Rockaway address," the cop decided. "We'll send someone out there right away."

The reporter called the police several times throughout the day, remembering different things Brian had said. He went to church a lot. Check the churches. He had friends in Florida. Check Florida.

By the end of the day everyone felt a little better. The police hadn't found a body.

*　*　*

Brian did not like his room at the Pine Motor Lodge. People in the lobby could see right into Room 1. There was too much traffic in the motel. Brian knew there would be an all points bulletin put out on his car. He didn't want to be discovered. Not yet, anyway.

Shortly before noon, a Suffolk County police officer cruised through the parking lot, looking for three men who had just robbed a cash machine. Brian waited until he saw the car clear the lot and then packed up his garbage bag. He left the motel, leaving his Honor Legion plaque behind.

"We figured he'd be back," said John Drake, a desk clerk who discovered the plaque. "A cop would want to keep it. It would be important to a cop."

By 12:30 Brian was back on the highway, heading further east. He drove until he ran out of highway, winding up in Southampton, on the eastern tip of Long Island. He pulled into a deserted motel parking lot.

"Are you open?" he asked, knocking on the door to the Southampton Motel.

"Yes we are," said Camille Gosiewski, the motel's sixty-three-year-old owner. "Come right in."

He registered as Daniel Grant, paying $37.65 in cash for his room. The motel's only guest was given Room 2. Brian asked Gosiewski for directions to a McDonald's and then headed back into town. He returned later, entering the room with his note pads and his uniform in a green plastic garbage can. He also carried a pint of Seagram's Seven Crown and a bottle of 7-Up. Brian liked the symbolism—Seven and Seven was the perfect drink for a cop from the 77th Precinct.

He sat at a desk and began writing again.

"I can't swim in a cesspool, can you?"

The cop spent the rest of the evening writing a one hundred page note, a rambling explanation of his life and times in the 77th Precinct. Brian watched television and saw that he had been indicted for crimes involving some eighty felonies and misdemeanors. He watched news footage of his friends being led to Central Booking in handcuffs. He fell asleep after watching the eleven o'clock news.

Brian woke at 5 A.M. on Thursday, November 7. It was still raining. He left the motel shortly before six and drove into town, buying two newspapers from coin-operated machines. He returned to his motel room and read the reporter's newspaper, studying the front page account of his own interview. Then he began writing and sipping from the paper cup filled with Seven and Seven again.

"I am guilty, but not as guilty as you understand."

As he sat at a dresser across from the bed, Brian occasionally looked up, studying his face in the mirror. He wrote that his stomach felt nauseous and that he did not like the face he saw in the mirror anymore.

"I look bad."

He was still writing at 9:20 A.M. He had changed into his blue "Alamo" T-shirt and turned on the television. He watched the Phil Donahue show as he wrote of his love for Cathy and of his fear of being caught by members of the Emergency Services Unit.

"Only have about $4. What a choice. Death or jail. Got no place to go. Do you think God wants me? Does it hurt to die?"

Brian's older brother Greg discovered a letter in the family's mailbox at about the same time. He found a handwritten note from his missing brother, postmarked November 6, the day Brian disappeared.

"I've always considered myself to be an honest upstanding

citizen," Brian wrote. "I was firmly convinced that nobody cared in the ghetto from the people that lived there to the police and the city. In short terms, they put us in a cesspool and expected us to swim. I'm sorry it had to happen this way but it did. I wish you only health and happiness in the future. Try your best to take care of mom."

Greg showed the letter to his younger brother Kevin and his mother.

"It was the type of letter you get from somebody you don't expect to see anymore," Kevin later explained.

Brian probably stopped writing shortly before 10 A.M. He placed the garbage bag containing his uniform near the bed and propped up his birth certificate and union identification on a nightstand. He noted that the motel's check out time, 12:30 P.M., was nearing. He wrote one last line before putting his pen down.

"Bye. This will be hard to do."

Brian turned out the lights, drew the shades, and lay down on the bed, the television still blaring. He raised a .25-caliber Titan automatic pistol with his right hand and pressed the chrome barrel to his right temple. Then Brian Francis O'Regan fired.

Camille Gosiewski discovered the body shortly before two o'clock. She knocked on the door several times first, yelling, "Mr. Grant? Are you in there, Mr. Grant?" She pushed open the door and saw a figure lying on the bed in the darkness. "Are you all right, Mr. Grant?" She stepped closer to get a better look and saw that there was a gun in the man's hand and a dark stain on the pillow. Oddly, she didn't scream. The scene seemed too serene to be disturbed. Gosiewski simply backed out of the room and closed the door. Then she called her son.

"There's a dead man in Room Two," she said.

The reporter learned of the cop's suicide shortly after three o'clock. He cried in the newsroom. Moments later, a clerk yelled across the copy desk, "Mr. O'Regan is on the phone. He wants to speak to you." The reporter thought someone was playing a sick joke on him. The caller was Greg O'Regan. He was calling from a pay phone in Huntington, Long Island. He had been out searching neighborhood churches for his brother.

"We were just wondering. Is Brian with you? We got a letter from him this morning, that, well, really disturbed us."

"No," the reporter replied. "But I wish he was."

The reporter told O'Regan to drive home. He told a white lie, saying he would come out and help search for their brother. Then he called the police. He knew they would be looking for Brian O'Regan's family now. He spoke to Frank Corcillo, the Deputy Chief of Internal Affairs.

Corcillo was upset.

"We can't get anybody out there in time," he said. "The media already has the story. I've never done this before like this, but I'm going to have to tell them about it on the phone."

The reporter hung up. He tried to picture Brian O'Regan's smile. He tried to recall his last words to him.

"See you around," Brian had said.

13

"Hey, Buddy Boy."

There was a wake and a funeral. That Sunday night, Brian was laid out in the same oblong room of the Moore Funeral Home where he had sat sentry over his father's body seven years earlier. Dorothy O'Regan sat in a folding chair near the front of the room, watching over the mahogany coffin. She would not leave her son alone.

The lid on the coffin was open. Brian would spend eternity dressed in blue. He wore a blue suit and a white shirt, a blue tie knotted firmly at the collar. The undertaker had wrapped a set of black rosary beads in the policeman's hands. Brian's brothers had taped pictures to the casket hood of him laughing with his family. Brian went to his grave looking innocent, his face suggesting the first hint of a smile.

Kevin O'Regan invited the reporter to the wake. He arrived in the early evening, walking past a group of cops from the 77th Precinct who were milling around outside, dragging hard on cigarettes. Having purposefully left his notebook at home, the reporter continued past an assembly of working newsmen. Kevin met him inside the front door. The dead cop's brother and the reporter shook hands. The reporter, a man who worked with words, simply shrugged. He had no words left.

"We wouldn't have been able to get through this if Brian had just left without telling us how he felt," Kevin said. "He never told us how he felt about that precinct. He never sat down with any of us for four hours to talk. He must have trusted you. We all feel that Brian was lucky to have met you. Someone else, well, they might have written the story differently."

The dead patrolman's brother smiled and reached out to embrace the reporter.

"I have my whole life to cry," Kevin said.

Brian's girlfriend Cathy sat in the third row, a police officer at her right side. She wore black and her blue eyes looked vibrant and clear. She handed her unused handkerchief to a woman weeping quietly on her left. One of Brian's relatives told Cathy that she looked strong.

"There's nothing else to be," she answered.

Most of the suspended cops attended the wake. They filed past the casket. Later, there was angry talk in the back of the room when someone mentioned the names Henry Winter and Tony Magno.

"The wrong guy shot himself," one cop said. Another nodded.

Accompanied by his wife, Robert Rathbun suddenly approached Brian's mother. There were tears in the ruined police officer's eyes. He spoke in a whisper.

"I worked with your son," Rathbun muttered in a voice so low that he had to repeat himself to be heard. The cop and his wife sat down. "If I didn't have a wife and kids . . ." Rathbun continued, his voice dying out in mid-sentence. The patrolman's wife, a slight but fiery woman, spit out a name. "Henry Winter," she said, trying to place blame for her husband's misdeeds on an absent cop. "He better move out of town. I don't know how he can stay here." Dorothy O'Regan nodded. Rathbun got up and left the room, moving on legs that wobbled as he walked. It was hard to imagine that he had ever worn new sneakers.

In a hunting cabin outside a small town in the Adirondacks, Henry Winter sat dazed before a fireplace. The investigators had taken away his service revolver on the day they found O'Regan's body. Henry had escaped to the woods with his friend Jimmy Leavy. They spent most of their day sitting on a stump talking, loaded rifles at their feet. A doe wandered by but neither man could find the strength to shoulder his gun. Later Henry drove into town and wired flowers to the Moore Funeral Home. He signed the card, "A friend."

Henry had spent one day searching for Brian in churches throughout Rockaway and Valley Stream. News of his death confused Henry. No one at Internal Affairs headquarters would talk to him about it. Searching for answers, he went to the reporter's home on the morning after O'Regan committed suicide. The men walked down a block near Prospect Park, reviewing what Brian had said and done. As he listened, Henry had wiped tears and rain from his face.

"They left him out there alone too long," he decided. "You can't let a cop sit in a room for six weeks wondering about jail. The prosecutors don't care about any of us as people. We're just cases. Now they have one less case to try."

Henry and Tony had already come to terms with their guilt. They didn't blame themselves for Brian's death. They hadn't entrapped O'Regan or forced him to commit crimes.

"If this was what Brian was set on doing then it didn't matter if we caught him or someone else caught him. I just wish I had called him."

William Gallagher did not attend the wake. After the viewing on Sunday, Greg O'Regan spoke briefly over the phone with Gallagher's wife. Eventually she handed the phone to her husband.

"I'm sorry," William Gallagher said. "I'm so sorry." He could be heard weeping into the receiver before handing it back to his wife.

Later Greg said of the conversation. "Billy feels it's his fault. I can't say that. That's not for me to say."

Charles J. Hynes told *The New York Times* that he would not take the blame for the policeman's death. He had been through this type of thing before. Brian O'Regan was the third defendant in one of Hynes's cases to take his own life. Hynes found no solace in numbers.

"It's very troubling," he said. "I feel very sad. But I don't feel guilty. Investigating cops is the saddest job I've ever had. It destroys lives. If you enjoy it, you're sick. But if it gets to the point where you have trouble sleeping at night, you ought to be out of it. It's something that has to be done. And done professionally."

Hynes would not second guess his tactics in the case either. The cases could not have been made, the corruption carved out of the body of the 77th Precinct, without the cooperation of Henry Winter and Tony Magno.

"The only way to catch a thief is to turn a thief," the prosecutor insisted.

* * *

Police commissioner Benjamin Ward attended a prayer breakfast on the morning of the wake and led a moment of silence for a cop who had "strayed." He described O'Regan as a lost member of the police family. "I'm not going to judge him. No court will judge him. A higher authority will judge him . . ."

Ward did not mention that he was already in enough trouble. On the day of the indictments, the commissioner had announced a foolhardy anticorruption plan, demanding that 20 percent of the department's work force of twenty-seven thousand cops be rotated into new precincts every year. He apparently believed that the best way to fight corruption was to make strangers out of cops. Ward eventually dropped the plan, but not before the union president demanded his resignation and city cops exerted a one-week job action where they simply refused to write tickets or make arrests. By the time the O'Regan family buried Brian on Wednesday, November 12, morale in the New York City Police Department had hit an all-time low. The cops called their affliction "the Blue Flu."

"The kids are yelling at us in the street now," said Lieutenant George Duke, the commander of the 77th Precinct's detective squad, the only unit in the station house untouched by the scandal. "They're saying, 'Hey officer, can you sell us some crack?' "

A polished silver hearse carrying Brian O'Regan's body was escorted by a police color guard from the funeral home to the Holy Name of Mary Church in Valley Stream. Officers from the 77th Precinct, all of whom would be either transferred, suspended, or indicted in the months ahead, stood at attention, their hands covered with white gloves. The cops saluted as the ex-Marine's flag-draped coffin was carried into the church.

Greg O'Regan left his seat during the middle of the service, walking down the right side of the church during the Sign of Peace to shake hands with one cop after another. With the glaring exception of Henry Winter and Tony Magno, all of the Buddy Boys were in attendance. Rathbun languished in a wooden pew next to his wife, moaning quietly. Having embraced his dead partner's oldest brother, Gallagher stood in the back of the church, a white-knuckled grip on the pew in front of him, his eyes leaking tears.

Once returned to the hearse, Brian O'Regan trailed a cluster of leather-jacketed police officers on motorcycles to his grave. Family members laid single red carnations at the foot of his grave and the ghetto cop was finally laid to rest in suburban earth.

Henry and Tony were assigned to Internal Affairs headquarters in Brooklyn Heights, Complaint Investigation Unit No. 3. They carried guns and badges to work but did not feel like cops anymore. Real cops drove patrol cars, and hung out in locker rooms. Their new cop world was devoid of laughter.

Henry tried to make new friends among the cops he worked with. At first he brought them coffee and told them jokes. The gestures of friendship didn't do much good. The officers sipped their own coffee and told each other their own jokes. Henry complained to his wife that there was no warmth or camaraderie in his new command and Betsy sent her husband off to work with even more love notes hidden away in his clothing.

"Just let us go out on patrol," Henry and Tony pleaded with their supervisors. "You can trust us. We won't do anything. Let us feel like cops again."

Henry tried to crack the icy wall during the Halloween

party. He painted whiskers on his face and walked around handing out cheese.

"What are you supposed to be?" a cop asked.

"A rat," Henry replied, laughing.

They were originally invited to the office Christmas party, but later told that they had been "uninvited."

"Nothing personal guys," a cop explained. "It just wouldn't be right."

"I wonder," Henry said to Tony later. "Is being uninvited anything like being unarrested?"

Tony befriended no one. He seemed to like the wall of silence. He had been forced to take an assignment with Internal Affairs, but the other cops there had volunteered to police other police officers. Tony decided he had no use for cops who liked sending other cops to jail.

"I'm finished as a person," Tony told Marianne later. "What's going to happen with me in life? All I know is how to be a cop. All my friends are cops. And now they don't call. What's going to become of me when I'm done testifying and they let me go? At least Henry has friends off the job. I respect him for that. But all I got now is my partner. Henry is all I got left."

The cops began to spend more and more time at home. Literary agents called Henry Winter, offering to buy the rights to his story. Former New York City police detective Robert Leuci, another cop who had walked among corrupt cops with a tape recorder, called Henry. Having already told his own story of police betrayal to author Robert Daley in the brilliant yet disturbing bestseller *Prince of the City*, Leuci now offered to help write Henry's book.

"I know what you're going through," he said. "You'll be all right. Things will pass."

Henry turned down the offer, but was later seen sitting

with his feet up on Bob Leuci's old desk in Internal Affairs, thumbing through a copy of *Prince of the City*. Some of the cops he worked with began asking, "Will I be in your book? Are you thinking about a movie too? If you are, you gotta get Paul Newman to play me."

Nineteen-eighty-seven broke with Henry and Tony continuing to sift through miles of tape. They reported to work at 7:30 A.M. and studied transcripts until signing out of their new office at 4 P.M. An investigative grand jury had been empaneled in December and continued to winnow through the secret testimony of no less than twenty-five police officers working in the 77th Precinct. Nearly all of the cops were talking now. Some rushed to put their retirement papers in, hoping to get out before they were incriminated in the scandal.

Prosecutors plucked cops out of the precinct one by one. A cop facing indictment was arrested after he walked into a smoke shop with his daughter and bought marijuana. Another was suspended after refusing to take a drug test. Figueroa was disciplined after he wrote down an attractive woman's license plate number and called her at home. The woman set up a meeting with him, but Figueroa was beaten by the woman's husband who explained to police that he suspected the cop of making obscene phone calls to his wife. It was later determined to be a case of mistaken identity.

Having transferred all of the 77th Precinct's 20-odd supervisors into new commands in October, Police Commissioner Ward made the decision in December 1986 to transfer each of the remaining 205 cops in the 77th Precinct into new station houses throughout Brooklyn. The precinct's law-abiding officers howled about the transfers, complaining that Ward was making them all look guilty in the public eye. Some cops were ostracized by the police officers in their new commands.

"You worked with the rats? How do we know you didn't give somebody up too?"

Henry and Tony read more and more about their cases in the city's newspapers, particularly the tabloids. A lot of information had been leaked. They were called in by their supervisors and questioned on the leaks. They were furious when confronted with the accusations.

"Are you guys crazy?" they asked.

Henry and Tony returned to their transcripts, marking time until the day in April when they would take to the witness stand and testify as members of the New York City Police Department against their indicted colleagues. They would also be asked to testify in the Police Department's own trial room against some twenty-five police officers brought up on departmental charges. Once clear of the witness box, they would be asked to turn in their guns and shields. The tapes themselves, the bitter legacy of Police Officers Henry Winter and Tony Magno, would remain with the department, packed away in a cardboard box and marked with the numerals "7" and "7".

On May 23, 1987 Sergeant Bernadette Bennett walked into their office carrying a cake with a single lighted candle. Henry was intrigued.

"What's this for?"

"Happy Anniversary. You became part of the team one year ago today. Make a wish."

Henry laughed as Tony glared at the sergeant, a curse on his lips.

"Henry, you make the wish," Bennett said. "Because if Tony gets his wish I may drop dead in my sleep."

"I left work early one day in February. I was supposed to take my daughter to a square dance out in Valley Stream. I was coming down Henry Street in Brooklyn Heights, country

273

music playing on the radio, and I was getting into it. The day started out pretty bad. A lawyer from the special prosecutor's office called to tell we'd be going to trial on Rathbun pretty soon. They gave me eleven tapes to go over. I kept listening to them over and over again. And you know, no matter how many times you listen to the tapes, you always hope to hear the guy say 'No thanks, I don't do that,' when you offer them the money. But they always take the money. That never changes.

"So I'm coming down Henry Street and I make the left onto Atlantic and then I hear it. My window is rolled down and I hear it, clear as a bell. 'Hey Buddy Boy.' I look to my left and it's Billy Gallagher. He was driving a step van, a bread truck. The sliding door to the van was open and my window was open. I just snapped my head and looked, because, I mean, nobody uses the word 'buddy boy' anymore. And there was Billy, sitting in the bread truck.

"I was just going to roll up the window and take off. I didn't know what to do. I was scared at first, my stomach felt queasy. I drove down the street another fifty yards and then pulled over. I had to talk to him. I said to myself, 'No, I can't run. I just can't run. I'm tired of running.' So I made a U-turn and pulled up behind him. I could see him through the side mirror of the truck, and I'm looking at his face and he's looking back at me. I'm waiting, like who's gonna make the first move. He did. He started to get out of the truck. Then I got scared. I didn't know if he had a gun. I thought maybe he could hurt me, maybe he can kill me. But I really didn't give a shit at that point. I figured if he's gonna hurt me, let him do it now. Now, instead of years from now. Whatever he's gotta do, let him do it now. So he gets out of the truck and he walks towards me. I got out and we met halfway. We stood there for a second or two just looking at each other.

"Billy had lost a lot of weight since I last saw him. He used to weigh about two-forty. Now he was down to about two-ten. He lost weight but he didn't dress the part. He still had on his old clothes. Before, Billy filled up his shirts. But everything was big on him now. He needed a shave. He had a cold sore on his lip and his hair was in disarray. Billy didn't look too good. He wasn't the Billy I knew. I'm used to seeing Billy and saying, 'Hey Buddy Bee, what are you doing? Let's go do this. Let's go do that.' And this time it was flat. There was nothing there. I was hoping—being naive, but still hoping—that it could be like that again. I looked in his eyes, he looked in my eyes. We were sizing each other up. And then I made a gesture with my hand, like to say I was sorry or something. He looked at me and said, 'Don't give me your shit.' And then we started to talk.

"He started out with, 'We went through a lot together. How could you do this to me?' and I said, 'You know, I have a family, Billy. True, I was thinking of myself too. I didn't want to go to jail. But I was thinking of my family, my kids.' And he comes back at me, 'Well sure, you weren't thinking of *my* kids, you weren't thinking of *my* family.' And you know it was bad, that part was bad. And then he said something like 'Sure, you're up there in IAD. You get to report to work every day. You get your paycheck every two fucking weeks. Meanwhile I'm out here working sixteen hours a day, seven days a week, trying to put bread on the table for my family, and it's hard because I'm going to jail. Every day I come home, I'm hustling out here to make money, and I come home and say, What for? Why? I'm going to jail. They offered me five to fifteen years. I'm going to jail.' So I said, 'Bill, don't say that, you got a lawyer, anything can happen, you got a good lawyer.' And he says, 'Yeah, but they got a strong case. I know what case I'm going in on. It's Tony's case with the heroin. My lawyer says it's strong. So I don't know what I'm going to do. I tell you, I'm not going to jail though.' I didn't know what to say. And then he brought up Brian.

"He said, 'We were close. We had good times and bad ones too. And after all that shit one guy's dead.' Meaning Brian. That really hurt me. I know I didn't kill Brian, but it's still inside of me. I didn't pull the trigger, but it wouldn't have happened without me. Then Billy says, 'You know, I don't mind losing the job, but I don't want to go to jail. I says, 'Billy, you've got a lawyer, I'll do anything I can to help. You need money? Take half my paycheck—I'll give it to you.' I didn't know what to tell him. He says, 'Yeah, you're full of shit. You know damn well you can't do that. You got a family just like I do. I know you're looking out for them. I probably would have done the same thing. And maybe if they give me the chance down the road, I will do the same thing.' I says, 'Well, maybe they will give you the chance. Do whatever you have to do. Nobody wants to go to jail. I didn't. Tony didn't.' And then he mentioned to me that he was having marital problems now. He said another indicted cop's wife had already left him. He says, 'You guys created hardship with everyone. You and Tony destroyed a lot of families.' I couldn't tell him that if it hadn't been me someone else would have caught him. And then he says to me, 'You know, you don't have to testify.' And I said, 'Billy, if I don't testify, what happens?' And he answers, 'You go to jail.' And I said, 'That's right, Billy. And I'm not going to jail just like you don't want to go to jail. It has to be done.'

"At some point we both cried. I think it was after he mentioned Brian's name. I turned my head and tried to hold it in. But Billy had broke down when I turned around, so I broke down too. I really wanted to grab him. I wanted to put my arm around him or something. But I couldn't. You see, I still wanted to be liked. I had been with these guys since 1980. I saw them more than I saw my family. They were my family.

"The thing that bothered me most about the whole investigation was the fact that the same guys who saved my life were the ones that I was burying. During the investigation Tony and I had an incident down on Buffalo Avenue. We arrived at a building and there's shots fired. An old guy comes out and shoots a kid in the foot. We didn't know what was going on, so we put out a ten–eighty-five [additional units required] over the air and guys rush to back us up. It's like, I don't know how to explain it. Here I am keeping myself out of jail but I need help. I call them and they're there. And that's what bothers me today. Here I am about to get my ass kicked or killed and the guy I'm recording, to get evidence on, comes racing in at sixty miles an hour to do battle for me. He's gonna save me and I'm killing him on the other end with the recorder. That's the worst part.

"That's what I was thinking about when I was talking to Billy on the street. I wanted him to like me. I just wanted to talk to him. And when we broke down, I wanted to put my arm around him and say I was sorry. But I kept quiet. I didn't reach out for him or anything. You know that feeling you get when you really want to reach something and it's just beyond your grasp? The frustration? Well, that's the way I felt then.

"Then we both got straight. He said, 'Look. I'm really hustling out here. I got no time to talk to you. If you ever want to talk to me, have your lawyer talk to my lawyer. I don't hate you guys. I just never want to see your faces again.' It may sound strange, but when Billy told me that

277

he didn't hate me, I felt better. It was like a divorce or something.

'He was ready to leave, but just before he turned, I wanted to shake his hand and say, 'Good luck,' or something. I guess he sensed it or saw me move, because he just looked down at my hand and said, 'What are you, fucking kidding me?' And with that, he turned around, got into his truck, made a left turn, and just drove away. I walked back to my truck and started crying as I pulled away. I drove until I couldn't see anymore. Then I pulled over and found a pay phone. I had to tell someone about this. So I called my partner. I told Tony what happened, and talking to my partner made me feel better. I don't know who Billy called.

"About a month later I read the news. Billy Gallagher cut a deal with the prosecutors. They walked him into court right before St. Patrick's Day and he pleaded guilty to one felony. They dropped all the other charges. Billy's deal is three years in exchange for testimony against all the other indicted cops. They may even count the time he's working on the cases as time served. If the trials go on long enough, Billy may never have to serve jail time. I felt happy for him in a way. Billy did what he had to do. Maybe now he even understands. We did what we had to do.

"I had the tape recorder in my jacket pocket when I met Billy on the street that day. I thought about turning it on too. But then, it hit me. I don't have to record cops anymore. There isn't any more for me to record. That part of my life is over. I threw the recorder out of my truck window on the way home. I felt pretty good after that. I turned on the radio and listened to country music again. It was like, 'End of story, end of life, end of everything.' "

Epilogue

I was watching the Brooklyn street from a Park Slope saloon named Clockworks, waiting to meet Henry Winter for the first time. I had been told to look for blond hair.

It was mid-October, 1986, three weeks after news of a corruption scandal in the 77th Precinct had exploded across the front pages of the city's tabloids. The saloon was nearly deserted. I nursed a beer and watched a storm hammer 12th Street, a rivulet of fouled rainwater rushing towards a sewer. A biting wind slapped sheets of rain against the windowpane. I wasn't sure what to expect.

In outlining the ground rules for our initial meeting, Winter had made a single request.

"No tape recorders," he said. "I don't do that anymore."

As I studied the street, a blond-haired man driving a blue Ford pickup truck pulled up and parked. He sat in the cab smoking a cigarette, the motor still running. For a moment I thought he might drive off again, taking his secrets with him. But after finishing his cigarette, Henry Winter emerged from the truck. He gathered his brown suede jacket against the cold and ran for the bar. He entered wiping the rain from his brow with the back of his left hand.

"McAlary?" he asked.

I nodded. Winter smiled and offered me his dry hand. The gesture was rushed and awkward. I guessed he had not shaken hands with anyone for a while. I looked at Henry's hand and the cop's face went flush. I rescued him with a handshake.

The bartender slid two bottles of beer at us and Henry pulled out his wallet. He insisted on paying, explaining it had been some time since he had bought someone a drink. We retired to an empty table in the back of the room and started talking. We've been talking ever since.

Over the next year, as I interviewed Winter and his partner, Tony Magno, for this book, we went through it all. We started out with names, dates, and times of crimes committed. We wound up with talk about fear, betrayal, and loneliness. Henry wanted to be liked, or at least understood. Tony wanted to trust someone again, or at least be trusted himself.

I guess they trusted me. At some point Henry began to end all our conversations with a chilling send-off. He called me Buddy Boy. "Talk to you later, Buddy Boy," he would say. I don't think I ever got used to that. It reminded me of something O'Regan had said before committing suicide. "Buddy Boy is his favorite word. If you want to see thirteen cops turn in their graves just go up to them, tap them on the shoulder, and say, "Hey Buddy Boy."

Steadily I came to recognize the paradox in Winter. He could be engaging and confident one moment, reluctant and bewildered the next. Sometimes I saw him cry. At other times, I heard him laugh. Mostly he seemed tortured by his own legacy.

"You keep calling me a 'rogue' in your newspaper stories," Henry had said that first night. "Do you know what the word "rogue" means? I looked it up in the dictionary last night with my wife. It's like calling someone a worthless animal. Do you think that's the way I'll be remembered?"

By the time Hynes announced his indictments, I was writing about the investigation every day for *New York Newsday*. And then one night O'Regan picked up the telephone, reaching me in the newsroom, saying he wanted to meet in a diner to talk about his case.

There was no choice but to go and meet him. O'Regan had been around long enough to know how it works with newspaper reporters: You call them. They answer the call.

When they found a copy of my article about O'Regan next to his body in the motel room, it bothered me for a long time. I had hoped the cop would read the explanation of his ruined career and turn himself in. But O'Regan, ever the Marine, had already committed himself to carrying out his final detail. I had become the cop's unwitting pawn—a writer to set a non-writer's suicide note to paper.

At first, no one would reveal the contents of O'Regan's own rambling notes. Much later I learned that his desperate jotting included the line, "McAlary wrote too much." There was no further explanation. Like the voices on the 77th Precinct tapes themselves, the meaning of O'Regan's message was left for the living to decipher.

The entry unnerved me, and forced me to ask questions about the responsibility for O'Regan's suicide. Eventually I reached the conclusion that O'Regan was responsible for his own death, just as he was liable for his own misdeeds.

By dying without giving me a chance to ask him to explain himself further, O'Regan put me in a vulnerable position. In rebuttal, a dead man's words put the living at a distinct disadvantage. But if I wrote too much, it may have been because he told me too much. I guess I can live with that. Cops still call me. I still answer the phone.

In the year following his suicide, each of the 77th Precinct's indicted cops managed to shoulder the same burden that O'Regan collapsed under. They arrived one by one in the mahogany-paneled Brooklyn courtroom of State Supreme Court Justice Felice Shea, sitting at a defense table, listening to the testimony of police officers Henry Winter and Tony Magno. They sat staring at an engraved inscription on the wall behind the judge. It read: "To be perfectly just is an attribute of the divine nature."

As the officer facing the most charges in the scandal, Gallagher arrived in Shea's courtroom on March 10, 1987 to plead guilty in a plea-bargain arrangement. He was dismissed from the force after pleading guilty to one count of selling cocaine, just one of eighty-seven counts in a series of indictments for burglary, drug sales, and grand larceny. In exchange for cooperation—Gallagher agreed to testify in departmental trials against the other suspended cops—he was given a three-and-a-half- to ten-and-a-half-year prison term. He remains free until his sentencing at the conclusion of the other trials.

"I think it's a very sad day for all of us," Hynes said after Gallagher entered his plea. "Not only has he disgraced himself, but he has dishonored other police officers, most of whom I believe are honest."

Gallagher left it to his attorney, Barry Agulnick, to explain his reasons for agreeing to help Hynes prosecute other cops.

"It's been the worst moment of his life," Agulnick told reporters. "His partner received a death sentence for this case. I think that weighed heavily on his mind. He wants to get on with his life."

As Gallagher went back to driving a bread truck, Robert Rathbun headed to trial. He used entrapment as a defense in answering a thirty-seven-count indictment. Rathbun's lawyer, Mark Summers, described his client as a "hero cop who became a tragic figure." He told the court that when Rathbun first heard his own voice on tape, he said, "I don't know that person." Summers added, "He could not identify the person on the tape as being him and the good cop he had been for thirteen years."

A jury found Rathbun guilty on all counts on May 14, 1987, after just three hours of deliberation. They gave no credence to the defense claims that Rathbun had placed stolen money in a church poor box and that he had been enticed to steal by Winter.

"His hand was in the cookie jar all along," said one juror, William Stills, an airlines courier. "Once his hand was in, he didn't know how to get it out." The jury foreman, Paul Heckler, was outraged. He told reporters, "He knew what he was doing all the time. He took an oath to uphold and protect the law and he broke it. He stole and he robbed— the tapes told it all."

Rathbun was sentenced to three-and-a-half- to-ten-and-a-half years in prison on June 29, 1987. Prior to his incarceration, Rathbun explained, "I was burnt out. I was between a rock and a hard place. I was depressed and I chose the wrong way out."

A week before Rathbun went to jail, another jury decided to reject Winter's testimony and simply disregard the voices of corruption on his tapes. Officer Frank Lauria, twenty-eight, was charged with breaking into a Brooklyn apartment on June 10, 1986 and stealing $280 from a drug dealer. Lauria claimed he had gone to the apartment looking for a cop killer and had not taken any money. The jurors sided with Lauria, declaring him innocent of all charges. They did this even as another indicted officer, Jose Villarini, was pleading guilty to burglary and theft. Villarini received probation.

Faced with a departmental trial on the charges he beat in court, Lauria quit the police force. In a post-verdict twist, his attorney, Bruce Smirti, told reporters that the best witness for the defense had been Henry Winter.

"One of the jurors said to me that Police Officer Winter, the rat, was the most immoral, disgusting individual they had ever come across and that they wouldn't have believed him in a thousand years."

The jury in *People vs. Day,* a case in which James Day was charged with stealing thirty-nine vials of crack and accepting a $160 payoff, was similarly unimpressed with Tony Magno. Asked by the prosecutor, Pamela Haynes, how long he had been a corrupt cop, a definition which she defined as including accepting gratuities like free cigarettes and coffee, Magno had replied, "My whole career." The jury lost interest in Magno and his tapes after that exchange.

Day was acquitted on July 8, 1987, after just ninety-six minutes of jury deliberation. During his summation, Day's attorney, Joel Winograd, told the jury that the prosecution had put the wrong cop on trial. Some jurors agreed.

"Magno was lying through his teeth," said juror Richard Anderson, a transit worker, who decided Magno had singled out Day for prosecution and refused to wear a wire on the precinct's most corrupt cops. "It was a case of a corrupt cop who wasn't burying any of his friends."

The most bitter trial resulted in the November 5, 1987 conviction of Crystal Spivey on corruption charges. The trial began with name calling—defense attorney Howard J. Herman referred to Winter as "slime" and "the Ayatollah of Corruption"—and ended with insults when Spivey's father called Winter a coward. In between the attacks on Winter, Spivey was described both as "incredibly naive" by Herman and the "Mata Hari of Corruption" by prosecutors.

Mildred Spivey, the ruined cop's mother, attended each court session but sat in a wooden pew for much of the trial with the headphones on her lap. "I can't always listen," she told reporters. The cop's former boyfriend, the street dealer named Understanding, testified against Spivey in exchange for immunity in a robbery case. "She's guilty," Understanding told reporters covering the trial. "But it's a shame. Crystal wasn't doing anything out there that all the other cops aren't still doing."

During his cross-examination of Winter, Herman insinuated that Henry and Crystal had once been lovers. He also tried to prove that Winter had only gone after Spivey because she was a black police officer and Internal Affairs had run out of white targets. A jury deliberated the case for eight hours before coming back with a split verdict. Spivey was acquitted of drug possession charges but found guilty of official misconduct and renting out her badge for $500. She faces four years in prison.

The best witness against Spivey turned out to be Internal Affairs detective Eugene Poulson, the fifty-year-old undercover narcotics dealer she had known as "Mo." Upon taking the stand, Poulson, who had also worked as an undercover agent in the case involving Henry's brother-in-law at the 75th Precinct, called the Spivey case "his toughest assignment." He explained that he had once worked with Crystal's father, Sergeant Leroy Spivey, and that he had known the defendant's parents for almost thirty years. "I broke in on this job with her father." Poulson testified. "I know her mother Mildred. They are fine people."

Sergeant Spivey would not condemn the same man he once shared a patrol car with. "Detective Poulson was just doing his job," Sergeant Spivey told reporters. "But I wouldn't want to be Henry Winter. I don't see how he'll be able to live with himself. He knows what he has done to his friends. Henry Winter is a coward."

By the winter of 1987, after a series of court appearances in which they testified against other cops, Henry and Tony had become the Police Department's reigning outcasts. They were assigned to a single room at Internal Affairs and were constantly watched. A supervisor had the only key to their office, and on those days when he was absent or late, Henry and Tony had to stand in the hall outside.

While making a return visit to their sector to locate witnesses in July, 1987, Henry and Tony spotted their old patrol car—No. 1491—stopped for a traffic light. The insignia "77" had been painted over with the letters "MT"—police shorthand for Motor Transport.

When he inquired about the status of the car, Henry was told that 77th Precinct cops had nicknamed it "The Ratmobile," and simply refused to ride in it. The car was shuttled off to a new command and is now used only as a patrol car of last resort—a fill-in for cops with broken-down cars.

In June 1987, thirteen months after the investigation began, Henry had made his first and last return trip to the 77th Precinct stationhouse. He had come along with two investigators from the special prosecutor's office to point out different areas of the stationhouse where he had divided up stolen drugs and cash with other cops.

One of the few remaining cops who had worked with Henry at the precinct, an officer assigned to community affairs, spotted Winter as he walked past the muster room. He yelled, "Quiet guys. Quiet guys. Fucking Winter is here. He might be wired." The precinct's new cops snapped to silent, sneering attention. The investigators walked away from Henry, leaving him to walk out of the precinct alone.

As Henry stood on the sidewalk, he felt the eyes of the precinct upon him. He turned around and saw a dozen faces pressed against the building's windows. Each cop wanted to get a good look at the type of cop who turns in other cops. The front door opened and Henry saw an elderly woman, a precinct secretary, standing before him. Once they had been close.

Henry smiled and asked, "You got a kiss for me?" The secretary replied, "Not for you," and slammed the door in Henry's face.

As the trials progressed Henry and Tony were forced to get their home telephone numbers changed to unlisted exchanges. A trickle of crank phone calls became a deluge of threats once the Rathbun verdict came in. On the night before Rathbun's sentencing, someone left a message on Henry's answering machine: "You better do yourself before someone else does you." One of the ruined officers' relatives called to add, "You might be free on us but you're gonna rot in hell."

In late September 1987, a year after the first suspensions were announced, Henry's mother telephoned her son, saying she had news for him. Hynes had lost the indictment against Albert Smolinski, one of twelve officers who had surrendered for arrest in November 1986. Originally charged with a break-in, Smolinski had returned to work in August, agreeing to a deal in which he forfeited eight months back pay in return for his job.

"I got to tell you something about Albert," Henry's mother told him.

"Albert?" Henry said. "What Albert?"

"The Albert that got arrested in the Seven-Seven," Mildred Winter said. "Albert Smolinski. That's your aunt Anna's son. She just called me."

"What?"

"Yeah. Albert Smolinski is your cousin."

Henry began to stammer. "What do you mean he's my cousin? I never saw him at anything with the family. I didn't know he was my cousin. You think I'd do this to my own cousin?"

The policeman's mother sighed.

"Of course not, dear," she said. "We know you're not like that."